Crash Course in Genealogy

Recent Titles in
Libraries Unlimited Crash Course Series

Crash Course in Genealogy

David R. Dowell

Crash Course Series

LIBRARIES UNLIMITED

AN IMPRINT OF ABC-CLIO, LLC
Santa Barbara, California • Denver, Colorado • Oxford, England

Library of Congress Cataloging-in-Publication Data

Dowell, David R.
    Crash course in genealogy / David R. Dowell.
      p. cm. — (Crash course series)
    Includes bibliographical references and index.
    ISBN 978-1-59884-939-4 (hardcopy : alk. paper) — ISBN 978-1-59884-940-0 (ebook)
  1. Genealogy.   I. Title.
    CS16.D68   2011
    929'.1—dc22   2011012144

ISBN: 978-1-59884-939-4
EISBN: 978-1-59884-940-0

15   14   13   12   11   2   3   4   5

This book is also available on the World Wide Web as an eBook.
Visit www.abc-clio.com for details.

Libraries Unlimited
An Imprint of ABC-CLIO, LLC

ABC-CLIO, LLC
130 Cremona Drive, P.O. Box 1911
Santa Barbara, California 93116–1911

This book is printed on acid-free paper ∞

Manufactured in the United States of America

CONTENTS

PREFACE

This book is intended to be a basic training course for library workers who need to absorb an overview of genealogy very quickly in order to help family history researchers who visit the libraries where they are employed. It will also be useful to individuals interested in researching their own families. As you read this book you will encounter some intentional redundancy as I emphasize key concepts. Although I tried to give credit to those whose ideas and words I used, the book is unapologetically written in an informal, almost blog-like, style. If that offends you, you probably should not be reading *Crash Course in Genealogy*. You probably are looking for a more formal and detailed treatise on the subject.

As a brief introduction to the subject, this book cannot make a library worker into an expert in any particular area of genealogical research. However, hopefully it can reduce the fear factor that you may now feel when a rabid genealogist confronts you at your service desk. In this book I will introduce you to the most important overarching principles of genealogy research; expose you to the most used resources, many of which may be available in your library or on the Internet; march you backward through U.S. history; give clues about destinations to which you can refer your patrons for additional information; suggest some of the approaches to the challenges of researching families of color; help you get a concept of how to start overseas research; help you begin to understand how DNA research can be applied to genealogy; and give suggestions for further learning.

I would like to acknowledge the following individuals who assisted me in my endeavor:

Blanche Woolls, the editor of the *Crash Course* series for inviting me to write this book and gently nagging me until it came to the top of my priorities list.

Ron Maas, VP Operations, Libraries Unlimited at ABC-CLIO, whose calm demeanor and sage counsel have been invaluable during all of my projects with Libraries Unlimited since 1998.

Emma Bailey, Senior Production Coordinator, Libraries Unlimited/Linworth, for efficiently guiding this manuscript through the publishing process.

Deborah LaBoon, Marketing Manager, Libraries Unlimited/Linworth, for cheerfully resolving all kinds of logistical and distributions problems over the years.

Dan Burrows, who graciously allowed me to include his genealogical glossary as an attachment to this book.

Martha Grenzeback, genealogy librarian of the Omaha Public Library, for suggesting the need for a chapter on beginning European research and for critically reading the first draft of that chapter.

Pete Petersen, retired genetics instructor and former colleague at Cuesta College, for reading the first draft of chapter 10 and making sure I did not stray too far from the scientific truth in my chapter on applying DNA testing to genealogy research.

Bill Forsyth for providing access to the wide array of databases marketed by ProQuest.

Kim Harrison and her colleagues at Ancestry.com for permission to use most of the census and other templates in the appendix.

Tom Kemp for providing access to GenealogyBank.

Bennett Greenspan of Family Tree DNA for granting permission to use the migration maps shown in chapter 10.

And most of all to Denise Dowell who tolerated, without too much complaint, my long absences to my basement office and who carefully proofread two drafts of this book.

CHAPTER 1

Introduction

Genealogy is the study of multigenerational family history. Jay Verkler, president and CEO of FamilySearch, describes its attraction: "[F]amily history research fulfills a need to belong or feel connected. Each new discovery into our family history provides immense satisfaction. What we learn can expand family relationships in the present and helps us better understand ourselves as we realize our ancestors struggled with similar or greater challenges."[1]

Pulitzer Prize–winning author and historian David McCullough describes the addictive nature of genealogy: "The more we know, the more we want to know. Curiosity is accelerative. There really is no such thing as the past. No one really lived in the past. They lived in the present, their present."[2]

Since I began writing this book in early 2010, family history seems to have exploded in the mass media. In venues as diverse as an episode of *The Simpsons* and series on PBS, BYU-TV, and NBC, it seems a lot of people are getting interested in knowing more about their ancestors.

In episode 13 of season 21 of *The Simpsons,* genealogy figures prominently in the story line.

When Miss Hoover asks her students to research their family history, Lisa is horrified to discover that most of her ancestors were bad people—a motley crew of horse thieves and deadbeats. But while rummaging through the attic, Lisa happens upon a diary kept by her ancestor, Eliza Simpson. As Eliza's story unfolds, Lisa learns that her family was part of the Underground Railroad, a group that helped slaves escape to freedom. Eliza recounts liberating a slave named Virgil, but when Lisa presents her findings at school, some of her classmates refute it, leaving Lisa determined to exonerate her family's name.[3]

Public television has explored the diverse family backgrounds of prominent Americans.

> What made America? What makes us? These two questions are at the heart of the new PBS series *Faces of America with Henry Louis Gates, Jr.* The Harvard scholar turns to the latest tools of genealogy and genetics to explore the family histories of 12 renowned Americans—professor and poet Elizabeth Alexander, chef Mario Batali, comedian Stephen Colbert, novelist Louise Erdrich, journalist Malcolm Gladwell, actress Eva Longoria, musician Yo-Yo Ma, director Mike Nichols, Her Majesty Queen Noor, television host/heart surgeon Dr. Mehmet Oz, actress Meryl Streep, and figure skater Kristi Yamaguchi.[4]

Viewers with access to BYU-TV on cable or satellite have been able to watch *The Generations Project* in which everyday individuals explored a part of their family tree with which they had long held a fascination.

> What secrets run in your blood? This new reality series answers this question as it follows real people traveling the country in search of clues about their family past. As they investigate their ancestors, they begin to understand that the best way to know who you are is to know who you came from.[5]

Perhaps the most important venue for raising the consciousness of the general public about the fascination of exploring one's roots has been a prime-time series on NBC. Patterned after the long-running BBC hit series of the same name, one celebrity each week tries to answer the question, who do you think you are?[6]

The last two series were rerun in fall 2010. They were judged so successful by the networks and their respective corporate sponsors, RootsMagic and Ancestry.com, that producers of both series are busy filming new episodes for a new season. For viewers who may have missed any of these televised offerings, all four were still available for viewing over the Internet in late 2010. In addition, fans can follow the chatter regarding these shows on Facebook and Twitter.

All of this media exposure seems to be creating a new wave of interest in genealogy. Libraries across the country are reporting significant increases in the numbers of patrons seeking to research their family histories. The greatest increase is in individuals just starting this process. Perhaps more important to continuing the media exposure,

> Ancestry.com reported subscriptions in its databases jumped. Gross Subscriber additions were 291,000 in Q2 2010, an 81% increase over Q2 2009 and a 4% increase over Q1 2010, driven by the continued success of marketing programs and the airing of *Who Do You Think You Are?* early in the quarter.[7]

Prior to this media blitz, activity in researching family history had been building more quietly for the previous decade and a half. Genealogy, until fairly recently, has been an activity that could be pursued comprehensively only by those who were retired or not fully employed. A primary reason for this was that so many of the most important resources were only available from 8:00AM to 5:00PM Monday through Friday. That's when the court houses, archives, and other repositories of records were open. The census, probate, property, and vital records generally were available for review only during business hours and even then only at one or two, often remote, locations. Most working folks had jobs that allowed visits to such places only on their precious vacation days. The Internet began to change this by the eve of the 21st century as more and more records were digitized and made available online. Although this process is still far from uniform and far from complete, it has dramatically changed genealogical research. As a result, everyone with an Internet connection can now research their family history at any hour on any day. As more people get the genealogy urge, library workers need to be prepared to assist them, but where to begin?

While all of this is raising the awareness of family history in your community, what is going on in your library? Recently, a librarian told me that all of her colleagues slithered for the exits when a genealogy patron appeared. Although this may be a bit of an exaggeration, many library workers do not feel adequately prepared to respond comfortably to the growing number of patrons who are now researching their family histories. Particularly bothersome can be the enthusiastic novice.

BACK IN YOUR LIBRARY

It's early Saturday morning. You have just finished your second cup of coffee in the library staff room and hurried out to the public part of the library. Jack Simpson describes the first minutes of what happens next:

You have just opened the reference desk, and already you have:

- a new resident on the phone asking about recreational sports leagues
- a regular at the desk looking for the new Elmore Leonard novel
- a computer freezing up

Into this scene strides a patron with a pile of disorganized papers in his hand and a confused expression on his face. He begins to speak, tentatively at first but with increasing fervor as he warms to his subject.

Um…Hi…I'm trying to get started on my family history, and I was told you have good resources here at the public library. I guess I'm mostly English and Scottish but maybe also German. The German was my Mom's side I think, and then the Irish was her dad's side. But I'm interested in my great-grandfather on my Dad's side because my Grandpa never really talked about him. There's some mystery there. He had the same name as me. He was a mine manager in Pennsylvania but also in West Virginia, but that side of the family is also supposed to be from Ohio, so I guess he moved around. He died when my Grandpa was young. Then, my Grandpa married my Grandma, who was also from Ohio, and her family had a general store.[8]

Figure 1.1: "The Lockhorns" comic. Used by permission of the LOCKHORNS © 2010 WM HOEST ENTERPRISES INC. KING FEATURES SYNDICATE.

Is this the same man you encountered at the Friends of the Library reception last night?

Whether or not he is the same person, it is now time to put up your hand and temporarily stop this spontaneous outburst. To do so, you might say, "Whoa, there. Slow down a minute and help me organize all this in my mind so that I'll be able to help you."

We will resume the encounter with this patron later. Novices like the fictional gentleman described by Jack Simpson, or his cousin who also suffers from attention deficit disorder, may live in your community. Actually, this is fairly typical behavior for a recent convert to the thrilling pursuit of genealogy. Finally, he has a captive audience with whom he can share his newfound excitement. But while we have temporarily paused this patron's story, let's take advantage of the interlude to stop and review some basics of genealogical reference service.

PURPOSES OF THIS BOOK

The purposes of this book are twofold:

1. If you are now working in a library open to the public, sooner or later you will have patrons request your assistance in extending their family trees—perhaps

even some as enthusiastic as the man just described. This book is intended build your confidence in your ability to meet such needs by giving you a process to organize your thoughts as you begin to help them.

2. If you want to climb in your own family tree, this same thought process will help you as well. Although the book is organized to focus on the former purpose, its value to help you explore your own family tree will also be obvious as you read further.

Reading this book will not make you an expert genealogy librarian. This is a crash course. As such, it is only a quick first step in your professional evolution. Mike McCombs, who has been a student in several of my genealogy research classes, describes my approach as taking you on a guided tour by flying over genealogy research at 20,000 feet. Hopefully, this quick overview will make you more familiar with the terrain and stimulate you to do later flyovers at 10,000 feet or 5,000 feet. Perhaps you will be motivated to actually put your genealogical boots on the ground and really specialize in a particular aspect of library service to family historians. Resources to assist you in further learning are discussed in chapter 11.

WHAT IS GENEALOGY?

At a macro level, genealogy is the process of learning and discovery of how, over the years and generations, the forces of both nature (DNA) and nurture (environmental factors) have shaped who you are and who the members of your family are. It is also about who your children and grandchildren are in the process of becoming.

The Board for Certification of Genealogists gives the following more systematic answer to the question, what is genealogy?

> Genealogy is the study of families in genetic and historical context. Within that framework, it is the study of the people who compose a family and the relationships among them. At the individual level, it is biography, because we must reconstruct each individual life in order to separate each person's identity from that of others bearing the same name. Beyond this, many researchers also find that genealogy is a study of communities because kinship networks have long been the threads that create the fabric of each community's social life, politics, and economy.
>
> Good genealogists use every resource and tool available, emphasizing original records created by informants with firsthand information. Genealogists have long studied economics, geography, law, politics, religion, and society in order to properly interpret records, identify individuals and relationships correctly, and place their families in historical context. The modern field of genetics has added another valuable tool to their intellectual toolbox.[9]

This definition is great for experienced researchers. I hope that you, as an information professional, will also embrace it. However, I would be the first to admit that the patrons standing in front of you are highly unlikely to be ready for you to give them as comprehensive a response as might be called for within the perimeters of the board's definition. However, it is important for you to keep all of it in mind as you struggle to meet the immediate needs of those who seek your assistance. But back in the trenches at the library service desk, you may require a more basic plan.

IT'S ABOUT THE NAMES, STUPID!

Let's try a simpler approach. Most of you remember the 1992 presidential campaign.

"It's the economy, stupid" was a phrase widely used during Bill Clinton's successful 1992 presidential campaign against George H. W. Bush. For a time, Bush was considered unbeatable because of foreign policy developments such as the end of the Cold War and the Persian Gulf War. The phrase, recently made popular by Clinton campaign strategist James Carville, refers to the notion that Clinton was a better choice because Bush had not adequately addressed the economy, which had recently undergone a recession.[10]

For genealogists at all levels, it's about the names. This is particularly true of novice researchers who may be interested in little else. Of course, the relationships among the names and the stories behind the names are also important, but it all starts with the names. Without them, there can be no successful research. Without finding more names, that research cannot progress further.

BASIC SERVICE TO GENEALOGISTS

The library profession through the Reference and User Services Association (RUSA), a division of the American Library Association, has established a policy statement about library services to genealogists. It says, in part, the following:

Public libraries have a responsibility to serve the needs of patrons interested in genealogical research by providing basic genealogical reference materials and how-to-do-it books in the library and by providing access to additional genealogical research materials through interlibrary loan or referral. Other libraries that wish to develop a genealogical collection and provide services may find these guidelines useful as well.[11]

Library workers carry out many activities in preparation for researchers to arrive at a service desk. Among them are the following:

1. Building and preserving collections
2. Organizing and cataloging collections

3. Digitizing unique records

Other activities continue as a way to make visits to the library more efficient for researchers or, in some cases, to provide assistance by alternative means:

4. Creating finding aids
   a. Handouts
   b. Websites
5. Providing short courses and other public programming
6. Information assistance
   a. In person
   b. E-mail, online chat (Web 2.0)

LIBRARY POLICY

It would be wonderful if all libraries serving genealogy researchers could allocate sufficient resources so that all the previously listed functions could be achieved in an outstanding manner. In real life, however, that is possible only in a few of the largest and most specialized genealogy libraries. The libraries where the rest of us work must prioritize their scarce human and other resources. The beginning of that process is to clearly enunciate a genealogy service policy.

What is your library's policy about helping genealogy researchers? Does it have a specific policy about assisting family history researchers? Is it a separate policy statement? Is it incorporated into a general services policy? Is that policy communicated to the library staff? How is it communicated to library users?

Such policies, if they exist, should be well understood before you begin to help genealogy patrons. Such policies may limit service to just assisting inquirers with finding and using in-house resources and externally linked databases. Some may call for extensive interlibrary loans to and from other libraries. Some may provide for actually conducting fee-based research—at least on a limited basis. Others may rely on group education activities and/or well-developed websites and handouts. Below are a few examples of such policies.

While the Genealogy Service Policy of the Glenview (IL) Public Library seems to limit its reference assistance more than some other libraries, it offers a wonderful web page of links to other resources of interest.

> The GPL genealogy collection supports lifelong learning in the areas of genealogy, family history, and local history. General assistance identifying resources in the collection and online is provided. Reference librarians cannot undertake genealogical research. Patrons may be referred to specialized genealogy libraries or services for further assistance.[12]

A different approach is taken by the Cambria (PA) County Library.

As staff time allows, the reference department can provide photocopies of obituary and marriage notices from the *Johnstown (PA) Tribune,* its successor, the *Johnstown Tribune-Democrat,* and the *Ebensburg Sky.*

Only a limited amount of other research can be provided by library staff. Pages from city directories, telephone books, local histories, etc. can be photocopied for a $5.00 research fee if an exact citation is given. When time must be spent in searching for a topic, a $20.00 per hour charge will be incurred.

Library staff cannot search census reels or birth, marriage, naturalization, and indexes of will books on microfilm.

If you wish, in-depth requests may be sent to a local genealogy researcher. Although the library does not endorse or recommend genealogical or historical researchers, a list of people willing to do local searches can be provided upon request.[13]

The Troy (NY) Public Library offers somewhat similar service.

Researchers are welcome to use the library's Troy Room, which houses our non-circulating genealogy and local history collection.

For those who cannot visit our library in person, we offer remote assistance for a fee of $25. The $25 fee must be paid in advance, and will cover up to one hour of genealogical research.

Please understand that we require payment of the $25 in order to begin searching. Genealogical research can be quite labor-intensive, and even in cases in which our searching turns up no information, payment is still required. Questions are answered in the order in which they are received. Response time will vary based on the number of questions received and may take up to one or two months.

If you require extensive research assistance (more than two hours of work), you should consult with a professional genealogist. Here is a *list of researchers* who work in the Capital District.[14]

Most libraries are only able to offer the kind of general assistance offered by the Glenview Public Library. Just as library staff do not research and write term papers for students, they rarely have the resources to do detailed research for genealogists.

BEGINNING THE REFERENCE INTERVIEW

Another RUSA policy statement discusses the reference interview.

4.1 Librarians should know how to ascertain the skill level of their patrons in regards to genealogical research, and how to provide to the patron both an appropriate orientation to the collection and services provided by the library and instruction in the evaluation of information...

4.3 During the reference interview, the librarian should learn the answers to the following questions from the patron, as appropriate: What are the research goals? What is known about the target ancestor-their name, children, parents, birth, marriage, death dates/places, etc.? Does the patron have pedigree and family group forms that include the target ancestor? Which sources has the patron already consulted?

4.4 As a result of the reference interview, the librarian should analyze the information needed by the patron (names, dates, places, etc.) and determine the types of sources that will provide the required data.[15]

You should begin the reference interview by helping patrons focus on what they want to find out *today*. Experienced researchers may already have this clearly in mind. With these patrons, your task will be to help them find anything available in or through your library that will help them answer the question they have already defined. Experienced researchers will be realistic about what they can accomplish and what may be available.

However, the novice researcher we met earlier will need a bit more guidance in coming up with a realistic expectation and devising a research plan to begin to address his needs. I have a feeling that if he were asked what he would like to find today he would say, without hesitation, "Everything!" Generally, the place for this kind of novice researcher to begin is with a pedigree chart, which begins with him in the box at the extreme left of the chart. If he is temperamentally capable of sitting down and beginning to organize his thoughts in the form of a pedigree, that might be the best way to help him begin his family history. However, I suspect it may not be that easy. We will examine pedigree charts in much more detail in the next chapter.

Another approach, if the activity level of your service desk allows, could be to tell him you are a visual learner and that it would help you to visualize his family if he could help you start filling out such a chart. When this has gone as far as is productive given his current state of family knowledge, it is time to decide what his next research step should be. If he is still all over the place and wants to jump on his horse and ride off in 19 research directions at once, you will have to ask him something like, "If we only have time today to find out *one* new thing about *one* of these people on your chart, who is it and what would you like me to try to help you find out?"

After you (and/or he) try to fill out a pedigree chart, it may become clear that there are other steps in the research process that he should be going through before you can help him with library sources of information. However, it will do wonders for his motivation to continue as well as his confidence in you as an expert resource person if you can help him find at least one record of his family that he can copy and take home with him.

BEFORE LIBRARY AND OTHER DATABASE RESEARCH

However, there are other processes that should have begun before the researcher came to the library. Unfortunately, these preliminary steps are not always intuitive to novice researchers. The diagram in Figure 1.2 was created to help genealogists think about their family research in a systematic manner. As you begin to formulate a search strategy to assist your patrons, the following cycle can be a useful reminder of steps through which your patron may need to be guided. Of course, this cycle was not created from the perspective of a library worker. However, its author did include libraries as a major part of Public Document Repositories—circle 6. Those of us who work in libraries know that

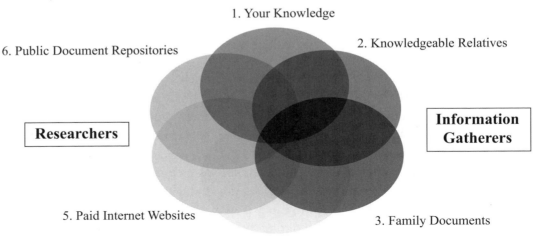

1. Your Knowledge

2. Knowledgeable Relatives

6. Public Document Repositories

Researchers

Information Gatherers

5. Paid Internet Websites

3. Family Documents

4. Free Internet Websites

Figure 1.2: **The circles of genealogy information. Used by permission of *OneGreatFamily.*** *Source:* "Where Can I Find More Genealogy Information to Add to My OneGreatFamily Tree? Are You an Information Gatherer or a Researcher?" *OneGreatFamily Newsletter,* http:// www.onegreatfamily.com/newsletters/Newsletter_Guests_2007_08_02.html (accessed January 23, 2008).

we are also an important provider of Paid Internet Websites—circle 5. Therefore, even though this model may not be as complete as we would like, it is a good starting point. One important point to remember is that a researcher should mentally rotate through this cycle, or an even more complex one, many times during the course of a research project. This is not a case where one can go through the cycle once and consider it done. It is often helpful to return to a model like this and use it as a checklist every time one begins to investigate a new family branch or a new surname attached to the family tree.

Steps your patrons will have to do on their own—perhaps with your gentle guidance—are as follows:

1. Are your patrons aware of all the relevant things they know about their family? Have they organized them in a way that documents what they know and that exposes what they should try to find out next? Clearly, our eager patron needs more than a little guidance on this process.
2. A knowledgeable relative may have already documented some of the family story. Some relatives may have stories and recollections that may not be recorded anywhere.
3. Family documents could be pictures, postcards, newspaper clippings, school annuals, scrapbooks, licenses, certificates, and so forth.

Steps in which you can be more directly involved will be discussed in more detail in subsequent chapters—particularly chapters 4 through 6.

4. Much research can be done at free Internet sites or through referrals from them.

5. Libraries often provide subscriptions to databases, which many patrons cannot afford.

6. Libraries, courthouses, historical societies, and archives are the most obvious repositories of such documents, but can you think of others?

HAS SOMEONE ALREADY RESEARCHED THIS FAMILY?

Sometime early in the research process, it may be useful to suggest to patrons that they try to find out whether someone has already attempted to document a part of their family history. In some ways, this is an extension of circle 2 in Figure 1.2. Perhaps a knowledgeable relative has already started recording elements of the family history. Perhaps it is a more extended family member or even an unrelated individual.

BUILDING GENEALOGICAL REFERENCE SKILLS

A number of approaches can be helpful. With practice, you will find the one(s) that works best for you. As with other kinds of reference transactions, all professionals will explore a number of alternative methods and find out which sources and processes seem to work best for them. Some major resources will be described here—particularly in chapter 3—but in this fast moving environment, new ones are constantly emerging and some older ones lose their relevance or disappear entirely.

NOTES

1. KCSG Television, "A Celebration of Family History Delights Thousands of Genealogy Enthusiasts," April 29, 2010, http://www.kcsg.com/view/full_story/7263938/article-%E2%80%9CA-Celebration-of-Family-History%E2%80%9D-Delights-Thousands-of-Genealogy-Enthusiasts?instance = home_stories1 (accessed December 16, 2010).
2. Ibid.
3. "The Color Yellow," *The Simpsons,* season 21, episode 13, http://www.watch-simpsons.net/ (accessed March 10, 2010).
4. *Faces of America with Henry Louis Gates, Jr.,* PBS, http://www.pbs.org/wnet/facesofamerica/ (accessed August 5, 2010).
5. *The Generations Project,* BYU-TV, http://www.byutv.org/thegenerationsproject/ (accessed August 5, 2010).
6. *Who Do You Think You Are?* NBC, http://www.nbc.com/who-do-you-think-you-are/ (accessed August 6, 2010).

7. "Ancestry.com Inc. Reports 2010 Second Quarter," Yahoo Finance, http://finance. yahoo.com/news/Ancestrycom-Inc-Reports-2010-pz-2435158211.html?x = 0&.v = 1 (accessed August 6, 2010).

8. Jack Simpson, *Basics of Genealogy Reference: A Librarian's Guide* (Westport, CT: Libraries Unlimited, 2008), p. xi.

9. "Certification: Frequently Asked Questions (FAQ)," Board for Certification of Genealogists, http://www.bcgcertification.org/certification/faq.html#5 (accessed April 19, 2009).

10. "It's the Economy, Stupid," *Wikipedia,* http://en.wikipedia.org/wiki/It%27s_the_ economy,_stupid (accessed August 6, 2010).

11. References and User Services Association (RUSA), "Guidelines for Developing Beginning Genealogical Collections and Services," June 1999, http://www.ala.org/ala/ mgrps/divs/rusa/resources/guidelines/guidelinesdeveloping.cfm (accessed April 19, 2010).

12. Glenview (IL) Public Library, http://gplgenealogy.blogspot.com/ (accessed July 14, 2010).

13. Cambria County Library Johnstown (PA), http://www.cclib.lib.pa.us/services_refer ence.htm (accessed July 14, 2010).

14. Troy Public Library (Troy, NY), http://www.thetroylibrary.org/?p = 25 (accessed July 14, 2010).

15. RUSA, "Guidelines for a Unit or Course of Instruction in Genealogical Research at Schools of Library and Information Science," January 2007, http://www.ala.org/ala/ mgrps/divs/rusa/resources/guidelines/guidelinesunit.cfm (accessed April 19, 2010).

CHAPTER 2

Backward Thinking and Other Keys to Successful Genealogical Research

Successful family history research requires a few small attitude adjustments to the way most people are accustomed to thinking. Most of us have been trained to follow the European tradition of reading from left to right. We are used to reading books from beginning to end and watching movies from beginning to end. We read histories that start with some early event and then move forward in time—perhaps to the present. Biographies start with the person's birth and move through their childhood and then adult life. That also may be the way one would publish a family history. However, successful genealogy research is done backward.

Some of you may remember how as kids in the 1960s we participated in a brief fad as we imitated NASA engineers by counting down everything, "10, 9, 8, 7, 6, 5, ..." Making a similar adjustment in one's mind-set is one of the keys to becoming an efficient genealogical researcher. You must learn to think backward.

Thanks to Letterman, it has also becoming a tradition for Dave to come up come with lists of 10 things arranged from 10 down to 1. The following 10 things are so important to successful genealogical research that I am going to run the risk of being redundant by repeating them more than once in this and following chapters. Here goes the first rendition of my top 10 list.

DR. DAVE'S TOP 10 RULES FOR SUCCESSFUL GENEALOGICAL RESEARCH

- *Rule 10.* When you are stuck, widen your net. Now is the time to ignore Rule 6 and follow the chickens: the siblings, the in-laws, the neighbors, the witnesses to legal documents, the fellow church members, the business associates, and so forth. (Isn't it fun to be given permission to violate a rule even before you know what that rule is?)
- *Rule 9.* Don't ignore the ladies. Often their lines are more challenging to trace because maiden names (or other married names) may be difficult to unearth.
- *Rule 8.* Look for records where they would have been recorded when they were created. Location, location, location! Location in place, location in time, location in record repositories of the governing body at the time of originating time and place.
- *Rule 7.* Plan your search strategy. This will help you prioritize your time online or on visits to records repositories such as libraries, courthouses, cemeteries, and so forth. Plan research trips by working online to identify those things of interest that are likely to be contained in the repositories you visit.
- *Rule 6.* Find a focus ancestor and research that person as far as you can go. Don't follow every chicken that runs across the road. However, you should document such sightings for future exploration—perhaps when you arrive at Rule 10.
- *Rule 5.* Organize your data on pedigree charts and family group sheets as you go—better yet, in a genealogy program on a computer. These building blocks really work to keep you focused and on track.
- *Rule 4.* Believe everything and believe nothing you are told or see in print. There are elements of truth in most oral traditions, so don't totally discard them. Paper and web pages will record any nonsense any fool writes down. Look for primary sources whenever possible—eyewitnesses and documents recorded at the time of the event. However, even primary sources are sometimes incorrect. Collect multiple sources, and weigh them against each other. Use common sense.
- *Rule 3.* Record where you found it and/or who told you. In the excitement of discoveries, this is easy to forget, but didn't I tell you that Rule 3 was *record* where you found it and/or who told you? Trust me. You will be glad you did.

- *Rule 2.* Interview living members of your family and examine any papers you or they have laying around including letters, diaries, scrapbooks, bankbooks, Bibles, photographs, loose papers, and any other kinds of memorabilia that may have passed through the hands of your ancestors. Record interviews if possible. It's hard to take in every nuance and clue the first time through. Temporarily borrow any papers and pictures you come across and run to the nearest Kinko's or come with your own portable scanner or copier. Sometimes a good digital camera will do the trick. Ask if they know of anyone else researching your family.
- *Rule 1.* Start with what you know (yourself) and build back to what you don't know—step-by-step. *Don't skip steps!*

20TH-CENTURY RESEARCH: THE STARTING POINT

A few of these 10 rules are my own creation, but most of them, in some form or another, would be in the top 10 of any serious genealogist. The latter would certainly be true of Rule 1. It is the first rule for a reason, but it is also a rule likely to be disregarded by individuals just starting to do their family history. That was certainly the case with the overly enthusiastic patron you met earlier in this book. Of course, he was starting off in all directions at the same time and therefore not going anywhere. Often people have heard that they had an ancestor on the *Mayflower* or that they descended from Napoleon or had relatives that were famous or notorious for other reasons. Trying to start with the list of persons arriving on the *Mayflower* and working down to the present is a real loser of a strategy—even if your patron has a surname in common with one of those on that ship. Tracing every descendant of even one of those Pilgrims through 400 years of history would be a lifelong undertaking, and even then, there would be no guarantee of success. So where should one begin the quest?

START WITH WHAT *YOU* KNOW

Generally, persons should begin their family history research at some point in the 20th century. That beginning point will vary depending on when your patrons have memories of events they have experienced themselves. This follows Dr. Dave's first rule.

- *Rule 1.* Start with what you know (yourself) and build back to what you don't know—step-by-step. *Don't skip steps!*

That means what you really know from your own experience. It does not mean things you have heard about as they passed down through the family second or third hand. We all know what happens as information is orally passed from one person to another. There may be a grain of truth in it. We will come back later to these oral traditions that every family has. However, we need to have a much firmer foundation from which to launch our family history research.

Those who are now walking into libraries to begin researching their family history have personal memories of their family in the 20th century. Therefore, that is where their research process should begin. However, as we noted in the previous chapter, there are other processes that should have begun before the researcher came to the library.

COLLECT EXISTING FAMILY INFORMATION

Steps 2 and 3 from the research cycle in the previous chapter work in parallel with Rule 2, which I am sure you remember says the following:

- *Rule 2.* Interview living members of your family and examine any papers you or they have laying around including letters, diaries, scrapbooks, bankbooks, Bibles, photographs, loose papers, and any other kinds of memorabilia that may have passed through the hands of your ancestors. Record interviews if possible. It's hard to take in every nuance and clue the first time through. Temporarily borrow any papers and pictures you come across and run to the nearest Kinko's or come with your own portable scanner or copier. Sometimes a good digital camera will do the trick. Ask if they know of anyone else researching your family.

I was a special investigative officer in the air force before I became a librarian. Some of the lessons I learned there have been very useful to me in reference interviews, and they are also useful when family history researchers interview relatives about the histories of their families. One such lesson was that everyone has more information than they think they do. For a variety of reasons, they do not divulge all that they know the first time they are asked about the topic. They may not think an item is relevant or important. They may think you already know more than you do. There may be information that they feel embarrassed to talk about for one reason or another. They may not want to brag. But the most important reason may be that the information may have slipped down into their subconscious and is not immediately accessible.

One example of this latter phenomenon took place more than a decade ago when an elderly aunt came to visit me for a week. As soon as breakfast was cleared from the table on the first morning she was there, I got out my laptop and systematically started going over our family tree with her. I asked what she knew and what she had heard about every person with whom she could have come in contact. About half the time she said, "I don't know." She said this even when one could reasonably have expected her to know something. For the next six days, she did not come down for breakfast any morning with less than three additional tidbits of information that had emerged from her subconscious overnight. In retrospect, I should have kept her with me for another month.

Library patrons are the same way when they start to document their family histories. In order to help them, you may need to interrogate them gently and repetitively on important questions—rephrasing the questions in different ways or asking them to help your faulty memory. Sometimes they may not realize that some item is important or may not want to bore you. In addition, patrons will often already have the raw ingredients in hand that can be used to answer the question they are posing to you. Sometimes it will be in their head, and sometimes it will be in documents they have already collected.

All of this effort is to establish where the starting point of the patron's search is going to be. Once the input of living relatives and the information from documents and realia found around the homes of the older generation of family members have been collected and analyzed, the gathering gives way to researching. Realia, in the sense used here, refers to three-dimensional objects—*real* things—and not pictures or documents describing them. Again, we continue the process of looking backward.

The most recent events should be documented first. If the gathering did not turn up evidence that backs up the recollections of the researcher, the process should start by searching for such documentation. The most likely events to be documented first are recent deaths. Because of privacy concerns, many records are not made publicly available until a person is dead. It is good to remember that *personally identifiable information* about living persons should not be published, particularly on the Internet, because of concerns about identity theft. Although there has not been much evidence of identity theft based on information derived on published genealogical information or even state vital records, it may be useful to remind your patrons it is considered bad form to publish information that is frequently used by financial institutions to verify the identities of their customers.

Deaths are commonly documented by obituaries, death certificates, funeral home records, church records, cemetery records, and tombstones. All of these records may have been created contemporaneously with the death. As a bonus, each of these sources may provide additional information. At a minimum, it is likely that one or more of these sources will provide information about the decedent's birth. It may also provide information about the person's parents, spouse, and sometimes other family members. Since information gathered from these sources was recorded at or near the time of death, the part of it relating to the death can be considered a primary source—a topic to which we will return later.

It is important to mine every nugget of information from each of these sources. Too often novice researchers will transcribe the date and place of death. Then they will close the image if it is a digital file or stick the page in a file folder if it is a paper copy. In their joy and the resulting adrenaline rush, they hastily move on to the next block on the pedigree chart. In so doing, they may overlook much potentially valuable data as well as important clues to help uncover further records about the family.

Death certificates are good places to look for the following pieces of data, which may be included:

1. The cause of death
2. The attending physician
3. How long the decedent lived in that community
4. Marital status
5. Spouse, if living
6. Date and place of birth
7. Occupation
8. Parents
9. Informant (or who went down to the funeral home and gave the information). This is an important clue as to how accurate the information is likely to be. How knowledgeable was the informant about the history of the decedent? We should remember that this information is usually requested at a very traumatic time when the informant may have many other pressing priorities that seem more important than some paperwork at the funeral home.

Cemetery records are very uneven in quality but can be a treasure trove of information—particularly when other sources are missing. For years, we had been trying to find out what had happened to my wife's Irish immigrant ancestor. His only official appearance that we had discovered was the 1860 census in Chicago. In it, he was listed as a 30-year-old from Ireland who had a 20-year-old wife and an infant son. City directories had listings for him in the early 1860s, and then he dropped off all radar screens. By the 1870 census, his wife was married to another man. All kinds of suggestions were made by various individuals. Most of these ideas centered on the Civil War. However, that path also turned up fruitless. Remember that the Great Chicago Fire of 1871 destroyed much of the city and its records. Then, almost by accident, I stumbled across records of a cemetery that had been transcribed by volunteers from a National Society of the Daughters of the American Revolution chapter who had deposited a copy of their work in the Family History Library in Salt Lake City. Even though the ancestor had been misindexed in the transcription, I am very grateful for their efforts. It turns out that the cemetery was outside Chicago in 1871 and thus was spared from the ravages of the fire. Today it is surrounded by the city. When we contacted the cemetery, they were able to tell us when he died, his cause of death, and even that an infant daughter (until then unknown to us) had been buried in the same plot. Although he does not have an extant tombstone, the records in the cemetery office allowed us to bring closure to his life. Perhaps others will be able to have similar success when searching in burned counties where records have been destroyed by courthouse fires.

Obituaries can be particularly useful to family history researchers. However, changes in the newspaper industry have made this source of information more uneven. Most still print brief death notices at no cost to the family, but lengthy obituaries now generally must be paid for by the column inch. At the same time, more funeral homes now post obituaries on their websites, or at Legacy.com, and sometimes add guest books for friends and family to use to share remembrances. It is too early to know how long these online sources will be archived. At the moment, it appears that they may start disappearing after a year unless someone pays to renew them. One would hope the funeral homes are archiving them in a more permanent form in some manner.

Tombstones tend to be more permanent; however, even they do not always survive the ravages of time and vandals. This permanence is sometimes a mixed blessing. Once something is chiseled in stone, it takes on a life of its own. I have an aunt who has unwittingly contributed to false or misleading information being placed on two different tombstones in two different states. In one case, she filled in the middle name for a family member who had only used a middle initial all his life. After the stone appeared, other family members asserted that she had not chosen the correct middle name. In another case, she had "Mother" and "Father" added to the tombstone of her dad who died in a state in which her mother had never even visited in her lifetime. To her, it was a simple memorial to her mother who previously had been cremated a thousand miles away. To future family historians, this inscription can be misleading. To counter such errors by survivors, an ancestor of my wife had a lengthy saga carved on his tombstone. This was done during his lifetime and while he could control his legacy. It detailed his service as a young cabin boy on a ship in the British armada that helped bring down Napoleon.

Finding death records is a way to bring closure to the life of a family member. However, to a genealogist they are a way to open up a life history by unearthing clues that allow the search to move on to the next backward step in time. From them, it may be possible to move back to marriage records, birth records, and even to the lives of the parents of the deceased ancestor. Then, hopefully, these additional records will give clues that allow the trail to be followed even further back in time—step-by-step without skipping steps.

Other tools for making this backward journey will be discussed later in this chapter. However, for the first steps of traversing the second half of the 20th century, the death records of recently departed ancestors can be invaluable. Most of all, they serve as a reminder that we need to think backward in order to pursue our family history most efficiently.

DOCUMENT IT!

Those of you who are aficionados of the television series *NCIS* probably realize the importance of remembering the rules of Special Agent Jethro Gibbs. If so, you probably remember Dr. Dave's Rule 3. For the rest of you, here it is again.

- *Rule 3.* Record where you found it and/or who told you. In the excitement of discoveries, this is easy to forget, but didn't I tell you that Rule 3 was *record* where you found it and/or who told you? Trust me. You will be glad you did.

I wouldn't think this rule would have to be stated for library workers. However, we all know better. It is very important for you to remind your genealogical patrons of this rule early and often. Not only does documentation lend credibility to research findings, but it also makes future research more efficient. Unfortunately, this may be the hardest of the rules for novice researchers to follow. Even experienced researchers too often have difficulty consistently putting it into practice.

Documentation, as I am using it here, refers to two different processes. The first and the most obvious, at least to library workers, is to record where you got every fact, picture, and story you unearth. This is just good practice in any kind of research. It also gives proper respect and acknowledgement to those who have contributed to your success as a researcher. I'll have more to say about intellectual property rights later. In addition, it will help you make an analysis later if another source is subsequently discovered that seems to contradict a fact you have previously recorded. Which is the most credible? If you haven't documented where you previously got your information, you will have no idea how much weight to give each reported fact. Also, you won't know where to backtrack to verify whether you initially copied it correctly. One of the principles of any kind of solid research is that it can be replicated by another researcher. Unless you establish a trail of documentation back to your information sources, others will not be able verify your results, and your work cannot be relied on as a foundation for the work of others interested in the same family.

In this book, I will make no pretense in trying to cover the proper format that documentation should take. That topic has already been covered on various levels by Elizabeth Shown Mills, the grande dame of documentation. The best thing I can do for you is to refer you to her prolific writings. Her magnum opus on the topic, *Evidence Explained: Citing History Sources from Artifacts to Cyberspace,*[1] runs almost 900 pages and should satisfy the detail lovers among you. For the rest of you, some of her shorter works and Quick Sheets may suffice. Or you can chose to take the easy way out and order the latest version of a good comprehensive genealogy software product such as *RootsMagic* or *Legacy.* At about the price that one of the shorter works will cost and at about half of the cost of *Evidence Explained,* you can get templates that cover almost any conceivable source you might encounter. Even better, these are bundled with database software that will store all your information about your ancestors. They also will help you organize and publish all kinds of reports. So there is no real excuse for researchers to fail to document except for laziness and perceived lack of time. However, if one continues researching a family for very long, the time factor will reverse and come out in favor of the researcher who documents. In other words, not documenting each fact, and so forth, as it is collected is penny wise and pound foolish.

The corollary to Rule 3 is to create and use a research log. In it, you should document every source you have consulted in researching each ancestor, whether or not you find anything useful. The log can be as brief or as detailed as you desire. However, this will be a useful way to keep from looking in the same sources over and over again for information. Even better, if you can convince your genealogical patrons to use such a log, it will save both of you an immense amount of time as you continue to work together as the family tree grows more complex.

EVALUATE THE CREDIBILITY OF EACH FACT

Now back to our earlier mention of family oral traditions. You and your patrons need to critically evaluate everything you encounter, whether it is told to you or whether you find it printed in what appears to be a reputable publication or on the web.

- *Rule 4.* Believe everything and believe nothing you are told or see in print. There are elements of truth in most oral traditions, so don't totally discard them. Paper and web pages will record any nonsense any fool writes down. Look for primary sources whenever possible—eyewitnesses and documents recorded at the time of the event. However, even primary sources are sometimes incorrect. Collect multiple sources and weigh them against each other. Use common sense.

Be very reluctant to disregard the seemingly far-fetched tale your Aunt Mary told you about what her grandfather had told her when she was a girl. There is probably an element of truth in it. The best policy is not to swallow whole any fact or tale that is presented to you. Rather, you should slowly and carefully examine it and weigh it against other evidence. Very few things in a family history are ever absolutely proved. Even eyewitness evidence is sometimes distorted and filtered through the prism of what that witness would have liked the event to have been. However, researchers must not become so timid or paranoid that they can make no progress whatsoever. The Board for Certification of Genealogists has created "The Genealogical Proof Standard" to strike a balance that can be accepted within the genealogical community.

Proof is a fundamental concept in genealogy. In order to merit confidence, each conclusion about an ancestor must have sufficient credibility to be accepted as "proved." Acceptable conclusions, therefore, meet the Genealogical Proof Standard (GPS). The GPS consists of five elements:

- a reasonably exhaustive search;
- complete and accurate source citations;
- analysis and correlation of the collected information;
- resolution of any conflicting evidence; and
- a soundly reasoned, coherently written conclusion.[2]

A fuller discussion of each of these elements is available on the board's website.[3]

After decades of research, I have come to the understanding that "acceptable conclusions" can be reached, but very few facts can be absolutely proved. To me, it is like the scientific method of proof that postulates that hypotheses cannot be proved. However, if a reasonably exhaustive effort fails to disprove a hypothesis, it should be shared with other researchers so it can be subjected to their scrutiny to be refuted or replicated. Unless and until it is disproved, it can become the foundation upon which we stand to examine other related aspects of our family story.

THE BUILDING BLOCKS OF GENEALOGY: FROM FLOOR PLANS TO BLUEPRINTS

- *Rule 5.* Organize your data on pedigree charts and family group sheets as you go—better yet, in a genealogy program on a computer. These building blocks really work to keep you focused and on track.

A pedigree chart can be thought of as a floor plan of a family history. It shows how all the units of the family fit together. It is an overview. Shown in Figure 2.1 is a template of a four-generation chart—perhaps the most common size. The accepted convention is for the paternal (father's) line to be on at the top of the chart and maternal (mother's) line to be below it.

Within each box on the chart, the following information is recorded if known (see also Figure 2.2):

- The full birth name of the individual. This is rather obvious for males. However, some neophytes may start out putting the married name of females. Although recording the married name of female family members is important, recording it on a pedigree chart, instead of the maiden name, will confuse readers who are at least somewhat familiar with genealogy.
- Date and place of birth.
- Date and place of marriage to the spouse with whom they are paired on this chart.
- Date and place of death.

As implied, one cannot include every important event about a family member in a pedigree chart. The purpose of the chart is to record information relevant to the person on the left side of the chart. Even for that person, the information recorded on the rest of the chart only relates to those who have contributed DNA to the initial person on that page. Other means will be needed to adequately record and display the more complex relationships of blended families and adoptions.

Actually, a pedigree chart can have any number of generations. Displaying more generations in one chart allows one to get an overview of the many lines that flow into

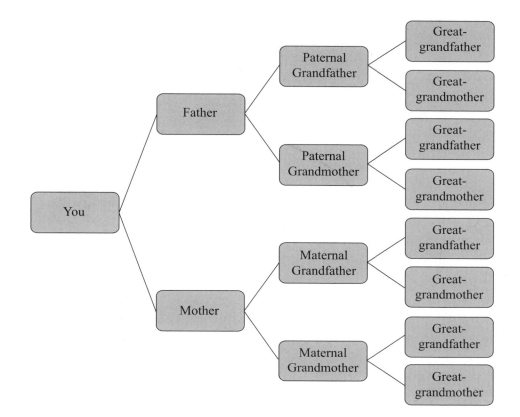

Figure 2.1: Four-generation pedigree chart showing the relative position of each of the family members.

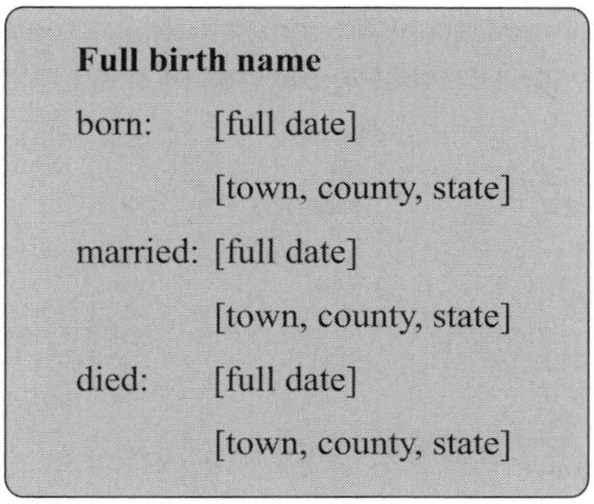

Full birth name

born: [full date]

           [town, county, state]

married: [full date]

           [town, county, state]

died: [full date]

           [town, county, state]

Figure 2.2: Data elements for boxes of pedigree chart.

a single individual. On the other hand, it becomes increasingly difficult to read the information on a chart as more than four generations are added.

As one's pedigree chart grows beyond the great-grandparents, it is usually best to start using cascading pedigree charts. Cascading pedigree charts are linked charts.

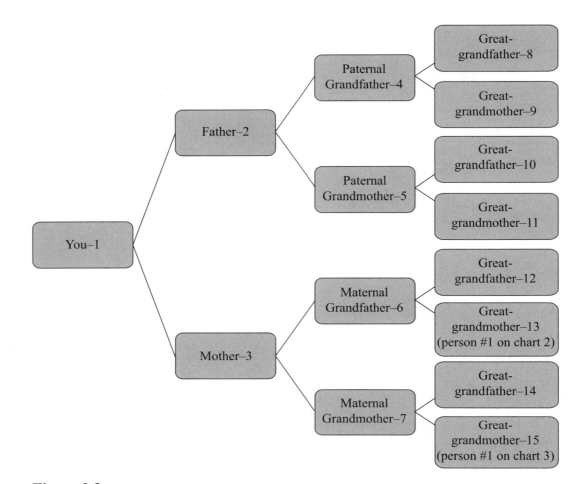

Figure 2.3: Numbering for individuals in chart 1 of a cascading pedigree assuming you only have information on the parents of two great-grandmothers—numbers 13 and 15.

Taken together, they can record any number of generations. They can be individual sheets linked together by a hand-numbering system. More commonly in the 21st century, these are the output of a computer genealogy program in which the program automatically numbers the charts with a system that guides the reader from one sheet to another.

Figures 2.3 and 2.4 show two different examples of the first page, chart 1, of a pedigree chart. In these pedigree charts in Figure 2.3, the boxes have been assigned a number between 1 and 15. Note that the numbering system runs from left to right and from top to bottom. This sequence is important to help readers follow the results when additional charts are added. For example, if information is known about the ancestors of the great-grandfather (8) in the chart, then he (8) will be duplicated at position 1 on the continuation sheet, which is called chart 2. A notation should be added in the margin to the right of him on chart 1 indicating that 8 is continued as 1 on chart 2. Likewise on chart 2, a notation should be added to the margin to the left of 1 indicating that more recent information on his line of descent is continued as 8 on chart 1.

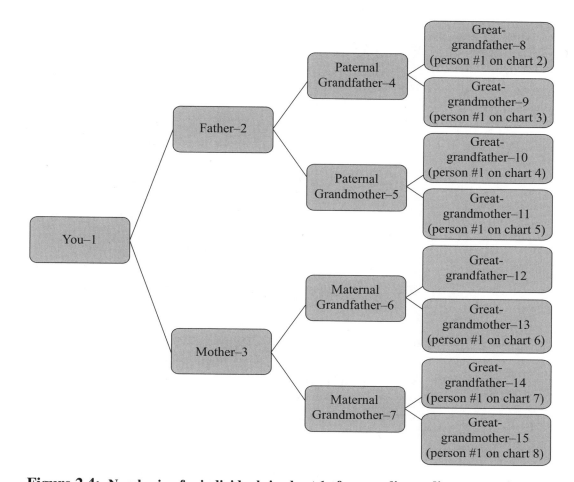

Figure 2.4: Numbering for individuals in chart 1 of a cascading pedigree assuming you have information on the parents of seven of your eight great-grandparents.

Additional charts can be added for any of the great-grandparents on chart 1 for whom information on their ancestors is known. However, the additional charts are added in the numeral sequence of their box numbers on chart 1. For example, if additional information is only known on the ancestry of the great-grandmothers in boxes 13 and 15 on chart 1, the information on the ancestry of the woman in box 13 would be continued as chart 2, and the information on the ancestry of the woman in box 15 would be continued as chart 3, the third page of the cascading pedigree chart.

It does not take very much foresight to realize that this whole numbering system can quickly become unwieldy if you are fortunate enough to find the parents of your great-grandparents 8, 9, 10, 11, and 14 in addition to 13 and 15. Then the numbers protocol would become as shown in the chart in Figure 2.4. Relatively inexpensive genealogy software eliminates this problem by formatting the charts automatically each time you wish to print them out. A template of a pedigree chart is included in the appendix.

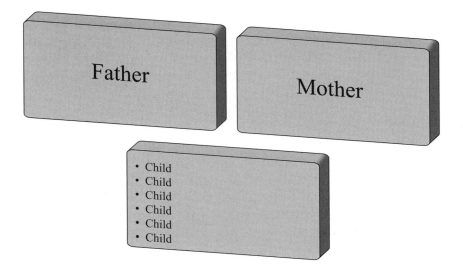

Figure 2.5: The structure of a family group sheet.

While the pedigree chart is certainly a great place to start recording family information, it has its limits. It is only two dimensional. Therefore, it cannot begin to convey the depth of any part of the family tree. Family group sheets add a third dimension to an individual family unit (see Figure 2.5).

This allows one to add information about all the members of a nuclear family unit. It fills in important details that begin to provide understanding of how that family unit is composed. It differentiates between the family in which I grew up and the one in which my mother grew up. While I grew up as an only child, my mother grew up as the 10th of 14 children who survived childbirth. These are two very different environments. It is also important to know if either of the parents in a family unit had multiple marriage partners and if the children all shared the same parents or if they grew up in a blended family. All these subtleties can be described in one or more family group sheets. It would be very difficult to begin to appreciate the lives of our ancestors unless such variations are understood and recorded. A template of a family group sheet is included in the appendix.

In some ways, family group sheets are more tedious than pedigree charts. Certainly, they are more time consuming. It takes at least seven family group sheets to support a four-generation pedigree chart (more if some of the parents had multiple mates). Some researchers prefer to work these relationships out on paper before they begin to enter them into a computer program. My own personal preference is to enter information directly into my computer program templates as I collect it. I only have to enter it once, and I can display it in a variety of ways. If I make a mistake, it is easy to correct. Typical word processing functions like cut and paste and spell-checker are built in. I do not run out of room to add new individuals or additional information.

From a researcher's perspective, the information contained in family group sheets is often necessary to differentiate between different couples of the same or similar names. Sometimes our ancestors were not very creative in naming their children. In one of my lines, there are several households where the male is named Samuel and his wife is Mary Ann. Some of these were in the same generation and lived in the same general area. I'm glad that my family members appreciated their ancestors to the extent that they honored them by naming offspring after them. However, this compounds the difficulty that genealogists face in differentiating among those who were similarly named. Well-documented family group sheets can help keep family units in their correct place in the family tree.

COUSINS

Cousins, in the broadest sense, are anyone with whom we share an identifiable common ancestor. In this sense, everyone else in an extended family would be one's cousin. However, when a more specific term is available, we tend to use it. Therefore, although siblings would technically meet the definition of being blood kin, they are generally called brothers or sisters. The same would be true of others within a family when terms more specific than *cousin* can be used. Some family historians have great fun and others have great agony trying to precisely identify specific degrees of cousinhood for everyone in the family. Figure 2.6 shows a chart that extends out far enough to cover cousins who are likely to be living simultaneously.

Basically, the way cousin relationships are counted is that you count the number of generations back to the common ancestor and then subtract one. In the simplest example, it is two generations from you back to your grandparents. Therefore, you are a first (two minus one) cousin with anyone who shares the same couple as grandparents. The *cousin once removed* or *cousin twice removed* comes in when the cousins are an unequal number of generations from their common ancestor. For example, your children would be one generation further removed from your common ancestor, so they would be a first cousin once removed to your own first cousins. Likewise, your grandchildren would be first cousins twice removed to your own first cousins.

Other charts showing cousin relationships often extend out to eighth cousins or beyond.[4] I find it much simpler to let my genealogy software figure out such relationships. I just select two individuals who are in my database, and it tells me whether they are related by blood and what that the relationship is—if any.

We tend to think that blended families are a recent invention, but they have existed for centuries. If you really want to go there, here are some extreme examples that can result:

Half cousins

Half siblings share only one parent. Extrapolating from that, if one of John's parents and one of Mary's parents are half siblings, then John and Mary are half first cousins. The half sibling of each of their respective parents would be their

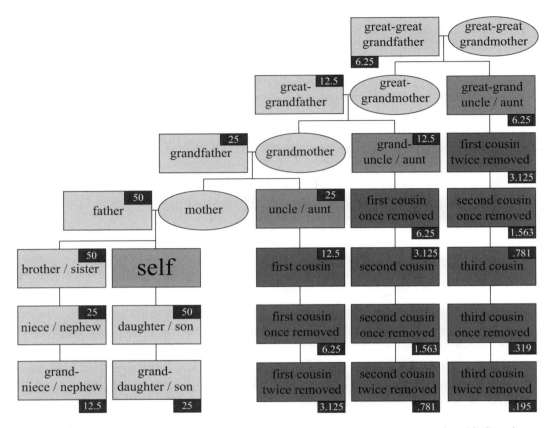

Figure 2.6: **Family tree showing the relationship of each person to one's self. Cousins are shown in the lower right quadrant. The genetic degrees of relationship are marked in boxes by percentage (%). This percentage is probably only relevant later in the book when we are discussing autosomal DNA**
Source: "Cousin," *Wikipedia,* http://en.wikipedia.org/wiki/Cousin (accessed July 29, 2010.) (The creator of this chart has released it into the public domain, so you can freely distribute it to your patrons.)

half aunt or half uncle, but these terms, although technically specific, are rarely used in practice. While it would not be unusual to hear of another's half brother or half sister so described, in common usage one would rarely hear of another's half cousin or half aunt so described and would instead hear them described simply as the other's cousin or aunt. Also, children of half first cousins are half second cousins to each other and so on because they would share only one common great-grandparent out of eight instead of two, and so on.[5]

One-and-a-half cousins

One-and-a-half cousins may be produced when two full siblings have children with two half siblings. However, if a set of half siblings has children with another set of half siblings, the resulting children would be double half first cousins and would have the same consanguinity as full first cousins. Furthermore, if a person's half sibling marries the person's half sibling from the other parent, assuming they are not stepsiblings, then the child of that couple and the child of the half sibling who is related to both partners in the married couple will likewise be double half first cousins.[6]

The day after I somewhat tongue-in-cheek included this definition in the first draft of this chapter, I was contacted by a distant cousin with whom I had previously had no contact. In a case that can best be described as life imitating art, I found that our exact relationship turned out to be that we are fourth half cousins through Peter Dowell and also fourth half cousins once removed through Moses Brown. We are both blood descendants of both Peter and Moses but not through the same wife in either case. Why did we think we invented blended families in the 20th century?

Stepcousins

Stepcousins are either stepchildren of an individual's aunt/uncle or children of a stepaunt/uncle. No blood relationship exists between stepcousins, although there does not need to be a blood relationship between cousins, as in the case of one or both of the siblings being adopted, their children would still be first cousins. First stepcousins once removed would be the stepchildren of your first cousins. A second stepcousin is the stepchild of your first cousin once removed.[7]

Cousin-in-law

A cousin-in-law is the spouse of an individual's cousin, similarly the cousin of an individual's spouse.[8]

As you can see, these relationships can be defined but doing so can become tedious and quickly get out of hand for the average family history researcher.

FOCUS ON ONE LINE

- *Rule 6.* Find a focus ancestor and research that person as far as you can go. Don't follow every chicken that runs across the road. However, you should document such sightings for future exploration—perhaps when you get to Rule 10.

For many beginning genealogists, particularly those who are male, the first ancestor to research will be the paternal line of their father. The curiosity about where his surname came from as well as testosterone may fuel this approach. It is, all other factors being equal, also the easiest line to research. In a vast majority of the cases, the surname will stay the same back many generations. Therefore, records should be easier to find than for maternal ancestors whose names tend to change at least once in every generation. They may even change more than once if the women are married more than once or if they go through a divorce and revert to a previous name. However, the point of Rule 6 is to focus research in one direction and stay on that course as long as progress is being made. The corollary to this rule is to take note of ancestors encountered along the way who branch off in other directions. This will give researchers starting places to begin researching auxiliary lines when research along the primary line bogs down. But in any case, the next rule will prove useful.

PLANNING YOUR RESEARCH

- *Rule 7.* Plan your search strategy. This will help you prioritize your time online or on visits to records repositories such as libraries, courthouses, cemeteries, and so forth. Plan research trips by working online to identify those things of interest that are likely to be contained in the repositories you visit.

Genealogical fieldtrips are a real treat for true family history researchers. Sometimes the experience is almost as much fun as finding new information. However, the experience if unfocused will diminish the possibilities of finding as much information as would otherwise have been possible. Fieldtrips will be discussed in more detail in a subsequent chapter. For now, the point is that if a researcher arrives with a plan that takes into account exactly what is expected to be found, much more can be accomplished than will be the case if half of the precious time available on site is taken trying to get organized. Even worse would be to find after traveling for a few hours or few days that the destination is not really the correct one for the needed data.

Talking with family members will be more productive if you have planned in advance what you would like to learn from each individual. Even Internet surfing at home will be more likely to yield results if it is done in a systematic way. Clear research priorities will help ensure that the most important items receive the most attention before your research time is gone.

LOCATION, LOCATION, LOCATION

- *Rule 8.* Look for records where they would have been recorded when they were created. Location, location, location! Location in place, location in time, location in record repositories of the governing body at the time of originating time and place.

Just as in real estate, the three most important things in finding information about your ancestors are location, location, location. The three locations to which I am referring are the following:

1. The *location* where they actually lived. In the 21st century, we might call this their *GPS* location or the precise place where they were physically situated.
2. The *location* in time when they were actually at that physical location.
3. The *location* of the records for the events that occurred at the intersection of locations 1 and 2.

Locations 1 and 2 should be intuitive. It is important that these be as precise as possible. Any information can be helpful, but to be really useful, you must refine it as much as possible. If you know that a great-grandmother was born in Wisconsin in the 1850s, that information may be a good starting place. However, unless you can narrow it down to a town or at least a county, you may not be able to find her birth record. Furthermore, unless she has an unusual name, you may need to know her exact birthday or at least birth year to make sure you have the right young woman. The logic for this should be obvious.

Not so obvious is the location of the record of that event. Birth records have been recorded in a variety of places. In early New England, such records were most commonly recorded at the town level. In many other parts of the country, such events were recorded by the county. By the early 20th century, most states had taken on this responsibility. Do not assume that these local jurisdictions are the same today as they were when your ancestors lived there. County lines have evolved considerably over the decades and centuries. State lines may have shifted particularly in colonial times.

For example, in the 18th century, some of my ancestors lived in Rowan County, North Carolina. At the time Rowan County was formed in 1753, it covered a wide expanse of territory that subsequently has been divided into about 20 current North Carolina counties. In addition, part of current state of Tennessee was also then part of Rowan County. In 1790, North Carolina ceded to the federal government seven counties, which became the nucleus for the state of Tennessee. Records remain in the repositories in which they were originally recorded. Already existing records generally have not moved with jurisdictional shifts that changed maps.

Then there are events recorded by religious bodies. In many European countries, religious bodies were required by the government to keep vital records in lieu of them being kept by the civil government. This tradition often continued until well into the 19th century. In some cases, this tradition was continued by colonists who migrated to North America. Be sure to investigate if there are church records that may be useful.

EQUAL RESEARCH FOR WOMEN

- *Rule 9.* Don't ignore the ladies. Often their lines are more challenging to trace because maiden names (or other married names) may be difficult to unearth.

Your female relatives contributed just as much to who you are genetically as did your male ancestors. They also helped shape the families in which your ancestors were reared. Beginning genealogists, for a variety of reasons, often fixate on tracing their paternal line to the exclusion of all others. This pattern is more likely to occur among male genealogists. Within limits there is nothing wrong with this approach. You will remember that Rule 6 can be taken too far. Sooner or later, most genealogists become interested in their maternal lines as well.

WHEN ALL ELSE FAILS

- *Rule 10.* When you are stuck, widen your net. Now is the time to ignore Rule 6 and follow the chickens: siblings, the in-laws, the neighbors, the witnesses to legal documents, the fellow church members, the business associates, and so forth.

Sometimes it is not possible to follow one's ancestors directly from one generation back to the previous one. No matter how hard one tries and how many records are consulted, the dreaded brick wall prevents discovery of the ancestors being sought. At this point, casting a wider net is a technique that often circuitously leads to the desired information. By following a sibling, or other family member, it may be possible to locate the desired information.

Sometimes it is the family of the spouse of a sibling that provides the clue needed to get past a brick wall. In one case, I was having difficulty tracing one line of my mother's ancestors. I knew where in Ohio they had lived in the early part of the 19th century. However, I couldn't find any information about where they had lived previously. I noticed that three of the siblings of my direct line ancestor had all married members of the Ruse family. I then discovered a published history of the Ruse family and found out that they had lived in North Carolina prior to moving to Ohio. I started looking around in the area of North Carolina from whence the Ruses had come. Voila! There were my Cashatts.

As families migrated west, they often did so in groups. Visualize the trains of covered wagons or ox carts. Some of these groupings were extended families. Others were members of the same religion. Still others were brought together by forces we will never uncover. However, it is not unusual for the same groups to migrate west together in a series of moves separated by stopovers of many years in interim locations. Often, some of the young people of the family married locals and did not continue the western migration when the rest of the group continued. Good researchers will keep alert for all these possibilities for following family migration patterns.

SUMMARY

These are just a few of the principles of successful genealogical research. However, if they are kept in mind, you should be ready to start helping your patrons with their family history research—even the one we met earlier at your service desk. In the following chapters, we will find practical applications for many of these rules, such as working backward in time to unravel the past of ancestors of those who come into your library to find clues to the lives of their family members. But first you need some databases to research.

NOTES

1. Elizabeth Shown Mills, *Evidence Explained: Citing History Sources from Artifacts to Cyberspace* (Baltimore: Genealogical Publishing, 2007).
2. "The Genealogical Proof Statement," Board for Certification of Genealogists, http://www.bcgcertification.org/resources/standard.html (accessed July 6, 2010).
3. Ibid.
4. "Genealogy Relationship Chart," *About.com,* http://genealogy.about.com/library/nrelationshipchart.htm (accessed July 29, 2010); "Cousin Chart," State Library of North Carolina, http://statelibrary.ncdcr.gov/genealogy/cousinchart.html (accessed July 29, 2010).
5. "Cousin," *Wikipedia,* http://en.wikipedia.org/wiki/Cousin (accessed July 29, 2010).
6. Ibid.
7. Ibid.
8. Ibid.

CHAPTER 3

Genealogy Speed Dial

Several megasites should be bookmarked on the computer of every library worker who helps genealogists. You may want to consider bookmarking them on public terminals as well for the benefit of your patrons. These are sites that offer resources that are both broad and deep. You will want to also add to your personal speed dial, places that are your own personal favorites as well as those that contain important local historical and genealogical information.

Of course, you know that I am not suggesting that you literally put these resources on your phone—even your BlackBerry or iPhone. However, I am suggesting that you will want to create a folder on your reference computer where you can bookmark them as favorites. If you work in a library that only occasionally gets genealogy questions, this will be particularly useful to use as a reminder. If you work at a reference desk that has lots of genealogy traffic, you are already familiar with many of them.

Once you have created such a list, you can find many ways to use it. You may want to create single page handouts to be able give to researchers when you are too busy to give them detailed assistance. This will give them resources to explore until you have a chance to spend more time with them. Such handouts may be not much more than a list of sites mentioned in this chapter supplemented with local resources specific to your service area. In addition, you may want to consider having a one-page flyer on each resource mentioned to give patrons a quick overview of that resource and a quick tutorial for getting started with it. Once you have created this information, you can consider adding it to a family history page on your library website and also using it as the basis for short genealogy classes for your local genealogy enthusiasts.

As you will see, I am listing these sites in alphabetical order. You will soon discover, if you haven't already, which of them you like to search for specific patron needs. Some of these sites are free, and others are commonly subscribed to by public libraries and/or local family history centers. Whole books have been written on how to take full advantage of just one of these resources. To be able to take advantage of all the features of them, you may want to add those books to your reading list. The subsequent descriptions rely heavily on information provided by these sites. If you read carefully, you may notice that more than one of them claims to be the biggest. I will not try to adjudicate those rival claims, because they are all very big and resource rich. If there were a way to measure which really was bigger, uploads or acquisitions next week or next month might reverse the rankings. Just enjoy what they each have to offer.

AMERICA'S GENEALOGYBANK (FEE)

Newspapers contain a vast amount of information of interest to those researching family histories. Accessing this information is often a challenge. America's GenealogyBank is a collection of newspapers specifically selected to appeal to genealogists. It is similar to but slightly different than GenealogyBank as librarian, genealogist, and vendor Tom Kemp explains.

We have two services:

1. GenealogyBank: which can only be purchased by individuals
2. America's GenealogyBank: which can only be purchased by libraries

The names are similar and the content is almost identical in both—but the individual service: GenealogyBank has more newspapers than the core America's GenealogyBank product.

Licensing agreements require us to use a different approach to newspapers we provide to libraries. Some newspapers are available for library use; some for only individual use and some for both. Libraries would license America's GenealogyBank and then add in the additional newspapers they want for their audience.[1]

GenealogyBank does not discuss its number of subscribers. It is a family-history-focused division of NewsBank, through which your library may have additional online periodical packages. Be sure to become familiar with it and with the other newspaper indexes available through your library. Newspaper indexes are notorious for returning false-positive matches. Some retrieve articles when the given name being researched appears in one article and the surname appears in an entirely different article perhaps even several columns over but on the same page. GenealogyBank mitigates this by defaulting to a search protocol that requires the names to be within two words of each other. Even this leads to many false-positive responses, but the number is greatly reduced. By using some of the advanced search features, experienced researchers can learn to get more precise results. GenealogyBank does include some government document sets, funeral sermons, and directories as well as traditional newspapers.

Of course, obituaries will be of interest to the family history researchers you serve. However, skilled use of the indexes to these products will yield far more of value.

> GenealogyBank's 4,500+ historical newspapers include letters, speeches, opinion pieces, advertisements, hometown news, photographs, illustrations and more. These unique primary documents go beyond names and dates, providing first-hand accounts that simply aren't available from census or vital records alone. With GenealogyBank, you'll get a glimpse into the triumphs, troubles and everyday experiences of your American ancestors.[2]

ANCESTRY.COM (FEE)

About 2,500 libraries subscribe to Ancestry Library Edition.[3] If you work in a small independent library, you may not have easy access. Ancestry Library Edition is not licensed for remote access. As a result it must be used in the physical library building. Ancestry offers a variety of packages to individuals, so it does not want the Library Edition to undercut these sales. The corporate genealogy of what is now known as Ancestry.com could easily fill a book by itself. A bit of that history is hinted at in a 2009 press release in which the corporate holding company announced it is returning to its roots by rebranding itself as Ancestry.com.

> Our company has a long and fascinating history, and we've been through several name changes over the years. But we started with Ancestry.com, and it now feels completely natural to let our company once again share the Ancestry.com brand with our flagship product," said Tim Sullivan, CEO, Ancestry.com. "We're proud that Ancestry.com has developed as the defining online brand associated with family history. Alongside Ancestry.com, we will continue to support our other brands, including Family Tree Maker, myfamily.com, MyCanvas, Rootsweb, Genealogy.com, Jiapu.com and of course, our international Ancestry sites.[4]

According to a press release in the summer of 2010,

> Ancestry.com Inc. (Nasdaq: ACOM) is the world's largest online family history resource, with more than one million paying subscribers. More than 5 billion records have been added to the site in the past 13 years. Ancestry users have created more than 17 million family trees containing over 1.7 billion profiles. Ancestry.com has local Web sites directed at nine countries, including its flagship Web site at http://www.ancestry.com.[5]

Fast Facts

Ancestry.com has more than 1 million paying subscribers. Ancestry.com aggregates a wealth of digital content that includes historical records, family trees, stories and publications, photos, and maps. Since July 2006, Ancestry.com members have done the following:

- Created more than 13 million family trees.
- Added nearly 1.4 billion people to those trees.
- Attached more than 30 million photographs, scanned documents, and written stories.

The Ancestry.com Historical Records Collection comprises the following:

- Census Records
- Immigration Records
- Jewish Family History Collection
- African-American Family History Records
- Birth, Marriage and Death Records
- Military Records
- Online Family Trees
- Newspapers
- International Records
- Photos and Stories[6]

It is difficult to contemplate doing serious genealogy research without having access to Ancestry.com. The census records alone can be worth the subscription price to anyone who is working on a family history at least two or three times a week. Demand for this database is so strong that some public libraries only allow a patron to have access for 30 minutes a day. While Ancestry is the Cadillac of genealogical databases, its DNA service does not enjoy that status among serious genetic genealogists.

Ancestry's search engine is its strength, but it is also sometimes a pitfall. The advanced search screen continues to evolve. At this writing, it offers more than 20 different places where search terms can be set to fuzzy or exact and includes almost that many boxes where parameters of the search can be added. In addition, it allows wild cards. In the hands of a trained professional this is indeed a powerful tool. At the same time, it can frustrate an amateur. It is too easy to add too much information or too much rigidity and therefore get no results or at least not the results sought. When editing a search or starting a different search it is easy to unintentionally leave search specifications in one box and carry it forward where it influences revised or new searches and thus compromises the results. Many times I have had to troubleshoot researchers' problems when they ask, "Why can't I get the same result I got yesterday? I put the same information in but don't get the same record." It's often as simple as placing a check mark or not placing a check mark in one of the many little exact boxes that control whether near matches should be displayed.

In spring 2010, Ancestry announced it was ceasing its print publishing activities, which had included *Ancestry Magazine* and two classic reference works. Most of the articles from the back runs can be found by choosing the "Article Archives" under the Learning Center tab of the website. *The Source: A Guidebook to American Genealogy* had been a standard reference source since the first edition published in 1984 when it received a "Best Reference" designation by the American Library Association. The content of the third edition (2006) has been digitized and is now available to Ancestry customers in wiki format.[7] This volume's 965 pages offer an encyclopedic coverage to most aspects of American genealogical research. It is known in some circles as the White Book.

That is to distinguish it from the *Red Book,* which also was published by Ancestry. The *Red Book: American State, County, and Town Sources* is organized by state and includes the following:

- Vital Records
- Census Records
- Internet Resources
- County Resources
- Background Sources
- Land Records
- Probate Records
- Court Records
- Tax Records
- Cemetery Records
- Church Records
- Military Records
- Periodicals, Newspapers, and Manuscript Collections
- Archives, Libraries, and Societies[8]

When the author toured Ancestry headquarters in Provo, Utah, in April 2010, it was interesting to see that every staff member who answered public inquiries in the phone bank had a *Red Book* and a White Book right next to their computer monitors in their workstations. Those who answer genealogy questions in libraries would be well served by having these titles handy either in print or digital format.

Ancestry is far too massive to describe fully in this Crash Course volume. Its aggressive acquisitions and regular uploads would make any static listing out of date before the ink was dry on the paper. However, patrons who want more in-depth coverage of the variety of resources available at Ancestry.com should be invited to explore George Morgan's *The Official Guide to Ancestry.com.*[9] Most researchers who visit your library do not know that parts of Ancestry.com are free. If you go to http://www.genealogybuff.com/ancestry_free.htm, you will find a hyperlinked list of 200 or so databases that are, at least at this writing, free at Ancestry.[10] To access these sites, researchers do not even have to sign up for a free trial.

CYNDISLIST.COM (FREE)

Cyndi's List is not a source of data. Rather, it is a categorized list of more than a quarter of a million links to other genealogical sites, many of which are data laden. Cyndi Howells told an interviewer in 1997

> that she once read that "the Internet is like a huge library with all it's book [sic.] strewn on the floor." With the help and encouragement from her husband Mark, she started to organize the genealogy section of this library in a helpful and unique manner.
> What makes this directory so different is the WAY that it is cataloged. Cyndi will dig deep into a single genealogy site and break it down into small, appropriately categorized links.[11]

This list has been a decade and a half in the making. At present, the biggest challenge to Cyndi Howells is to keep repairing all the broken links that naturally occur on the fast-evolving Internet. However, many genealogists also see the site as a challenge.

> It's intimidating: Cyndi's List is a massive online directory that has over 330 pages of links to websites related to genealogy. There are over 120 categories on four types of indexes, and each category contains an index for countless websites on that topic. So searching for what you need on Cyndi's List might at first seem unapproachable, confusing, and yes, even downright intimidating.[12]

Patrons can be referred to Rick Evin's "Using Cyndi's List for Genealogy Research: A Guide to Exploring the Largest Online Directory" for assistance in getting started with this massive gateway to genealogical information.[13]

FAMILYSEARCH.ORG (FREE)

FamilySearch is a family history service provided by the Church of Jesus Christ of Latter-Day Saints. In the vernacular, this church is generally referred to as the LDS or the Mormons, and its members "believe that family and marital bonds can last eternally. The primary purpose of their temples is to 'seal' or unite families together for eternity, and that their ancestors who have died may also be sealed and united with their spouse and family for eternity."[14] As a result of this belief, the LDS Church, through its FamilySearch arm, has invested untold billions of dollars in collecting, organizing, preserving and making available family history, family tree, and genealogy records and resources from more than 100 countries around the world.

Most of the services of FamilySearch are made available totally free to both church members and nonmembers alike. For those services for which there is a nominal charge, photocopies, shipping of microforms, and so forth, the fees are kept very low and probably do not recover the cost of providing the service. For example, their photocopy fees are consistently lower than those charged by public institutions. Nor do nonmembers need to worry about proselytizing. I, a nonmember, have been a regular user of many of the services of FamilySearch for at least three decades. The only time I was slightly uncomfortable was the first time I was asked to which *stake* I belonged as I entered a family history center. However, I quickly learned that the question was asked just so a tick mark could be entered in the gate count, which recorded how many members and nonmembers were being served that day. My church membership status has never caused me to be treated differently in any way.

Traditionally, the services of FamilySearch could be divided up into those available online and those available through its worldwide network of more than 4,500 local family history centers, which are technically branches of the Family History Library (FHL) in Salt Lake City. Since most of you have worked in library systems that have branches, you understand that some are bigger than others and some are able to offer a more complete array of services than others. Most of the branches are staffed by volunteers who are willing to assist but may not have the expertise to answer highly technical genealogy questions. Through these centers, researchers can often get free in-house access to subscription databases such as Ancestry Library Edition or Footnote. As a library worker serving genealogy researchers, you would do well to familiarize yourself with family history centers within a reasonable distance of your library. If you are familiar with the hours and services available there, you will know when a referral may be in the interest of your patrons. Although regional family history centers may have substantial print collections, most local centers have very small collections of such materials.

Interlibrary loan of microforms is the other big service offered by local family history centers. Any item that has been converted to microfilm or microfiche in Salt Lake City can be requested for a small fee. The items must be viewed in the local center and will be retained for the use of the requestor for several weeks. Through this service, a vast portion of the collections of the FHL can be viewed by researchers in their own communities. Researchers can explore the online catalog of the FHL from any Internet connection. Then items of interest can be ordered through the local branch family history centers. At this writing, the holdings of the FHL are not displayed when one does a search for an item in WorldCat, which will be discussed later. Thus, if you want to cover all your bases, a search of the FHL catalog must be conducted separately and in addition to a search for a book in WorldCat. The FHL will be discussed in chapter 9 on research fieldtrips.

Many useful online databases are made available by FamilySearch. These include data of two different types. The LDS Church has made very aggressive efforts to copy and preserve records from around the world that are of interest to genealogists. These are often copies of official records. As such, they are almost as good as the original records.

In some cases, these copies are now the only surviving records of events due to natural disasters, wars, or other destructive events that occurred to the originals after they had been filmed. These records should generally have good credibility for family history.

The other major resource accessible online through FamilySearch is a massive collection of genealogies submitted by church members and other researchers. There seems to be a widespread misconception that these records have been verified by expert genealogists in the LDS Church. While many of these pedigrees have been carefully researched and documented by competent researchers, some of them have been submitted by novices who have little research training or experience. In fact, new converts to Mormonism are required to submit at least a four-generation family tree if at all possible. So basically, these pedigrees are no more credible than those found elsewhere. The policy of consumers should be, "Buyers beware." While these pedigrees can be very helpful in suggesting possible avenues for investigation, they should never be accepted as absolute fact until the family historian has carefully evaluated each fact and weighed all available documentation.

When a researcher performs a search in FamilySearch generally the results will be grouped as follows:

1. Ancestral File (pedigree charts)
2. Census records (transcriptions and not the actual images)
   a. 1880 United States
   b. 1881 British Isles
   c. 1881 Canadian
3. International Genealogy Index for various regions of the world (individual events)
4. Pedigree Resource File (pedigree components but not in chart form)
5. U.S. Social Security Death Index (described elsewhere in this book)

FamilySearch is going through a very dynamic rebirth, which is much more extensive than a simple redesign of its web presence. By the time you read this book its online persona may look very different from what I am describing. Eventually, it will all have a unified appearance, but at this writing, it is still separated into distinct components that must be accessed separately:

1. familysearch.org (the original website).
2. labs.familysearch.org (new products under development).
3. wiki.familysearch.org (research guidance).
4. familyhistoryarchive.byu.edu (publications including thousands of printed genealogies that are out of copyright and have been digitized and can be searched by key word).
5. familysearchindexing.org (information on ongoing indexing projects being done by thousands of volunteers).
6. pilot.familysearch.org (an early version of a new site search engine). As this manuscript was being written, radical advances were emerging in the availability of digitized information.

FamilySearch is now the most comprehensive free location for genealogical research. When the new FamilySearch emerges, it will be an even more powerful tool for family historians.

FOOTNOTE.COM (FEE)

Footnote is relatively new, but due to its close partnership with the U.S. National Archives and Records Administration (NARA), which is discussed later in this chapter, this site has quickly become a major resource for family history researchers. Footnote.com was purchased by Ancestry.com in the fall of 2010. For now at least, the plan is to operate each separately. That means users must subscribe separately to each service. Footnote claims to already have more than a million members and bills itself as the number one website for historical content—71,460,737 documents in late 2010 and counting.[15] Although Footnote's best feature may be the digitization of records from the U.S. Archives, much other content of interest to genealogists is provided. Historic newspapers and city directories are just two of the types of additional information available.

GOOGLE.COM (FREE)

No matter how much you think you know about searching with Google, you will be able to learn some new tricks to teach your patrons or to save for yourself by reading *Google Your Family Tree* by Daniel Lynch.[16]

Although you may never have used these exact terms, you probably know that good database searching is the result of being able to find the optimum balance of *precision* and *recall.* Maximizing both of these simultaneously is difficult if not impossible. As one increases, the other generally decreases. Statisticians would say they have an inverse correlation. In this context, I am defining *recall* as finding everything possible that is relevant to your search. On the other hand, *precision* is not retrieving anything that is irrelevant to your search. As you can see, the perfect search would find everything relevant and nothing irrelevant. Such searching perfection is rarely achieved. Generally, the more you maximize one, the more you minimize the other. You can visualize a linear continuum that stretches from recall to precision (see Figure 3.1). One is not better than the other. It all depends on the purpose of your search.

The tools used to achieve greater recall or greater precision are based on the concepts of Boolean logic, with which you may be familiar.[17] The primary Boolean operators are AND, OR, and NOT. AND reduces recall but increases precision. *All* terms *and*ed together must be present. It is a way to narrow search results and impose greater specificity. On the other side of the equation, OR reduces precision but increases

Figure 3.1: Two opposing goals when searching.

recall. Only *one* (not all) of the terms *or*ed together must be present. It is a way to cast a wider net when you are not finding enough.

In the following example, the search terms "George" and "Washington" are entered. How they are entered makes all the difference. First, Google searches for "George" and finds more than 500 million records. That would represent the circle on the left in Figure 3.2. Then Google searches "Washington" and finds more than 980 million records—represented by the larger circle on the right. This is clearly too many for a person to look at. Even when both are included and enclosed with quotation marks (i.e., "George Washington"), 17 million records are found. In the diagram in Figure 3.2, that 17 million records would be represented by the dark area where the circles overlap. In Boolean terms, that would be a special kind of a "George AND Washington" search.

NOT terms reduce recall by eliminating false matches but increase precision. *Not*ed terms cannot be present. However, they may also remove matches that you would like to view.

When I mentioned that searching for "George Washington" was a special kind of AND search, what I meant was that it was a search for an exact phrase and as such was also a special kind of a proximity search. *Proximity* searching means that search terms must be next to or near each other to eliminate irrelevant matches and improve *precision*. One of my greatest frustrations is databases that will pick up one word in one article or part of a page and a second word in an entirely different article or part of a page. This most often seems to occur in automatic indexing of old newspapers and directories.

In a Google Search an asterisk (*) is used as a *wildcard*. This will retrieve additional results when any word or part of a word can be inserted in the place of the wildcard to increase *recall*. For example, when searching for an individual, inserting * between the given name and the surname will allow retrieval of occurrences when a middle name or middle initial are used in source documents. An example is shown in the next section.

Googlize Your Research

Any words listed in a Google search must be present—at least in some form. Listing too many terms can lead to no results (too much *precision* and not enough *recall*). Listing too few terms can lead to too many results (too much *recall* but too little *precision*).

Google uses AND and OR as Boolean operators, but they must be in all capital letters for Google to recognize them as Boolean operators.

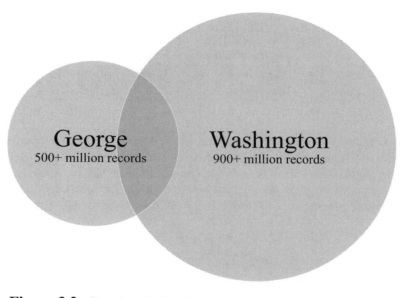

Figure 3.2: **Results of a Boolean search on George Washington.**

- The minus symbol (–) is the Google command for NOT. There must be no space between the minus symbol and the term being *not*ed.
- The tilde (~) is the Google command to find similar words. Again, there must be no space between the tilde symbol and the term being *synonym*ed.

Google also uses the following symbols:

"" to group words that must appear adjacent to each other. This can be an exact name or a phrase.

"*" as a wildcard, which means any word or phrase can appear at that spot in the document. For example, a search for "Barack * Obama" should return the following: Barack Obama, Barack H. Obama, and Barack Hussein Obama.

To experience a small taste of what you can glean from Lynch's book, complete the exercise in Figure 3.3. You really will not understand the full benefit of this exercise unless you try it with a surname of interest to you or to one of your patrons.

Remember, when you are doing an obituary search, your person's name may be listed in the obituaries of family members who precede or who follow them in death. So adjust your date range in such searches to cover the range of possibilities you wish to retrieve.

HERITAGEQUEST.COM (FEE)

HeritageQuest Online combines digital, searchable images of U.S. federal census records with the digitized version of the popular UMI Genealogy & Local History col-

"Googling Your Genealogy" Worksheet

Step 1: Pick a name and locations from your own family that you are interested in researching and enter the relevant information in the boxes below.

Given Name (First Name)	Surname (Last Name)	Town 1	Town 2	State

Step 2: Substitute your information from above in the Google search box of your browser as requested for the generic search query terms below and record the number of "hits" Google returns in the "Results" column. The **bold** term in the search query is the one to be added in that search. It does not need to be **bold** in your search box. Ignore the words in (parentheses) and [brackets] below. They are hints and not part of your search.

Search Query (in Google search box)	Results (# of hits)
surname (last name) [should be a single word in most cases]	
surname **family** [use the word "family"]	
surname family **state** [pick a state of interest]	
given name(s) surname family state	
"given name surname" family state	
"given name surname " **OR** "**surname, given name**" family state	
"given name * surname" family state	
"given name surname" OR "surname, given name" **OR** "**given name * surname**" family state	
"given name * surname" family state **~genealogy**	
"given name * surname" family state ~genealogy **town1**	
"given name * surname" family state ~genealogy town 1 **OR town 2**	
surname "new york" OR boston OR baltimore site:immigrantships.net	
"given name surname" filetype:ged	
given name surname born	
"given name surname" born	
"given name * surname" ~born	
given name surname obituary	
"given name * surname" obituary	
"given name * surname" obituary date range [e.g. 1890…1940]	

Figure 3.3: Exercise in refining a search statement. While this example uses Google, the principles apply to other databases.

lection and other valuable content. Like Ancestry.com Library Edition, HeritageQuest Online is marketed to libraries by ProQuest. Unlike Ancestry.com Library Edition, HeritageQuest is licensed to allow libraries to allow remote access to registered library card holders who use their library card barcode number as their password. About 7,000 libraries subscribe to this product.[18]

Generally, HeritageQuest is not sold directly to individual subscribers. According to ProQuest, the vendor for both Ancestry.com Library Edition and HeritageQuest to libraries, the collection consists of six core data sets.

> *U.S. Federal Censuses* feature the original images of every extant federal census in the United States, from 1790 through 1930, with name indexes for many decades. In total the collection covers more than 140 million names.

> *Genealogy and local history books* deliver more than 7 million digitized page images from over 28,000 family histories, local histories, and other books. Titles have been digitized from our own renowned microform collections, as well from the American Antiquarian Society via an exclusive partnership.

> *Periodical Source Index (PERSI),* published by the Allen County Public Library, is recognized as the most comprehensive index genealogy and local history periodicals. It contains more than 2 million records covering titles published around the world since 1800.

> *Revolutionary War records* contains original images from pension and bounty land warrant application files help to identify more than 80,000 American Army, Navy, and Marine officers and enlisted men from the Revolutionary War era.

> *Freedman's Bank Records,* with more than 480,000 names of bank applicants, their dependents, and heirs from 1865–1874, offers valuable data that can provide important clues to tracing African American ancestors prior to and immediately after the Civil War.

> *LexisNexis U.S. Serial Set* records the memorials, petitions, private relief actions made to the U.S. Congress back to 1789, with a total of more than 480,000 pages of information.[19]

NARA.GOV (FREE)

The National Archives of the United States is the official repository for all the documents created by federal government agencies in the course of doing business. Officially, it is the National Archives and Records Administration (NARA). The amount of information contained in this treasure trove is mind-boggling. Almost any of these records could, in the right context, have some value to some family history researcher. However, the records most requested according to NARA are probably those of the greatest significance to most genealogists.

- Census Records
- Military Service Records
- Immigration Records
- Naturalization Records
- Passport Applications
- Land Records
- Bankruptcy Records[20]

More will be said about many of these types of records in other chapters. A much more complete list of records of genealogical interest can be found on NARA's website.[21]

In October 2010, it was announced that the process for ordering documents from the U.S. National Archives had gone digital. You can now get access to the digitized documents you seek at http://www.archives.gov/order and get your digitized National Archives records faster and at no extra cost. The new Collector in Chief, as archivist David Ferriero calls himself, promises many other changes to make the agency service oriented in the 21st century.

In addition to the main location in Washington, D.C., there are regional facilities around the country. These branches each have some items in common with others such as the microfilms of U.S. censuses. In addition, they each house unique records such as records of naturalizations completed in U.S. courts in their region. You should know where the branch is that is closest to your community.

ROOTSWEB.COM (FREE)

RootsWeb is a totally free site, but it is hosted on servers owned by Ancestry. This tangled relationship provides many worthwhile services to the genealogical community. However, it also can be confusing. This partnership, along with one between Ancestry and FootNote, can cause unwary searchers to end up in a cyberlocation without being aware of how they got there. This occurs because search boxes for associated services are also prominently displayed on RootWeb's search page in locations that may confuse novice (or even experienced) searchers. Since RootsWeb is a free site, it must pay the rent some way. However, it is not always clear which of the search boxes will allow visitors to complete the free search they probably were anticipating and which boxes will lead to pay sites. Again, researchers need to beware.

RootsWeb grew out of one of the earliest mailing lists for genealogists, Roots-L. It was soon on its way to becoming the earliest megasite for family history researchers. Its grassroots growth was so phenomenal that it probably would have collapsed under the weight of its own rapid growth if corporate sponsorship had not emerged in 2000.

RootsWeb has many things to explore. Only the highlights of the site will be mentioned here. A more complete discussion can be found in *The Official Guide to rootsweb.com*.[22] The message boards and Listservs that were the features that launched the site still remain. They can be accessed in a variety of ways, but the most common approaches are through surname searches and locality searches. Your patrons may subscribe to lists whereby they will receive an e-mail every time someone posts information about the relevant surname or location. Alternatively, they can search the archives of those lists to look for information previously posted.

The WorldConnect feature is probably the most popular single part of RootsWeb. Through this part of the site, your patrons can find a huge number of pedigree charts that have been posted by other researchers. As I was writing this chapter, WorldConnect hosted 428,605 charts, which in aggregate contained 5,345,207 surnames and 616,470,429 names of individuals. Even when the obviously large amount of duplication is factored in, this is a very potent source of information. Some of the same files found here have also been uploaded to Ancestry.com's Family Tree section. However, some of the trees in WorldConnect allow downloading of information as a GEDCOM file for closer examination in the patron's genealogy software—a feature not allowed on Ancestry's site. Of course, as has been said elsewhere in this chapter, this kind of information is only as good as the individual who submitted it. Uploading it to the Internet does not improve the accuracy of incorrect information. So patrons should be advised to critically evaluate every aspect of such information.

WorldConnect can be searched independently or in conjunction with the other 45 databases on the site. Those other databases include the Social Security Death Index, which will be discussed in detail in a subsequent chapter. Also included are various state vital records indexes. Occasionally, one will be found that provides more data fields or more ways to massage the search results than the parallel database in parent site Ancestry.com. The California Death Index is one example of such a data set. But all the time you are searching here, you will encounter mouse overs and other enticements to tempt you to sites that operate for a fee instead of the free information provided at RootsWeb.

Also of note on RootsWeb are the links to various regional projects, which provide local databases of genealogical value. These will be discussed more fully in the following section.

USGENWEB.ORG (FREE)

The opening page on the website of the USGenWeb Project sets out its ambitious plan: "We are a group of volunteers working together to provide free genealogy websites for genealogical research in every county and every state of the United States."[23] Later, the site explains the organizational structure of this extensive grouping of local sites.

Although the basic unit of organization for The USGenWebProject is at the county level, State Websites include very important information as well, including such resources for postings of unknown county queries, family reunion bulletin boards, state histories, and maps showing the changing county boundaries, among others.[24]

It is easy to confuse the county resources offered by RootsWeb and those offered by GenWeb. This is in part because some county GenWeb project web pages have sometimes been hosted at RootsWeb. However, RootsWeb is just a hosting service for some of these local projects. GenWeb is a content provider, and most of the sites are hosted on servers other than those of RootsWeb. To make sure you have tapped into most of the resources for a county of interest to your patron, it would be best to try both sources. If there is only time to search one of these county sources, I would suggest GenWeb.

As is mentioned elsewhere, all-volunteer efforts like this can offer a richness of resources created by workers for whom creating the files was truly a labor of love. At the same time, you will find huge gaps resulting from the lack of such inspired effort. Also, the quality of the records will vary from some that appear to have been dreamed up to others that appear to be nothing short of perfection. That is the range of volunteer efforts. Willingness to help is not always combined with knowledge, skill, and attention to detail. However, often something is better than nothing. On the other hand, the more times information is transcribed, the more chance human error will find its way into the result.

You will want to get familiar with the GenWeb site for your county and perhaps for surrounding counties as well. Your own patrons may or may not be researching local ancestors. However, sooner or later you will attract visiting researchers who will need directions to local resources and sites. Incoming telephone, mail, and e-mail queries will be based on the assumption that you can provide such local guidance.

WORLDCAT.ORG (FREE)

As a library worker, you are probably already familiar with WorldCat.org. World-Cat is a service of OCLC, the world's largest cooperative database of library cataloging records. However, it may not have occurred to you to pass this resource along to your patrons. I am continually reminded that most genealogy researchers are very impressed that a tool like this can, if they enter their zip code, show them the closest library holding a sought-after book. As library workers, we tend to see this as a tool to locate an item being requested through interlibrary loan. In that case, geographic distance is not necessarily a determining factor as to which holding library to contact. However, for a genealogist, distance is often a more important consideration. Many of the items of interest are not available to be loaned outside the owning institution because of their age, condition, or frequency of use. As result, the researcher may have to travel to the item in order to benefit from it.

I tend to forget that it is called WorldCat for a reason: "WorldCat contains 54.1 million holdings from non-U.S. national libraries all over the world. In addition, OCLC plans to upload more than 250 million records from national libraries and major institutions into WorldCat in the coming year."[25]

In the summer of 2010, as I was writing this chapter, there were already 1,625,977,496 total holdings in this resource. To see how big WorldCat is at any given time, one can check the live counter at http://www.oclc.org/worldcat/newgrow.htm.[26] This counter can be an interesting site to show patrons. It is important to note that these numbers refer to holdings and not unique bibliographic items. Nevertheless, it is still impressive to be able to identify the physical location of that many items.

As noted elsewhere, not all libraries of interest to genealogists have entered their holdings here. These missing libraries tend to be specialized libraries, which are not embedded in a general library collection. Most depressingly, these nonparticipants include the coveted resources of the FHL and the National Society of the Daughters of the American Revolution Library. As a result, the online catalogs of these institutions must be checked individually, in addition to WorldCat, for hard-to-find materials. You will need to verify whether specialized genealogical and historical collections in your region have included their holdings in WorldCat.

LOCAL HISTORICAL AND GENEALOGICAL SOCIETIES

Until recently, I would have said that anyone helping family history researchers should become familiar with their local county historical society. Then I had the opportunity to broaden my horizons. You may be surprised, as I was, about how many such societies exist. Like me, you might expect states, counties, and large cities to have historical societies. However, small towns may have them as well. For example, there are at least 10 such organizations just in the northern part of San Luis Obispo County, California. As I am writing the first draft of this chapter, nine of them are cooperatively sponsoring a treasure hunt.[27] Check out what is available where you live and also in any communities in which the ancestors of your patrons lived. You never know what tidbit/treasure you may find about ancestors until you look! Be nice to the volunteers at these societies. Much of the relevant information may exist only in their heads or in files that only they have access to or know about. If your library does not already have an up-to-date list of such societies in your area, I would suggest that it would be time well spent for you to create/update such a handout for your patrons or to post to your library website. This is but one kind of resource that you should think about providing to your patrons.

I had an embarrassing experience along these lines more than a decade ago. At least it was embarrassing to me as a librarian. I was looking for a small rural cemetery where my great-great-grandfather was buried. I didn't think it should be hard to find. I knew the name of the cemetery and approximately where it was located. So I headed out that way. I stopped at several farm houses, but no one knew anything about the cemetery. I went to a small town just three or four miles away and stopped at the post office thinking a rural mail carrier would know. Later, I called the sheriff's office and several undertakers. No one could help. Finally, I called the county library. "Just a minute, let me check our card file." Voila! In their 3 x 5 card file there were precise instructions on how to find that cemetery. I had been within half a mile of it six months earlier and could not find it until I asked a library worker! So the moral of this story is that if your local historical or genealogical society has not compiled a list of local points of interest for genealogists for your local county GenWeb, you would serve your patrons well by starting such a resource. If they already have compiled such lists, these should definitely be on your speed dial.

Local historical and genealogical societies can offer rich resources for family historians. Be sure to encourage your patrons to check out the holdings and services of such organizations in any locale where their ancestors lived. Their collections and services vary so much that it will be necessary for you to carefully investigate each as you encounter them. Some are merely museums. Others sell detailed local histories and offer access to carefully created files such as obituaries, cemetery lists, and so forth. Since most of the societies are dependent on the efforts of volunteers, they do what the volunteers are interested in and able to do.

ON TO THE RESEARCH

With these resources now coded into your genealogical speed dial, we will begin our journey backward in time that will take us through the next several chapters. Let the research begin!

NOTES

1.   Tom Kemp, e-mail to the author, October 6, 2010.
2.   "About GenealogyBank," GenealogyBank, http://www.genealogybank.com/gbnk/information/about_us.html (accessed December 19, 2010).
3.   William Forsyth, personal communication with the author, June 25, 2010.
4.   "The Generations Network Becomes Ancestry.com," http://corporate.ancestry.com/press/press-releases/2009/07/the-generations-network-becomes-ancestry.com/ (accessed March 8, 2011).
5.   "Ancestry.com Helps Americans Discover Their Patriotic Roots with Launch of New Collection of Revolutionary War Records," Ancestry.com, http://corporate.ancestry.com/press/press-releases/2010/06/ancestry.com-helps-americans-discover-their-patriotic-roots-with-launch-of-new-collection-of-revolutionary-war-records/ (accessed March 8, 2011).
6.   "Fast Facts," Ancestry.com, http://corporate.ancestry.com/library/media/Fast%20Facts%20One-Sheet%202.19.10.pdf (accessed March 8, 2011).

7. Loretto Dennis Szucs and Sandra Hargreaves Luebking, *The Source: A Guidebook to American Genealogy* (Provo, UT: Ancestry Publishing, 2006), http://www.ancestry.com/wiki/index.php?title = The_Source:_A_Guidebook_to_American_Genealogy (accessed March 8, 2011).

8. Alice Eichholz, *Red Book: American State, County, and Town Sources* (Provo, UT: Ancestry Publishing, 2004), http://www.ancestry.com/wiki/index.php?title = Red_Book:_American_State,_County,_and_Town_Sources (accessed March 8, 2011).

9. George G. Morgan, *The Official Guide to Ancestry.com,* 2nd ed. (Provo, UT: Ancestry.com, 2008).

10. "Handy Tool: Free Ancestry.com Databases," GenealogyBuff.com, http://www.genealogybuff.com/ancestry_free.htm (accessed March 8, 2011).

11. Robert Ragan, "Classic Interview with Cyndi Howells, Creator of Cyndi's List," in *Treasure Maps Genealogy: Genealogy and Family Tree How-to Help,* http://amber-skyline.com/treasuremaps/cool-genealogy-stuff/cyndislist-interview.html (accessed September 3, 2010).

12. Rick Evin, "Using Cyndi's List for Genealogy Research: A Guide to Exploring the Largest Online Directory," Suite101.com, April 29, 2009, http://genealogy.suite101.com/article.cfm/using_cyndis_list_for_genealogy_research (accessed March 8, 2011).

13. Ibid.

14. Paul Larsen, *Crash Course in Family History,* 4th ed. (St. George, UT: EasyFamilyHistory.com, 2010), p. 85.

15. "Total Images: Millions Added Monthly," Footnote.com, http://www.footnote.com/documents/ (accessed December 19, 2010).

16. Daniel M. Lynch, *Google Your Family Tree: Unlock The Hidden Power of Google* (Provo, UT: FamilyLink.com), 2008.

17. Boolean logic is based on the ideas of George Boole, a 19th-century British mathematician.

18. Forsyth, personal communication with the author, June 25, 2010.

19. "Heritage Quest Online," ProQuest, http://www.proquest.com/en-US/catalogs/databases/detail/heritagequest.shtml (accessed March 8, 2011).

20. "Genealogists/Family Historians: Most Requested," National Archives, http://www.archives.gov/genealogy/ (accessed November 1, 2010).

21. "Research Topics of Genealogical Interest," National Archives, http://www.archives.gov/genealogy/topics/ (accessed November 1, 2010).

22. Myra Vanderpool Gromley and Tana Pedersen Lord, *The Official Guide to rootsweb.com* (Provo, UT: Ancestry Publishing, 2007).

23. "Keeping Internet Genealogy Free," The USGenWeb Project: Land of the Free . . . Genealogy, http://usgenweb.org/ (accessed July 25, 2010).

24. "About the USGenWeb," The USGenWeb Project: Land of the Free . . . Genealogy, http://usgenweb.org/about/index.shtml (accessed July 25, 2010).

25. "National Library Participation in the OCLC Global Cooperative," OCLC, http://www.oclc.org/us/en/worldcat/catalog/national/default.htm (accessed August 8, 2010).

26. "Watch WorldCat Grow," OCLC, http://www.oclc.org/worldcat/newgrow.htm (accessed August 8, 2010).

27. Lon Allen, "North County Historical Societies Sponsor Summer Treasure Hunt," *Tribune,* July 5, 2010, http://www.sanluisobispo.com/2010/07/05/1205243/north-county-historical-societies.html (accessed August 8, 2010).

CHAPTER 4

20th-Century Research

Generally, researchers should begin their family history research with their focus on some person/event in the 20th century. This follows Dr. Dave's Rule 1: "Start with what you know (yourself) and build back to what you don't know—step-by-step. *Don't skip steps!*" Unless the research is being done for a grade school project, those who are now walking into libraries to begin researching their family history have personal memories of their family in the 20th century. Therefore, that is where their research process should begin. It is now time to start verifying and documenting those memories. Again, reversing our normal thought patterns, we want to think backward. This means we want to start with the deaths of our departed ancestors and work back through their lives to their births.

VISUALIZE TIME LINES FOR AVAILABLE RECORDS

The following time line of some representative records of genealogical significance is provided as a means of giving you library workers (and your patrons) a way to visualize how to proceed, step-by-step, in the process of researching a family history. In the next few chapters, we will be examining some representative and commonly available resources by looking at segments of history roughly in chunks of a century at a time. The time line for the 20th century extends slightly into the 21st century. In subsequent chapters, we will look at resources that are available to explore the 19th century and then U.S. colonial periods. Of course, not all of your patrons will need the entirety of the time spanned by these time lines to trace their families back to their arrival in North America. However, my real intent here is to help you to begin to think in terms of the following questions: When would answers to those questions have been documented? What resources cover that particular time period? Finally, we arrive at the critical question, Where are those records housed?

With you visual learners in mind, Figure 4.1 is a time line of some of the resources for navigating backward through the 20th century. In no way is this intended to be an exhaustive list of the resources you should consult. It is only intended to provide a framework for you to find appropriate starting points for finding resources to answer patron questions. As I mentioned, it is not the intent of this book to teach you about every nook and cranny where information may be available to answer questions your patrons may bring to your desk. The intent is to give you entry points throughout American history where you can begin to find the names your patrons are seeking.

Ideally, we might want to start with U.S. census records. These records, when available, offer one of the most valuable resources for establishing the history of a family. Census records for the 20th century are particularly valuable to family history researchers. However, because of privacy concerns, they are not yet available to assist us backward through the last half of the 20th century. Therefore, researchers must turn to other avenues to bridge the gap back to the period for which U.S. census records are now available.

SOCIAL SECURITY DEATH INDEX (SSDI)

A great place to start documenting the life of ancestors who lived in the 20th century in the United States is with a good SSDI. Since Social Security death records are created by the federal government, the records themselves are not subject to copyright. Therefore, several different companies harvest them, create indexes, and provide access online. The most efficient of these companies usually have the information online and fully indexed within 30 to 60 days of the death. Since most Americans in the last half of the 20th century have had Social Security accounts, these records offer very comprehensive coverage of those who died in the latter 20th and early 21st centuries. Therefore, these records are an excellent starting point for documenting the lives of recently departed family members. In addition to giving us the date and often the place of residence at the time of death, they give us a date of birth and the state in which the person applied for the account. Therefore, these records exist for the vast majority of those who have died in this country for the last half century, and they will help us move backward through time as we seek the location of earlier events.

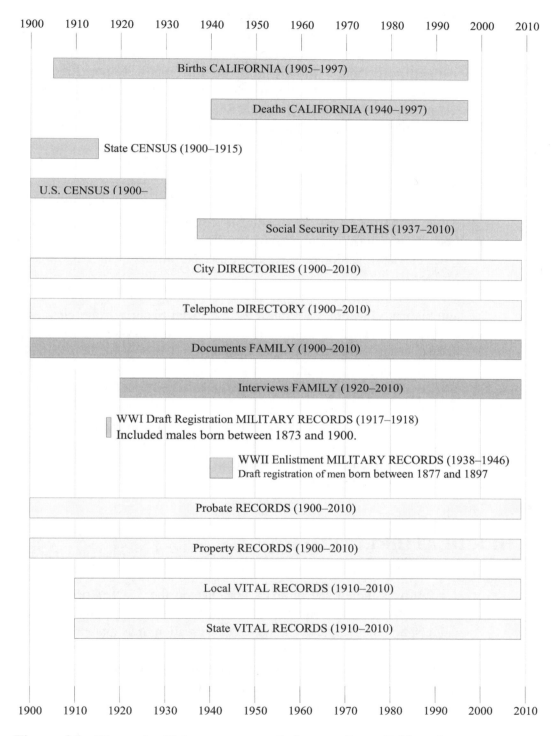

Figure 4.1: **Illustrative 20th-century records that may be available to document events that occurred at specific times.**

It is important to remember that although we tend to think of Social Security covering everyone, this is not quite true. About 98 percent of all workers are now covered, but membership has not always been so universal. After the law creating this program was signed by President Franklin Delano Roosevelt in 1935, a massive enrollment effort resulted in more than 35 million employees being registered by the time the program first started collecting taxes on January 1, 1937. Spouses and dependents were not included until 1940. At that time, the program only provided benefits to about half of all workers. For example, self-employed individuals like most farmers were not covered. After 1950 amendments were enacted, the program was expanded to cover almost everyone. So from that time on, SSDIs should cover virtually everyone who was in the workforce. Of course, at the time this did not include most homemakers. Another major exception would be some public employees: "More than six million public employees work outside the Social Security system, including roughly 1.7 million teachers in California, Illinois and Texas, and nearly two million employees of all types in Alaska, Colorado, Massachusetts, Nevada and Ohio, as well as Louisiana and Maine."[1]

Some online versions of SSDI allow family members of the decedent to almost automatically generate a request to the Social Security Administration. For a fee, a copy of the individual's initial application form will then be provided. Among other things, it may show the applicant's address and next of kin at the time of application.

One should not assume that persons not found in the SSDI must still be alive, although that is generally the case. A death record might not show up for a deceased individual for a number of reasons. Very few deaths that occurred before 1962 are included. If a person has a spouse, a minor, or an infirm dependent who is still drawing benefits on that account, the decedent may not appear. For other reasons why deceased individuals may not be included, read the "Social Security Death Index: Getting Started" page at RootsWeb.[2]

OTHER DEATH RECORDS

As was mentioned in an earlier chapter, the SSDI is only one of a number of records that tend to be created at or near the time of a person's death. For most individuals, no other single event leads to the creation of as many records as the death and burial process. Good researchers will take advantage of any and all of these that can be found. Even if the ancestor being traced is found in the SSDI and a birth date is found, researchers should collect data from as many of these documents as possible. Each of them has the potential to have an item not present in other records. This is also a good way to catch typographical errors. However, even if an item is repeated many times, that does not necessarily make it true. Information recorded at or near the time of death about the death itself can generally be relied on. It tends to be recorded by those who had firsthand knowledge of that event.

All other information, included with the actual facts of the death event, is not nearly as reliable. Just because something is written on an official death certificate does not make it true. It only means that the person who provided the information thought at the time that it was true. Check to see who the informant was who provided the information that became the official record. Generally, a medical doctor provides the cause and time of death. However, the rest of the information is usually provided by a family member. That person may be an extended family member who is trying to help out with arrangements. Sometimes that family member really doesn't know when or where the decedents were born or who their parents were. Even if they do know, the grief of the moment may lead to confusion. However, glean as much information as possible and move on to other sources.

U.S. CENSUS RECORDS

U.S. population census records are one of the best friends of family history researchers. As you probably know, these censuses have been conducted every 10 years beginning in 1790. The primary purpose of these massive efforts is to apportion political power among the states by determining how many members of Congress each state is entitled to. Over the decades, these censuses have expanded to collect much other information that the government thought it needed to know about its citizens. Although there is no evidence that our forefathers were prescient enough to foresee the needs of genealogists, the census records that have resulted have become invaluable to tracing our families back through time.

In a couple of decades, genealogists may look back fondly at the wealth of information collected in the censuses of the first half of the 20th century. Starting with the 1940 census, which is scheduled to be released about a year after this book is published, stratified sampling was used. As a result, many questions were only asked of a relatively few individuals. In this case, only those individuals who by chance had their names fall on lines 14 and 29 of the primary enumeration form were asked some questions that had been standard for several pervious censuses. For example, beginning in the late 19th century, everyone was asked where their father and mother were born. The answers were often important clues as genealogists traced families backward to the next earlier generation. This information was not thought to be important enough to ask of everyone in 1940. This could have happened because immigration had begun to subside or because statisticians convinced the Census Bureau that a stratified sample would yield reliable data. Possibly, the census was approaching the point at which it was judged that people would not comply if too many questions were asked. In any case, the census of 1940 was the beginning of the long form and the short form that became prevalent later in the 20th century. This trend is a reminder that the future needs of genealogists were not the primary concerns of these massive census efforts.

A major reason why census records are so valuable is that they are one of the few documents that treat the family as a unit. Most other official records are focused on an individual or on a married couple. Census records are focused on households. That usually includes two generations—parents and their children who are living at home. Sometimes extended family members are also living in the same household. In this case, three generations may be connected in a single document. Other extended family—siblings, parents, or married children—may be living next door or nearby. Sometimes the first clue to the maiden name of a female is when an older woman in the household is identified as mother-in-law to the head of household.

The information about the neighborhood is also valuable in getting a flavor for the environment in which the family lived. Was it a community of farmers, professionals, blue collar workers? Was the rent paid or the house owned by the family more expensive, about the same, or less than the average for the community? What was the ethnic composition of the neighborhood?

One of the biggest challenges of working with novice family researchers is to get them to absorb the totality of information about their family that can be uncovered in 20th-century census records. It will probably be easy to get them to notice the names and ages of family members. But these records have so much more to offer. Often the digital images of the census records make it difficult to realize what information is recorded because the column headings are difficult to read. That is why I have included templates of all U.S. census forms in the appendix of this book. Each census is different. Unless the column headings are taken seriously, researchers can easily jump to the wrong conclusions. For example, the 1930 census takers asked how old married individuals were at the time of their first (not necessarily their current) marriage. In earlier censuses, couples were asked how long they had been in their current marriage. It is very important to understand just how questions were asked.

Since U.S. census records have a 72-year delay in release for confidentiality reasons, the most recently released census at this writing is that enumerated in 1930. This creates a 72- to 82-year gap from the creation of the last publicly available census records to the time researchers are able to view them. April 2, 2012, will be an exciting day for genealogists as it will be the date of the release of the 1940 census. This time gap from the present back to U.S. census records can be bridged in part by SSDIs. The death indexes generally provide date of birth and the state in which the applicant lived at the time of application. Of course, for ancestors still living, this data will have to be collected more personally.

For individuals whose death records, or other information in hand, tell us they were born or were in a particular place in the United States before 1930 (soon to be 1940), we can begin to explore U.S. census records. Similar to SSDI records, almost everyone was enumerated in these census records. When they cannot be found, it is generally because the census takers wrote down what they thought they heard but may have misinterpreted it. Also, indexers sometimes misread the handwritten records of the census takers. When you do not find a researcher's relative in a census in which they were expected to be included, check to see if that census has also been indexed by someone else.

FROM FATHER'S DEATH RECORD TO THE BIRTHPLACE OF GREAT-GREAT-GRANDPARENTS IN ONE RECORD

Let's stop for a minute and help another patron who just wandered up to your service desk. He also wants to find out more about his family heritage. What he has with him are a fairly recent printed program for the memorial service for his father and the wedding band of his mother who predeceased his father. The memorial program gives the father's date of death as August 2, 2006, and the mother's wedding band has an inscription inside that reads "April 19, 1940." Here is one scenario of how you might help him get started in his research.

Reviewing the 20th-century time line in Figure 4.1, you mentally overlay the life span of the patron's father to see what resources from the time line might be helpful. The SSDI and the 1930 U.S. census records seem the most obvious starting places because you know the father was fairly recently deceased and that he was married in 1940. The latter is a good choice because he was, in all probability, more than 10 years old when he got married. You also consider the World War II enlistment records but discard the idea when the patron tells you his father didn't serve in the military.

Building backward, you check the SSDI to confirm the date of death of the father (see Figure 4.2).

This search confirmed the date of death and place of last residence. You were also able to confirm the date of birth listed in the memorial program. In addition, you noted a Social Security account number and the location where the father was when he applied for that account. Building backward in time, you then locate in Ancestry.com a U.S. census record for a Clarence Dowell of the appropriate age. This leads to a census record for Shiloh Township, Neosho County, Kansas, which was enumerated on April 28, 1930. (No index entries for this Clarence Dowell, or his father Arthur Dowell, were

Social Security Death Index about Clarence Dowell	
Name:	**Clarence Dowell**
SSN:	512-01-8084
Last Residence:	64601 Chillicothe, Livingston, Missouri
Born:	15 Mar 1913
Died:	2 Aug 2006
State (Year) SSN issued:	Kansas (Before 1951)

Figure 4.2: The Social Security Death Index confirmed the date of death of the client's father and provides additional information.

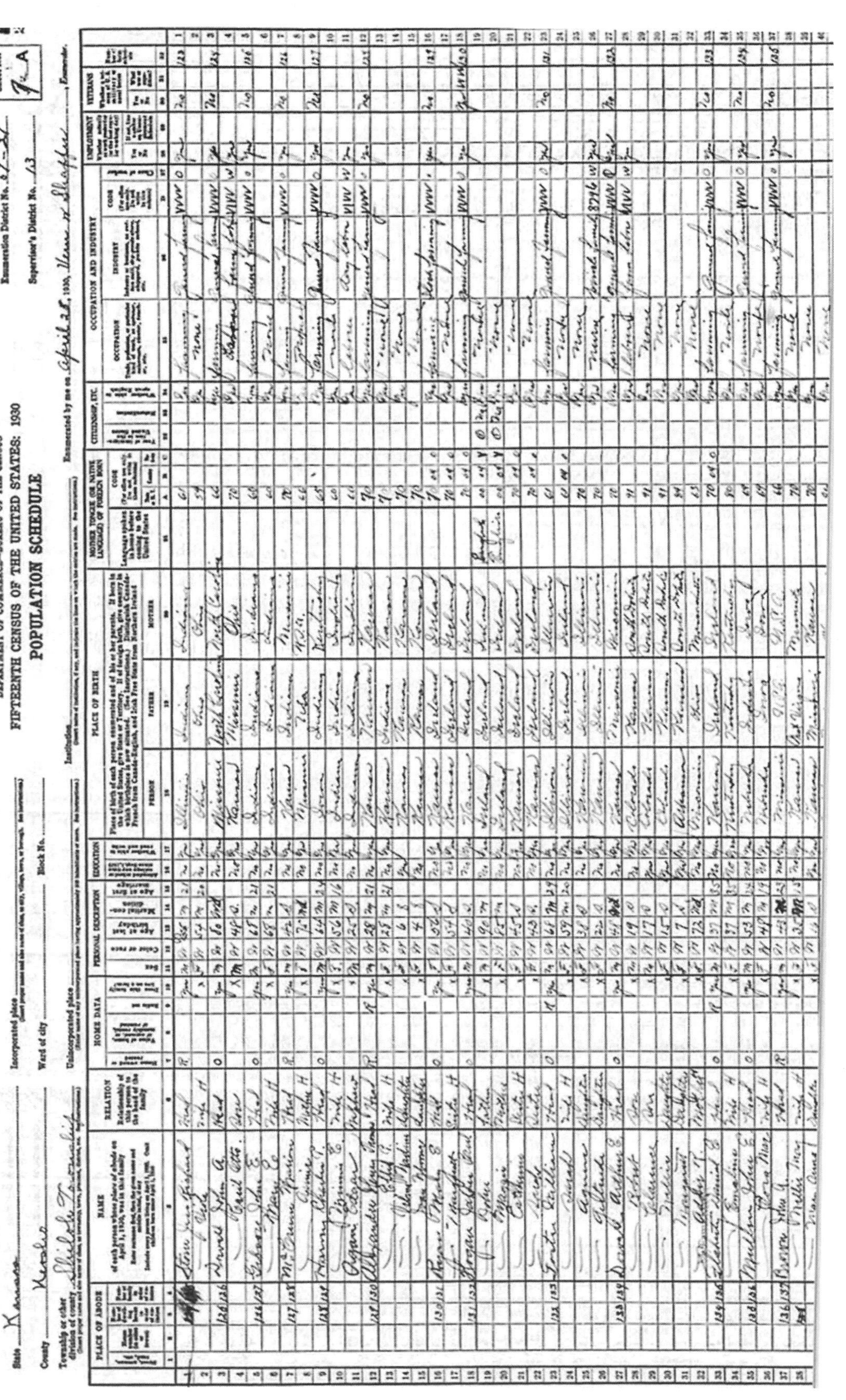

Figure 4.3: The 1930 census of Shiloh Township, Neosho County, Kansas, showing Clarence Dowell listed on line 29 with his family.

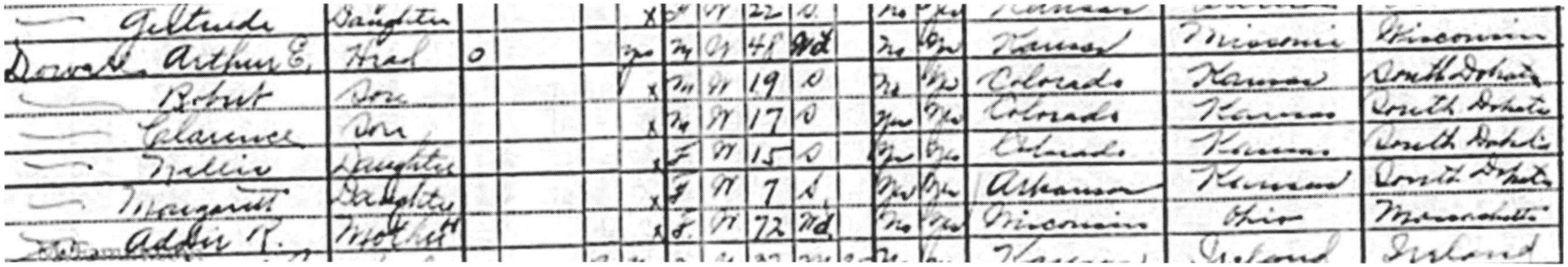

Figure 4.4: Blowup of a portion of lines 27–31 of Figure 4.3 showing Clarence Dowell and his family.

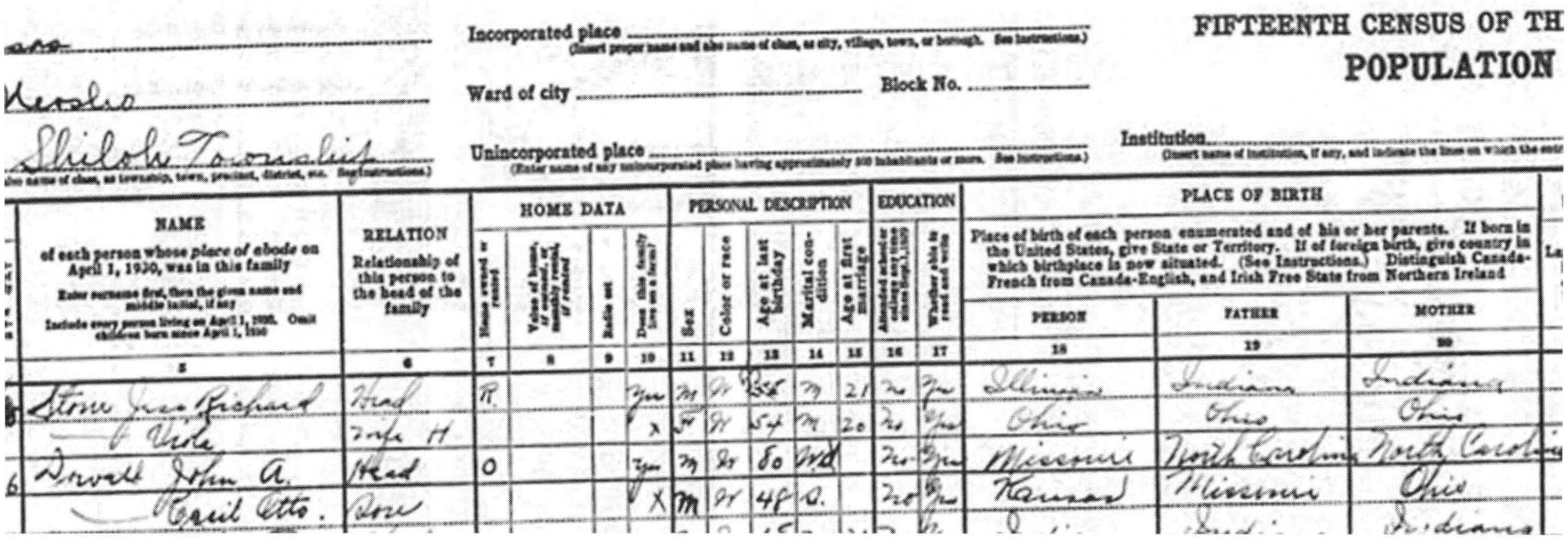

Figure 4.5: Blowup of line 3 of same census page showing "Uncle John" A. Dowell whose parents were born in North Carolina.

63

found in any 20th-century census record at HeritageQuest. The reason for some of this omission may become apparent later. However, if you do not find a person in a census, check any other versions of the same census that has its own index. The indexes are added by the vendors. They are not provided by the Census Bureau.)

From this one record, he was able to find out quite a bit about his family (see Figures 4.3 to 4.5). On this page is information about the birth location of his father, two of his grandparents, and two of his great-grandparents, although the latter fact needs a little support not found on this page. On line 29 of that record, Clarence is listed at the age of 17, which matches the date of birth given in the SSDI record. Note that it is important to record the actual date, not just the year, of the census enumeration. Clarence was listed as being 17 because he had celebrated his birthday about six weeks prior to the census. Living with him in the family unit were his father as head of household, his three siblings, and his father's mother who would be your patron's great-grandmother. She is listed as the mother of the head of household and was a 72-year-old widow. We are also told that she was born in Wisconsin, that her father was born in Ohio, and that her mother was born in Massachusetts.

From this record, you find that Clarence was born in Colorado. This matches what the patron had been told. Two of his three siblings also were born there. His youngest sibling, Margaret, was listed as having been born in Arkansas. Your patron had known all of these siblings as aunts and uncles, and the information shown seems to match the oral tradition of the family. The patron's grandfather was listed as owning his own home, and the record also tells us that the family lived on a farm. The census taker, Vern Shaffer, did not bother to list the value of any of the properties he visited that day, although his instructions were to do so. Shaffer also neglected to fill out columns 1 and 2 on the extreme left of the census sheet. In rural areas such as where the Dowells lived, these columns were commonly not filled in. In most towns and cities, the street name was written vertically in column 1, and the street number was listed in column 2. In large city buildings having several apartments, the census taker customarily only listed the street number for the first household in that building. Arthur was listed as a widower aged 48 who had been born in Kansas. The ages of his four children are also listed. Although the mother of the children was dead, we are told that she was born in South Dakota.

In this census and no other, families were asked if they owned a fairly new piece of technology called a radio. The Dowell family did not, but a few of their neighbors did.

One neighbor who was listed a few families removed from this one also had the name Dowell. When you brought John A. Dowell, aged 80, to your patron's attention, he recalled hearing stories about an "Uncle John" who lived on a nearby farm. Your customer speculates that this John was the older brother of his then recently deceased great-grandfather. Although this connection has to be supported by evidence not in this census record, it needs to be noted for some clues that will help push to family history back another generation or two. John was born in Missouri. Further investigation will be needed to establish that the patron's great-grandfather, John's brother, was also born there as the patron had been told. The record does show that John's parents both were born in North Carolina. Therefore, if he is able to establish from other documents that this is the "Uncle John" of family tradition, the patron probably will know where two of his great-great-grandparents were born. This is quite a lot of information to be found in a document that was not specifically focused on his family. Finds like this are why experienced genealogists love census records.

The right half of the census record, for which I did not give you a blowup, records other information that could be invaluable in many cases. There were columns for recording "Mother tongue (or native language) of foreign born," "Citizenship," "Whether able to speak English," "Occupation," "Industry," "Class of worker" [owner or employee], "Employment: Whether actually at work," and "Whether a veteran of the U.S. military or naval forces mobilized for any war or expedition." For the Dowells listed on this page, there is little remarkable information. Both they and most of their neighbors were native born and were also the children of native-born Americans. Perhaps that in and of itself is noteworthy. The single household in the neighborhood who were foreign born or the children of immigrants were Irish and were probably from Northern Ireland since they listed their native tongue as English. Since they lived on a farm, the Dowells were listed as employed as there was always work to be done. Placed in the context that this census was taken just a few months after Black Friday marked the official start of the Great Depression, this also may have been more important than it seems when first looking at the census sheet. None of them were veterans. Again, that may not seem to be important to note, but perhaps that will become important to know when we analyze our search later.

Let's stop for a minute and take stock of where we are and what our next step(s) should be:

1. Clarence:
   a. We can follow Clarence back to the 1920 census. In 1910 he would not yet have been born, but several of the family members shown in the 1930 census should have been listed.
   b. Make a note to check Clarence in the 1940 census when it is released in April 2012. At that time, he should still be single since his marriage, as recorded on his wife's wedding band, occurred two weeks after the official enumeration date for that census.
   c. Check list of compiled pedigree charts for Clarence.
      i. Ancestry.com
      ii. FamilySearch.org
      iii. RootsWeb.com
2. Arthur:
   a. Arthur should have been enumerated in the 1920, 1910, and 1900 censuses.
   b. He should also have registered for the WWI draft unless he already had enlisted. However, since he reported on the census record that he was not a veteran, we definitely will want to check for his draft registration record at some point.

    c. Check list of compiled pedigree charts for Arthur.
      i. Ancestry.com
      ii. FamilySearch.org
      iii. RootsWeb.com
3. Addie:
    a. We should be able to find her in the 1920, 1910, and 1900 census records.
    b. Check list of compiled pedigree charts for Addie.
      i. Ancestry.com
      ii. FamilySearch.org
      iii. RootsWeb.com

1920 CENSUS

The 1920 census found but tried to hide Arthur Dowell under the name "Aurthur Dalnell." This record was found using only "Arthur" with the default setting on the given name search in Ancestry along with the county and state set with the exact setting and spouse set at exactly "Mary." Of the four records that were returned, it was obvious which one was the right family. This was cheating a little since the search included information not yet discovered in our strict chronological backward march through time. At this time, Arthur was operating a farm and lived on that farm on Bentonville Road in Flint Township, Benton County, Arkansas. It may be worth noting that nearby Bentonville came to prominence a few decades later as the location of Sam Walton's first Five and Dime store, which was the beginning of Wal-Mart.

We find that Arthur's wife and Clarence's mother was named Mary. We confirm that she was born in South Dakota and note that her parents are said to have been born in Illinois and Wisconsin (see Figure 4.6). Note that the birthplace for Arthur's mother is incorrectly recorded as Missouri. The birthplaces of parents are one of the items most commonly listed incorrectly on census records. Age is another commonly incorrect item. In this case, Mary's age is given as 27—an age we will want to scrutinize when we find earlier records.

Pictures add another dimension to a family history. Ancestry.com is one of the sites that encourage subscribers to upload family pictures and scans of other documents to link to family trees. The picture in Figure 4.7 is of the Dowell family at about the time of the 1920 census. While the census record is interesting, it does not begin to bring the sense of connection that is engendered by photos like this one.

Looking at it, I wonder what is going through the minds and emotions of the various family members. I know from sharing family stories with a cousin that the two young boys in this picture would grow up with very different conceptions of what kind of man their father was. The oldest felt he could never meet his father's expectations, and the younger had a much more benign and positive view. What drew the two parents together when they came from such different backgrounds? How did Mary Jane Pierce, who was born with a silver spoon in her mouth, adjust to a mate who was a poor

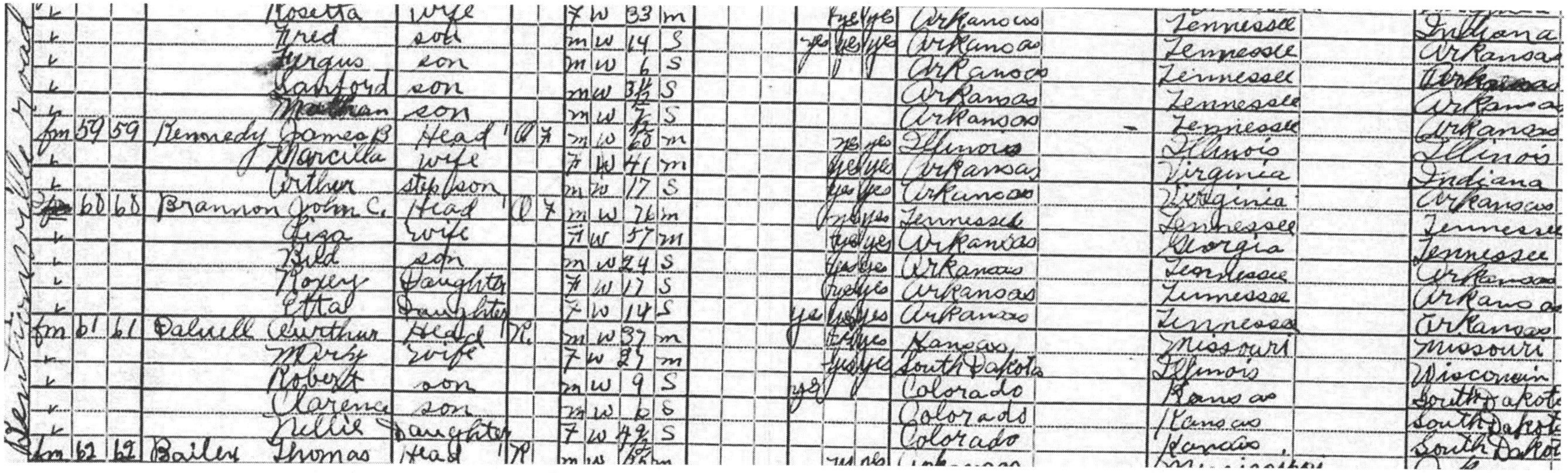

Figure 4.6: The 1920 census for Flint Township, Benton County, Arkansas, where the census taker misspelled both the given name and surname of Arthur Dowell and recorded him as "Aurthur Dalnell."

Figure 4.7: **From left: Nellie, Mary Jane, Arthur, Robert, and Clarence Dowell.**

ditch rider and later a dirt farmer who oral tradition said rarely wore shoes even in the wintertime? Mary had an aunt who in 1888 became one of the first female physicians in the United States and had other family members who traveled widely and abroad.

While pictures like this may bring pleasure to many when they are posted on the web, there is a certain protocol that is appropriate. Sometimes there are copyright issues as well. The picture in Figure 4.7 is just old enough that it barely escapes any concern about copyright. It was taken before 1923. However, in spite of that, good practice or even common courtesy would suggest that one should ask for permission before posting someone else's pictures on the open Internet. At the very least, one should acknowledge where items like this came from. This is a picture I posted on a password-protected website in 1999. It was a site for family members only. The person who uploaded it to Ancestry.com is usually careful to acknowledge the source of pictures, but that is not always the case.

Most novice genealogists have no idea that almost *everything* posted on the Internet or recorded in any other way is automatically covered by copyright law at the time it is expressed. For the last two decades, a person has not been required to apply for copyright to enjoy such protection. It is helpful, however, in seeking the most severe sanctions, if the owner of the copyright has formally made such an application. Certain items are automatically in the public domain and therefore free for use by us all. There are other exceptions when someone chooses to waive these rights. *Wikipedia* is an example where everything is shared with the understanding that any adaptation of content is to be shared in the same manner and that the origin of the content will be acknowledged.[3]

WORLD WAR I DRAFT REGISTRATION

Within weeks of the entry of the United States into World War I, Congress authorized a draft. Eventually, all men, regardless of their citizenship status, who were born between September 6, 1872, and September 12, 1900, were required to register. That comprised about 24 million men. Arthur Dowell, having been born in 1882, fell into the category of those called to the third and final registration in the fall of 1918. He was then included on a very comprehensive list of great genealogical potential. Patrons are usually impressed if you can show them the actual signature of their ancestors on the front of the card and their physical description on the back. Other little tidbits sometimes turn up as well as the expected information about date of birth, address, citizenship status, employer, and next of kin.

In the fall of 1918, when Arthur registered, he was employed as a ditch rider for the Arkansas Valley Sugar Beet and Irrigated Land Co. (see Figure 4.8). Ditch riders were about as popular as game wardens are now. It was their job to ride the irrigation ditches to ensure that no one was getting more that their allotted amount of water to irrigate their fields. Ditch riders were also responsible for removing debris that might have fallen (or been dumped) into the ditches and thus impede the flow of water.

1910 CENSUS

This record for Arthur E. and Mary J. Dowell and their one-month-old son Robert was almost impossible to find because Ancestry.com indexed it as "E. Dowell Arthur." It was really the fault of the census taker who did not list Arthur in the customary last name, first name format (see Figure 4.9). If the searcher did not know exactly where the couple was living, this record might not have been found. However, the Ancestry.com search engine is very flexible and can be massaged in many ways to overcome errors like this.

Once the record is found, it tells us that Arthur and Mary J. had been married during the previous year, and Mary's age on the census date was correctly reported as 19. Their son Robert P. was one month old. Note the coincidence that both of Robert's grandmothers (the far-right column in Figure 4.9) were born in Wisconsin. Arthur's mother really was born in Wisconsin as this census and the 1930 census recorded, and not Missouri as the 1920 census listed. I sometimes say, somewhat tongue in cheek, that I start believing information when I see it consistently reported in three consecutive censuses. This kind of inconsistency is why it is imperative to continue to research until all records have been reviewed rather than stop the first time information is discovered.

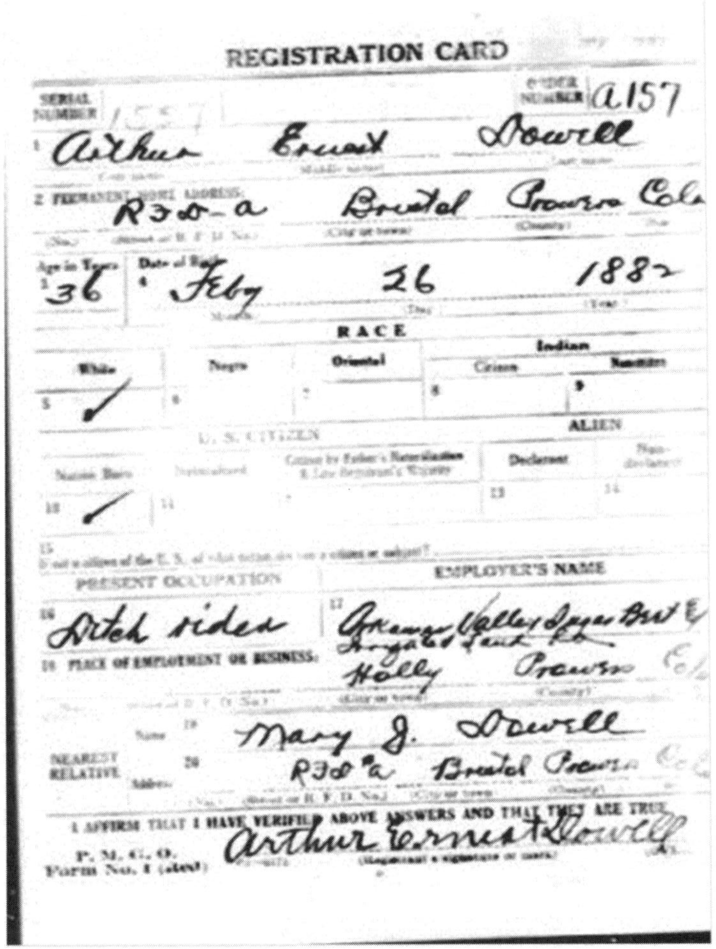

REGISTRATION CARD

SERIAL NUMBER 1557 | ORDER NUMBER a157

1 Arthur Ernest Dowell

2 PERMANENT HOME ADDRESS: R30-a Bristol Prowers Colo

Age in Years 3 36 | Date of Birth 4 Feby 26 1882

RACE

White	Negro	Oriental	Indian Citizen	Indian Noncitizen
5 ✓	6	7	8	9

U. S. CITIZEN Native Born	U. S. CITIZEN Naturalized	Citizen by Father's Naturalization Before Registrant's Majority	ALIEN Declarant	ALIEN Non-declarant
10 ✓	11	12	13	14

15 If not a citizen of the U. S., of what nation are you a citizen or subject?

PRESENT OCCUPATION: 16 Ditch rider

EMPLOYER'S NAME: 17 Amity Valley Sugar Beet & Irrigated Land Co

18 PLACE OF EMPLOYMENT OR BUSINESS: Holly Prowers Colo

NEAREST RELATIVE: Name 19 Mary J. Dowell; Address 20 R30 a Bristol Prowers Colo

I AFFIRM THAT I HAVE VERIFIED ABOVE ANSWERS AND THAT THEY ARE TRUE.

Arthur Ernest Dowell (Registrant's signature or mark)

P. M. G. O. Form No. 1 (Red)

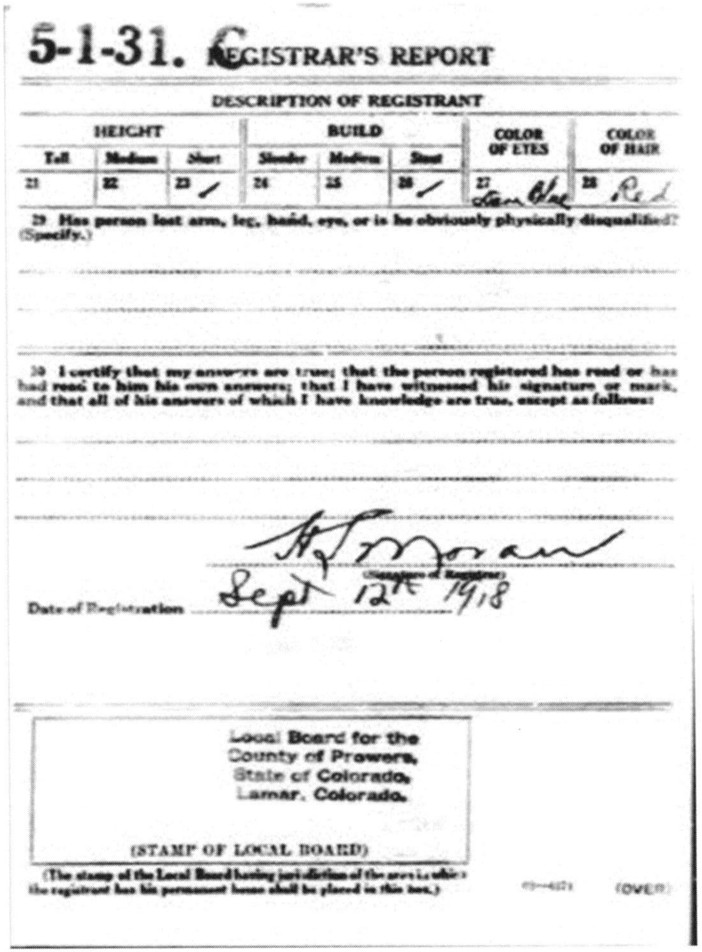

5-1-31. REGISTRAR'S REPORT

DESCRIPTION OF REGISTRANT

Height Tall	Height Medium	Height Short	Build Slender	Build Medium	Build Stout	Color of Eyes	Color of Hair
21	22	23 ✓	24	25	26 ✓	27 Lgt Blue	28 Red

29 Has person lost arm, leg, hand, eye, or is he obviously physically disqualified? (Specify.)

30 I certify that my answers are true; that the person registered has read or has had read to him his own answers; that I have witnessed his signature or mark, and that all of his answers of which I have knowledge are true, except as follows:

H J Moran (Signature of Registrar)

Date of Registration Sept 12th 1918

Local Board for the County of Prowers, State of Colorado, Lamar, Colorado.

(STAMP OF LOCAL BOARD)

(The stamp of the Local Board having jurisdiction of the area in which the registrant has his permanent home shall be placed in this box.)

(OVER)

Figure 4.8: Front and back of the registration card of Arthur Ernest Dowell created September 12, 1918, including his signature and physical description.

Source: Ancestry.com, World War I Draft Registration Cards, 1917–1918 [database online] (Provo, UT: Ancestry.com Operations, 2005), http://search.ancestry.com/iexec?htx=View&r=an&dbid=6482&iid=CO-1561787-0816&fn=Arthur+Ernest&ln=Dowell&st=r&ssrc=&pid=28554627 (accessed March 8, 2010). Registration Location: Prowers County, Colorado; Roll 1561787; Draft Board: 0.

1900 CENSUS

By 1900 we have traced Arthur Dowell back to where we first found him. We have traced him backward to the Kansas farm to which he had returned by the time of the 1930 census. The 1900 census has one little feature of special value to genealogists that is found in no other U.S. census. Census takers were instructed to record the month and year of birth for each person. This item may not be a primary source of evidence for this information. However, it may be as close as we are able to come for some individuals who were born in a time and location where births were not officially recorded or where such records were subsequently lost. This information turned out to be useful half a century later when individuals were beginning to apply for Social Security retirement benefits. It may not be the best source for establishing age, but it is certainly better than none. On this basis, we assume that Arthur ("Ernest A" according to Figure 4.10) Dowell was born in February 1882. This census also allows us to confirm that Arthur's paternal grandparents were probably born in North Carolina, which we have suspected since we found the previous record for "Uncle John" back in the 1930 census.

In this census, the family is hard to find because of an ink smudge and a census tabulator overwriting of the family surname. The indexer guessed the name was "Deafell." At least until this is corrected, it will be an easy record to find again because it is the only Deafell family in the entire 1900 U.S. census. Actually, this is the only record among the billions at Ancestry.com where that supposed surname appears. In some ways, using the Dowell family has been a poor choice for this book. My purpose is really to show you how easy it is to help people find their ancestors. However, three of the four 20th-century census records involving Clarence and Arthur Dowell have been problematic to locate. Usually, it is not this hard to find ancestors in census records. However, the records of this family have provided some teaching opportunities. They are an excellent example of why it can be very important to record additional information about where information was found in case someone needs to look at it again. The official way in which the 20th-century U.S. census records are documented follows a protocol shown in Figure 4.11. With this information, the record could be found again even without an index because these numbers are how the census records are actually arranged: "Enumeration districts are geographic areas assigned to each census taker, usually representing a specific portion of a city or county."[4]

Note that Addie/Adda, had given birth 10 times, but only 4 of those children are still living. The parents have been married 20 years. A similar question in the 1930 census had been asked slightly differently, so you need to pay attention to what question is being asked. Since the column headings are notoriously hard to read in these images, clean copies are provided in the appendix. More explicit lists of questions the census takers were supposed to ask and other instructions they were given are available.[5] In this census, the two oldest sons are listed by names other than the ones they used later in life. Arthur is listed as "Ernest A" and Ralph is listed as "Andrew R." This kind of

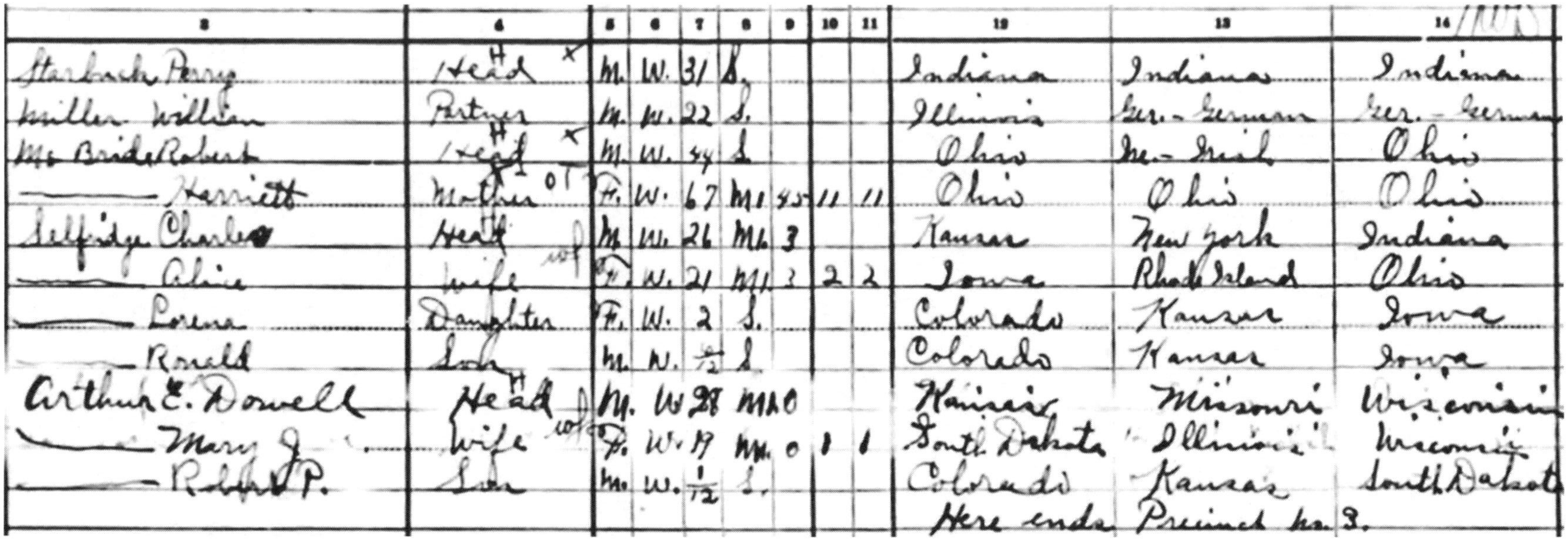

Figure 4.9: In this 1910 U.S. census record for Granby, Prowers, Colorado, the census taker listed "Arthur E. Dowell" rather than "Dowell, Arthur E." As a result indexers filed it as "E. Dowell Arthur."

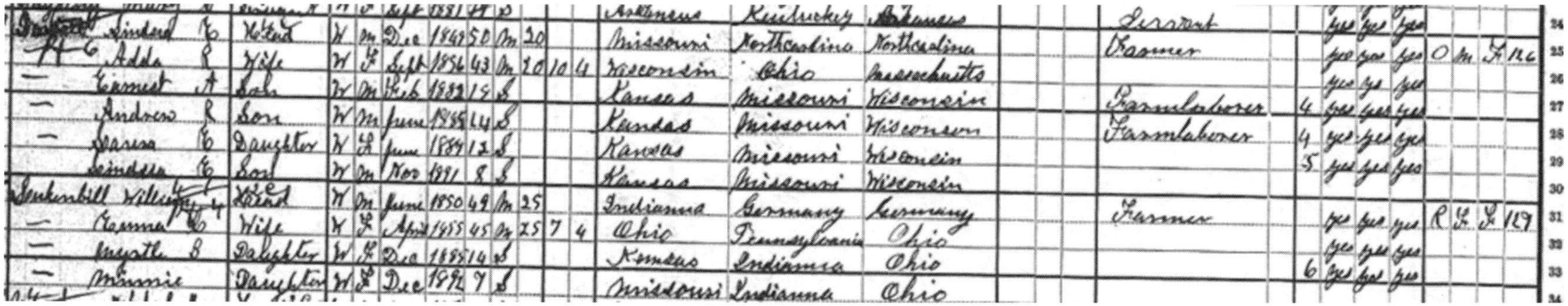

Figure 4.10: Census record for Shiloh Township, Neosho County, Kansas, for 1900 showing the Dowell family.

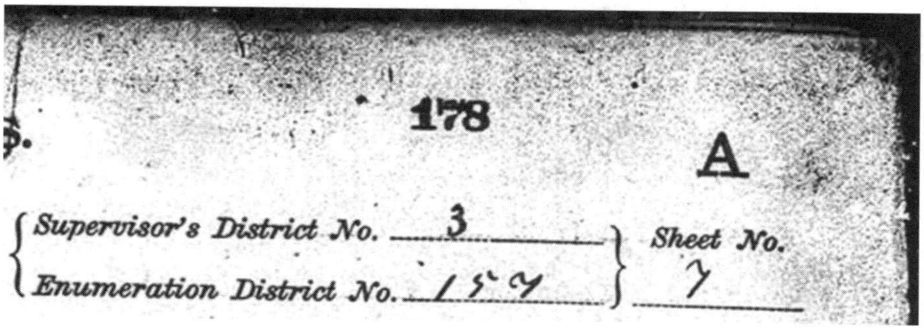

Figure 4.11: **Upper right corner of this census record showing that it is Sheet 7A of Enumeration District 157 of Supervisory District 3. The number 178 is a page number. Often two or more page numbers were assigned to a given page in the process of compiling the census results at different hierarchical levels of assimilation.**

switching is very common when you are trying to follow a family through the decades. It appears to be most common when one child is named after the father or mother. Then, in order to avoid confusion, the child is called by his or her middle name. However, that would not have been the case in this household.

This backward thinking gets confusing sometimes. I expect you and your patrons will want to write your family histories from beginning to end, but effective research is done backward. The journey we began with the death of Clarence Dowell in 2006 has now continued with the life of his dad to the beginning of the 20th century. We will look at 19th-century research in the next chapter. But first let's look at a resource that, like many other resources, can span both centuries.

COMPILED GENEALOGIES

Your patron might ask, "Why should I do all this work if someone has already done it?" That's a good question. Compiled genealogies are available on several sites on the Internet, on CDs, in printed books, and in other media. We all rely on the efforts of others when we do genealogy research. Even when we collect copies of official records or photograph tombstones, we are assuming that they got it right. Well, at least that they got it mostly right. Compiled genealogies are not much better and not much worse than other documents one could consult. They are at the very best secondary or tertiary sources.[6] But are they accurate? Are they useful? It depends on who compiled them.

If they were compiled by a careful and experienced genealogist, they could be better than original documents. How could they possibly improve on the original you ask? Any experienced genealogical researcher has encountered original historical documents in which some of the facts are known to be incorrect. If an experienced genealogist has conducted "a reasonably exhaustive search" followed by a thorough "analysis and correlation of the collected information"; resolved any conflicting evidence; and reached "a soundly reasoned, coherently written conclusion,"[7] the result could be better that the original in that specific instance. On the other hand, we know that every time humans copy information they introduce the possibility of typos and other errors of commission or omission. Such is the case with information found in compiled genealogies where sometimes the information being reviewed is the copy of a copy of a copy of a copy…

With all this in mind, I searched for public family trees that included a Clarence Dowell. There were a couple of brief items at FamilySearch, RootsWeb had eight trees, and Ancestry had six trees. It is highly probably that there was some overlap between the trees at RootsWeb and those at Ancestry.

I compared seven data elements in the six trees at Ancestry. I have no reason to believe such trees found in other locations would be better or worse. Figure 4.12 shows the data elements that I extracted from each of these trees.

Would it be in the interest of a library client to use this information? Absolutely! But which information? The spelling of the names was most likely to be correct. All six spelled Clarence Dowell correctly, and five of the six correctly added his middle name. All five that listed his parents got the right ones, although there was a difference of opinion about how the father's middle name should be spelled. For the purposes of this exercise, I decided to go with the way he signed his name on his draft card. Of the five that listed his spouse, four spelled her name correctly, and the three that listed a date of marriage got it right. All of the trees got the date of birth correct, but two got the place wrong. The only one to give a place of marriage got it wrong and also got the place of death wrong. However, it was the only tree to give the complete place of birth. Overall in my very unscientific sample, I judged 65 percent of the information to be complete and correct, 8.3 percent partially complete and correct, 6.7 percent incorrect, and 20 percent not offered. Removing consideration of the fields in which no information was offered, I adjusted my scores to 81 percent correct, 11 percent mostly correct, and 8 percent incorrect. So compiled genealogies can be helpful, but someone could be spending some wasted and perhaps cold days researching in Montana or Michigan if they relied on some of this information because Clarence Dowell never lived there and only very rarely passed through.

This was a quick trip backward though the 20th century that only used a very few of the available resources—primarily death records, U.S. censuses, and compiled genealogies.

Remember this is just an introduction. If the subjects of our search had been city folk, we probably would have made more use of both city and telephone directories. If your library owns or has access to such older directories for your region, these often can fill in the gaps by providing information about where your ancestors were between the decennial censuses or in the latter part of the 20th century when such records have not yet been made available. One thing that you should remember is that more recent census records can be made available in certain circumstances: "The Census Bureau

Data on Clarence Dowell, My Father	My Grandparents
Clarence Dowell BIRTH: **15 Mar 1913** - Powers, Menominee, Michigan, United States DEATH: **2 Aug 2006 - Chillicothe, Livingston, Missouri**, United States	**Arthur Ernest Dowell** **Mary Jane Pierce**
Clarence Ray Dowell BIRTH: **15 Mar 1913 - Prowers, Colorado**, USA DEATH: **2 Aug 2006 - Chillicothe, Livingston, Missouri**, USA MARRIAGE: **19 Apr 1940** SPOUSE: **Lucille Ruth Adams**	**Arthur** Earnest **Dowell** **Mary Jane Pierce**
Clarence Ray Dowell BIRTH: **15 March 1913 - Prowers, Colorado** DEATH: **2 Aug 2006 - Chillicothe, Livingston** County, **Missouri** SPOUSE: **Lucille Ruth Adams**	(Name Unknown) (Name Unknown)
Clarence Ray Dowell BIRTH: **15 Mar 1913** - Powers, Menominee, Michigan, USA DEATH: **2 Aug 2006 - Chillicothe, Livingston, Missouri** USA	**Arthur Ernest Dowell** **Mary Jane Pierce**
Clarence Ray Dowell BIRTH: **15 Mar 1913 - Bristol, Prowers, Colorado**, USA DEATH: **2006** - Livingston, MT, USA MARRIAGE: **19 Apr 1940** - MT, USA SPOUSE: Lucile **Ruth Adams**	**Arthur Ernest Dowell** **Mary Jane Pierce**
Clarence Ray Dowell BIRTH: **15 Mar 1913** -, **Prowers, Colorado** USA DEATH: **2 Aug 2006 - Chillicothe, Livingston, Missouri**, USA MARRIAGE: **19 Apr 1940** SPOUSE: **Lucille Ruth Adams**	**Arthur** Earnest **Dowell** **Mary Jane Pierce**

Figure 4.12: Information extracted from six public family trees posted on Ancestry. com. Information I judged to be absolutely correct is in bold font. Information extracted on August 7, 2010.

can release details from recent files in the form of official transcripts, but only to the named persons, their heirs, or legal representatives."[8]

CONTINUING THE BACKWARD JOURNEY

In the next chapter, as we continue our journey backward in time, we will examine some additional record types that can be useful in any period of historical research. While almost all of your patrons will follow very similar paths back through the 20th century, their paths will begin to diverge in the 19th century. Those researching recent immigrants will need the guidance of chapter 8 about taking research to another country. Others will not need this path until further back in the history of their family. People of color will also begin to seek other paths at different points in the 19th century as discussed in chapter 7. European Americans whose ancestors arrived in the 17th and 18th centuries will continue backward in time through chapters 4 and 5. All these researchers will face challenging but different tasks as they go further into the past to reveal the histories of their families.

NOTES

1. Mary Williams Walsh, "Payback Time: Maine Giving Social Security Another Look," *New York Times,* July 20, 2010, http://www.nytimes.com/2010/07/21/business/economy/21states.html (accessed March 8, 2011).
2. "Social Security Death Index: Getting Started," RootsWeb.com, http://helpdesk.rootsweb.com/ssdi/index.html#reasons (accessed August 2, 2010).
3. For another genealogist's take on this subject, see Dick Eastman, "Copyrights and Other Legal Things," *Eastman's Online Genealogy Newsletter,* http://blog.eogn.com/eastmans_online_genealogy/copyrights-and-other-lega.html (accessed August 2, 2010).
4. "Census Enumeration Districts," About.com: Genealogy, http://genealogy.about.com/cs/census_ed/ (accessed August 9, 2010).
5. "Enumeration Forms," Minnesota Population Center, *IPUMS-USA,* http://usa.ipums.org/usa/voliii/tEnumForm.shtml (accessed August 8, 2010).
6. "Primary, Secondary and Tertiary Sources," University of Pennsylvania Libraries, PORT: Penn Online Research Tutorials, http://gethelp.library.upenn.edu/PORT/sources/primary_secondary_tertiary.html (accessed August 8, 2010).
7. "The Genealogical Proof Statement," Board for Certification of Genealogists, http://www.bcgcertification.org/resources/standard.html (accessed July 6, 2010).
8. "Factfinder for the Nation: Availability of Census Records about Individuals," June 2008, U.S. Bureau of the Census, http://www.census.gov/prod/2000pubs/cff-2.pdf (accessed August 8, 2010).

CHAPTER 5

19th-Century Research

Nineteenth-century research in the United States starts out with a big challenge. How do you trace a family back from 1900 to 1880? That was a period when lots of families were moving around and many others were arriving from overseas. It would be interesting to know how many people were in exactly the same location in 1880 that they were in 1900. If the ancestors of your patrons were, then the two of you are ready to take the next step on your backward journey up their family tree. However, if they moved—even in the same city—your task is going to be a little more challenging.

If you have been paying attention, you may be wondering, "Why did he say 1880? Didn't they take the census every 10 years?" I must have forgotten to put you on the distribution list for the memo about the 1890 U.S. census. Well here is the condensed version. Due to a fire at the Department of Commerce in 1921, almost all of the census records for 1890 were destroyed. Only the listings for a little more than 6,000 persons have survived. These fragments are for individuals spread over 11 states.[1] As is often true in fires in records repositories including libraries, it wasn't fire that destroyed the documents. It was the mold, and so forth, that resulted from them getting wet as the fire was being extinguished.

In a 20-year gap like this, children can be born and move out of their parents' household, making it more difficult to establish the familial relationship between them. Families that move can fall off our radar screen entirely, making it difficult to establish that the family we found in the 1900 census is the same one we find in the 1880 census. If husbands die and wives remarry, the remnants of the family may be under completely different surnames in the more recent of the censuses. Of course, some of these challenges can occur even in a 10-year gap. However, a gap of two decades more than doubles the challenge.

1890 CENSUS SUBSTITUTES

A number of ways are available to bridge this 20-year gap. Of course, the easiest way is to jump directly to the 1880 census and hope you didn't miss too much of the family history that may have occurred in the interim. A number of states conducted their own enumerations in 1895 and 1885. Szucs and Wright provide a complete list of state censuses that have been conducted.[2] The variety from state to state and from one census to another in the same state is too great to try to describe here. In general, the state censuses conducted in the last half of the 19th and early 20th centuries were conducted in years ending with 5—in other words, halfway between federal censuses. More and more of these state census are being indexed and placed online at Ancestry. com. Other ways to bridge this gap are records constructed and maintained at the local level. These include city directories, land records, voter registration lists, and so forth.

EARLY 19TH-CENTURY CENSUS RECORDS

As you go back through the 19th-century censuses, you will notice that the amount of information recorded was less and less each 10 years until 1840 when there is a great change. At that time, they will become considerably less useful for genealogy purposes. From 1840 back to 1790, only the heads of households were listed. Note that I did not say that only men were listed. Women were listed if they were the head of a household, and men were not listed unless they were considered to be the head of a household. Actually, everyone is still accounted for even in these earlier enumerations. They just were not listed by name, and their ages were given within ranges of years instead of an exact age. One example of this is shown in Figure 5.1.

The 1830 census was the first in which standardized reporting forms (see Figure 5.1) were used. In prior enumerations, census takers were expected to provide their own paper, and this led to wide variation in the appearance of the results from one census worker to another.

On this census sheet from the 1830 census, "Peter Dowel" is listed as head of a family. Written horizontally on the extreme left of the document is his location, "Surry Co." Five lines below Peter is "Moses Calton" who is related to Peter's wife Mary. A researcher just viewing this document would not know that the Dowells and the Caltons/Carltons had a relationship deeper than just living in the same neighborhood. Further research, not shown in this book, will show that there was a

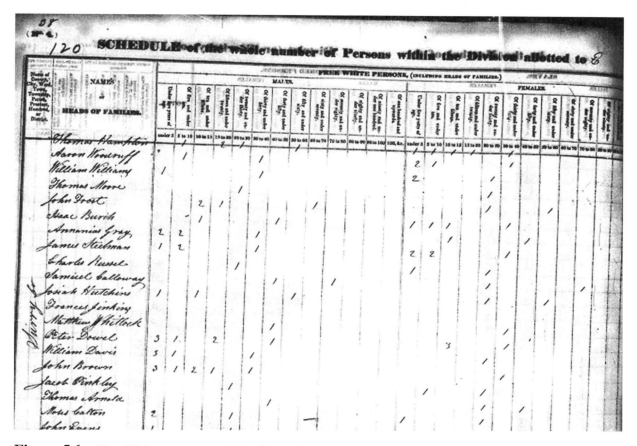

Figure 5.1: The 1830 census record for Surry County, North Carolina, including "Peter Dowel" and "Moses Calton."

blood relationship between Moses and Peter's wife Mary whose maiden name had been Carlton. At least two lessons should be learned from this record besides the information about the members of Peter's household. Good researchers always pay attention to who is in the vicinity of the family they are researching. When the same names start to show up repeatedly, this may be much more than a coincidence. Also, spelling was not as important as phonetics when documents were recorded in earlier centuries. Oral communication and oral tradition played a much greater role in daily life than did the written word. "Dowel" sounds very much like "Dowell" and "Calton" sounds very much like "Carlton," particularly when regional accents are taken into account. Also in days when not everyone knew how to read and write, census takers may have been more reluctant to ask people to spell their names. Instead, they may have been more likely to try to write down what they thought they heard.

What initially looks like stray marks or even scratches added by the photocopy machine is really the information about the approximate ages and genders of family members. A careful examination of the line on which Peter is listed will allow you to decipher the information presented in Figure 5.2.

About a fourth of the families in this North Carolina neighborhood owned at least one slave, and there was one family of six "free colored persons" living nearby.

Free White Persons	Males Under 5	3
"	Males 5 thru 9	1
"	Males 15 thru 19	2
"	Males 40 thru 49	1
"	Females 10 thru 14	3
"	Females 30 thru 39	1
"	Under 20	9
"	20 thru 49	2
"	Total	11
All Persons (Free White, Slaves, Free (Colored)	Total	11

Figure 5.2: Data that can be extracted from the 1830 census about the household of "Peter Dowel."

As you and your patrons try to trace ancestors backward through the decades, careful examination of these early 19th-century records can certainly eliminate many possibilities. A family that only had young girls of the age range you are seeking for a male ancestor certainly does not work. Likewise, the heads of households and their apparent mates can obviously be of the wrong age to fit into the family you are researching. However, it is rarely possible, unless the head of the family has an unusual and almost unique name, to confirm that you have the correct family just on the basis of one of these census records alone. Therefore, I am going to shift our attention to other kinds of documents that are particularly valuable to genealogists in finding 19th-century information about their ancestors.

LOCAL HISTORIES

Novice family history researchers are often tightly focused on following the names, as we have been doing so far through the early parts of the book. In addition to family histories, the other major source of information is local histories. Although these are unlikely to have large sections devoted to the persons who make up the family of interest, often individuals are liberally sprinkled throughout works that are written about the communities in which they lived. It may be nothing more than listing the ancestor among the 200 men who mustered in to a local regiment that was forming to take part in the Civil War.[3] Even this can document where an ancestor was at a particular time and suggest it might be profitable to look for accounts of that unit, for military service records, and for pension files.

Around 1876 there was a wave of patriotic fervor generated by the centennial of the Declaration of Independence. It became in vogue to write a history of counties (see Figure 5.3). If you notice in the 1870 census that an ancestor owned a significant amount of land or was listed as serving in a respected profession, look to see if that county has a surviving county history that was written a few years later. The year 1876 is not always an exact imprint date for all of these works. Some took longer to compile than others. Many of these were vanity publications. If you contributed to help defray the cost of publication, your sketch was more likely to be included. Others may not have been. Most tended to look for the good side of every biographee. Be all that as it may, these histories often give information on those covered that is hard to come by in any other source. Sometimes a very concise genealogy of the featured individual is given and even a portrait. If you are lucky, the local historical society, or some other public-spirited individual or group, will have created a name index to the original book.

Another wave of such publications was created by county history societies around the time of the bicentennial a century later. These were often created with two distinct sections of short articles. The first part was a collection of items about different local institutions (e.g., schools, churches, employers) and important events in the history of county. The second section was made up of short sketches about families in the community usually written by a family member. Sometimes, considerable information of a genealogical nature can be found in these sketches. Although these are usually indexed, be sure to check whether the numbers in the index refer to page numbers or to item numbers. Practice varied.

Other histories at varying times have been written with different purposes about institutions and events in a community, town, township, and county. They are very worthwhile for your patrons to investigate for any locality in which their ancestors spent any considerable amount of time.

LIBRARIES, COURTHOUSES, AND OTHER ARCHIVES

Before the Internet, genealogists conducted their research in libraries, courthouses, and other archives. Guess what? There is still a lot of information of genealogical interest in libraries, archives, and courthouses that is not on the Internet—at

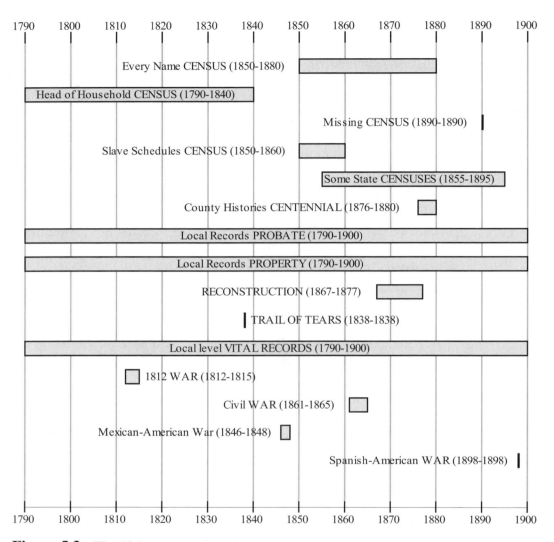

Figure 5.3: **The 19th-century time line of selected resources and major events of interest to genealogists.**

least not yet and not for the immediate future. Many of your patrons are afraid of the Internet, do not know how to search it effectively, or already suspect that not everything can be found there. So they may be ready to let you help them understand what one would expect to find in each kind of repository.

Since you work in a library, you probably know that libraries generally do not create the documents they make available to their patrons. They generally acquire books, newspapers, other periodicals and databases that have been produced elsewhere. The unique value of libraries to society is that they can pick and choose from a wide array of sources and location. We generally call it selecting the items that we believe will be of most value to those in our communities who use our libraries. Then we organize those items, create finding aids, and personally assist people to find and to use what they need. We could choose only things that support school curricula. We could choose only things that support local businesses. We could select only things that support genealogical research. Most libraries select all of these and much, much more.

On the other hand, you probably know an archive is the repository of documents that are created by an entity as a by-product of doing its business. The National Archives houses documents that were created by the federal government in the process of conducting its ongoing operations. In like manner, the archives of Ford Motor Company contain the documents created by that company in the course of business operations.

Courthouses are a special kind of archive because they are repositories of the records that document the lives of local people and events. In the 19th-century, records that documented the lives of our ancestors literally from cradle to grave and beyond were generally created and stored in courthouses. In some cases, these records or copies of them were forwarded to state archives. By the early 20th century, most vital records became available at the state level through agencies that might be called state archives, state bureau of vital statistics, state department of health, or other similar titles. Depending on local practice, they may have also been recorded at the county level as well.

FOUR IMPORTANT CATEGORIES OF ARCHIVAL RECORDS

Vital records make up the second of what have been called the Big Four of record types with which even semiserious genealogical researchers must become familiar. These four record types are as follows:

1. *Census records,* which we examined in some detail in the previous chapter, can exist at both the national level and the state level.
2. *Vital records* include official death, marriage, and birth certificates.
3. *Probate records* exist mainly at the county level and also can show family relationships.
4. *Land records* also exist mainly at the county level. They can show exactly where your family lived, when they bought and sold their land, how well off they were, and the identity of their neighbors.

Even though many of these records have been posted on the Internet in the last decade and a half, a majority of them remain only available in paper form in the location where they were created. Some of them have been abstracted and are available in major genealogical libraries and local history library collections that focus on those jurisdictions.

If your patrons are researching their 19th-century ancestors, sooner or later they are going to have to access the records of one or more county courthouses—but which one? The answer is not as simple as it may seem. Counties have evolved just as families have evolved over time. Some counties have genealogies as interesting and complex as those of most families. In the early 19th century, many counties still kept vital records, probate records, and land records in ledger books. Events were entered into the books chronologically as they were brought to the attention of the clerks responsible for recording them. This was roughly in the order that they occurred. These events, in the early days, may all have been recorded in the same ledger book, or separate books may have been used for different types of events. For now, I want you to focus on the physical ledger book itself. With that thought in mind, we will return to begin to answer the question posed in the first sentence of this paragraph.

County maps become very important in answering that question. Current maps are useful, but they must be compared with maps that are contemporaneous with the time the ancestors lived there. More specifically, it is necessary to find maps showing county borders at the time each event in the life of your ancestors might have been recorded. Confusing this matter even further, printed genealogies often confuse us when they give a county in which someone lived. We do not know if they have recorded the county in which that physical place (GPS location) is now located or whether they have recorded the jurisdiction of which that physical location was a part at the time events occurred in the life of that ancestor. It is entirely possible that the death record of a 19th-century ancestor could be recorded in one county, the marriage record in another, and the birth record, if it exists, in a third county. This was the ancestor who was born, lived all his life, and died in the same house on the same farm. How is this possible?

County lines changed over time. When Europeans first settled North America, they lived along the coast. As more and more settlers arrived, some of them had to move farther and farther inland to find land cheap enough for them to acquire it. This migration inland in search of affordable land also took place as younger sons, who did not inherit the family farm, wanted land of their own. The first counties were also organized along the coasts. However, initially their jurisdictions extended infinitely inland. They had no clearly defined inland boundaries. As new arrivals settled farther and farther inland, it became difficult to travel back to the coastal town or city to take care of official business. In response to this difficulty, new counties came into being. Remember my example in chapter 2 of 18th-century Rowan County, North Carolina, evolving into what are now 20 current-day counties in North Carolina and much of present-day Tennessee. Even if you know the current county in which your patron's ancestors lived in the 19th century, you may need to research further to find where the original copy of their records are on deposit. Traditionally, librarians and patrons have consulted either *The Handybook for Genealogists*[4] or *The Red Book*[5] to determine the genealogy of counties. However, a relatively inexpensive software program, *AniMap,*[6] easily can show these boundary changes year by year in a manner that is easy for patrons to comprehend. If your library does not have access to it, a free sampler of many states can be found in the Rotating Boundary County Maps feature at Family History 101 (http://www.familyhistory101.com/maps.html#county).

Christine Rose has written a good overview of courthouse research. One important thing she points out is to make sure it is really the county courthouse that is the repository of the records you seek. In some jurisdictions, some records have been recorded at the town level, and researchers must access them there. Once the appropriate repository has been identified, the patron will need to decide whether to visit it or to request assistance remotely. If the decision is to visit the courthouse (or town hall), Rose states, "preparation is the key" to whether the trip will be a success or a big disappointment.[7] She suggests that the first critical question is, Will they be open when the researcher arrives? Her book and those cited in the previous paragraph will be of great assistance to your patrons that you refer to local record archives to continue their research.

If you have a patron looking for a small out-of-the-way place or a place that seems no longer to exist, of course one can Google it. A more traditional resource that is often useful in finding 19th-century locations is the *Rand McNally Commercial Atlas.* This source, even in older editions, can often locate places that have been absorbed by annexation into another jurisdiction or have disappeared for other reasons. This source is the outgrowth of a tool originally created by railroad shipping clerks to help them locate places to which their customers wished them to make deliveries. Therefore, they often needed to be able to find very obscure locations. As a result, this commonly available atlas often can be useful when other sources have failed.

PROBATE RECORDS

Probate records are some of the most prized of those to be found in courthouses. Although these records are valued in any century, they become particularly valuable as research extends back into the first half of the 19th century as a way to tie children back to their parents when census records have ceased to list the names of all family members. Probate records also document how land and other property were passed on—generally from one generation to the next. In such documents, one can often find the married names of daughters of the deceased and sometimes the names of grandchildren as well.

Generally, we think of wills when we consider probate records. However, probate records come in many forms. The briefest of these only contain the date of the will and the date it was filed for probate. In the absence of a death or a burial date, such information narrows down the possible date of death. Still, it can be several years between the time ancestors wrote a will and the time they died. Likewise, it can be several years between the time of death and the time the will was entered into the probate process. More typically, these two events occurred fairly close together and can help establish an approximate date of death.

Another form of will record is an abstract, which typically lists the date of the will, the date it was entered into probate, and the names of those mentioned in the will. Some will abstracts are more complete than others and include the bequests that are made by the document. Researchers are much more likely to be able to find abstracts of wills in printed sources available in libraries or on the Internet than they are to find the complete wills.

Next comes will transcriptions. These typewritten versions are much easier to read than most handwritten originals. For that reason, they are often preferred by novice researchers. Actually, experienced researchers like to find them also. The handwritten scripts used even in the early 19th century often appear to be a foreign language to 21st-century eyes. However, these transcriptions are not primary documents. The transcribers, diligent though they may have been, may have misinterpreted some key words in the original documents. For that reason, it is always best to seek out the original document or at least a photographic reproduction. These photographic representations should contain the actual signature of the ancestors or show that they signed legal documents with an *X*.

However, the courthouse may have much more than a will in the probate package. The whole probate package can contain a detailed inventory of the assets and obligations of the decedent. It may be of interest to find out to whom the ancestors owed money and who owed money to them. If an estate auction is held, those who buy items may have familial or other ties to the deceased. If there are minor children, the probate package may document any arrangements made for their care. Even if the ancestors died intestate (left no will), the court may have commissioned an inventory of the estate, which could contain much information of interest.

Also remember Dr. Dave's Rule 9, "Don't ignore the ladies"—particularly when they survived their husbands. Very often they left an estate that needed the court's blessing to be settled. Figure 5.4 shows some of the documentation of the settlement of the estate of Mary (Carlton) Dowell, widowed wife of Peter. In this case, it appears that the children reached a settlement among themselves and then asked for the blessing of the court to recognize the legitimacy of that agreement. Mary had died more than two years before the date of this document. Even though Mary apparently left no legal will, the probate records link her to her surviving children. When in doubt, check the surviving courthouse records. Also read them carefully. In the record reproduced in Figure 5.4 it appears that Mary may have died June 29, 1870. Other contemporaneous documents record that it was January 29, 1870, of cancer. Can you see how one could get either interpretation from Figure 5.4?

PROPERTY RECORDS

As we are reminded in the *Oxford Companion to the U.S. Supreme Court,* "From the beginning of European settlement in America, land was the principal basis of wealth."[8] The possibility of owning land was the motivation for some of our ancestors to migrate to North America, and it also prompted them to follow the frontier as it moved west. This was particularly true for younger sons in cultures where the ancestral

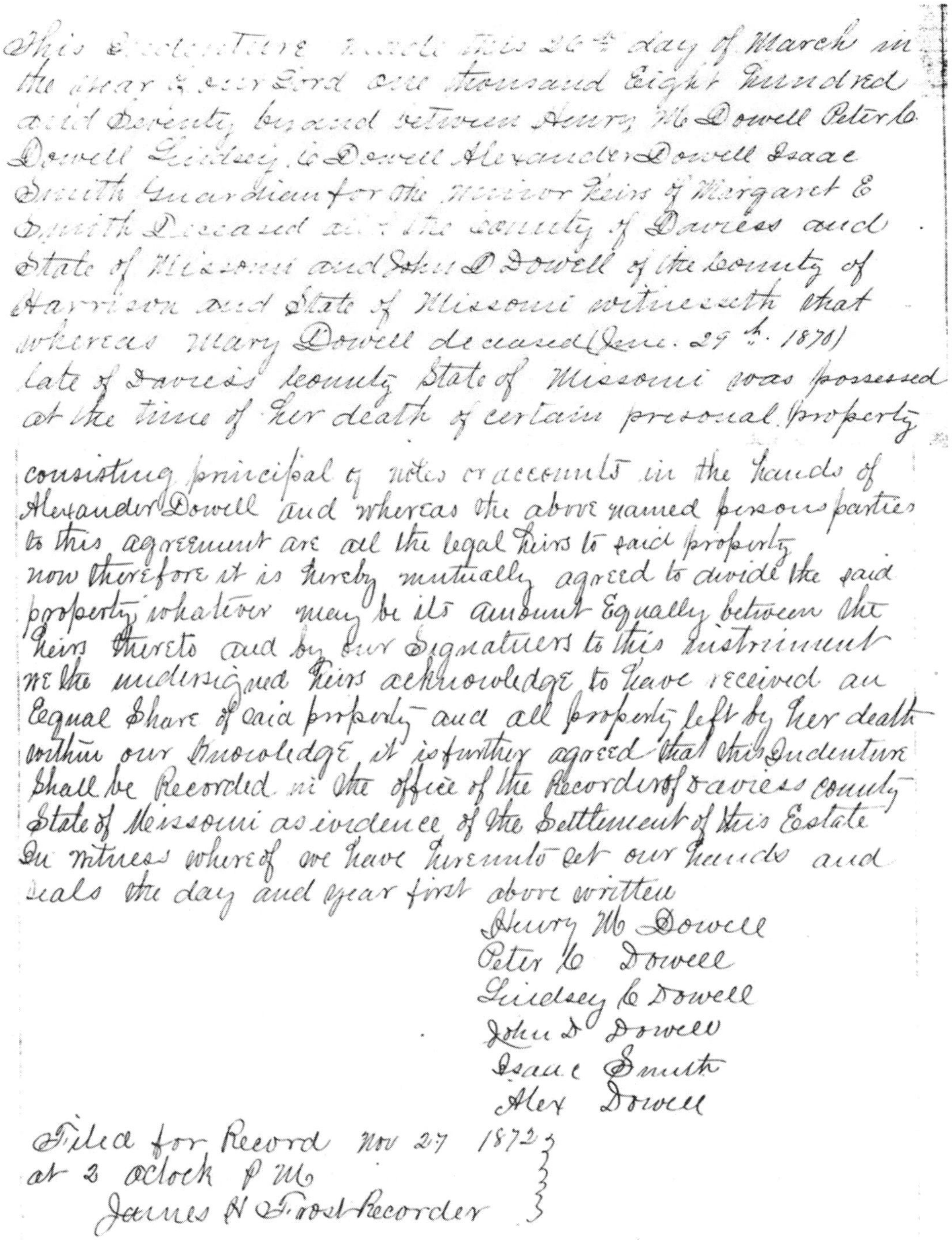

This Indenture made this 26th day of March in the year of our Lord one thousand Eight hundred and Seventy, by and between Henry McDowell Peter C Dowell Lindsey C Dowell Alexander Dowell Isaac Smith Guardian for the minor heirs of Margaret E Smith Deceased all of the County of Daviess and State of Missouri and John D Dowell of the County of Harrison and State of Missouri witnesseth that whereas Mary Dowell deceased (June. 29th. 1870) late of Daviess County State of Missouri was possessed at the time of her death of certain personal property

consisting principal of notes or accounts in the hands of Alexander Dowell and whereas the above named persons parties to this agreement are all the legal heirs to said property now therefore it is hereby mutually agreed to divide the said property whatever may be its amount Equally between the heirs thereto and by our Signatures to this instrument we the undersigned heirs acknowledge to have received an Equal Share of said property and all property left by her death within our knowledge it is further agreed that this Indenture shall be Recorded in the office of the Recorder of Daviess County State of Missouri as evidence of the Settlement of this Estate In witness whereof we have hereunto set our hands and seals the day and year first above written

Henry McDowell
Peter C Dowell
Lindsey C Dowell
John D Dowell
Isaac Smith
Alex Dowell

Filed for Record Nov 27 1872
at 2 oclock P M
James H Foost Recorder

Figure 5.4: From Book X, pp. 432–33, Daviess County, Missouri, Recorder's Office. Note that the ink in the first part of the document (bottom of the first page of the ledger) has faded more than the ink at the top of the following page.

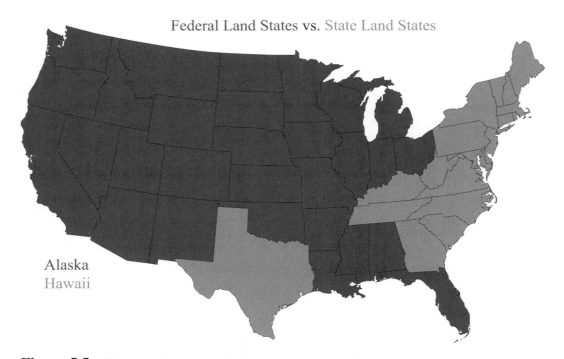

Federal Land States vs. State Land States

Alaska
Hawaii

Figure 5.5: The state land states in light gray and the federal land states in dark gray. Alaska is a federal land state and Hawaii is a state land state.
Source: "The Land Acquisition Process," FamilySearch Wiki, https://wiki.familysearch.org/ en/United_States_Land_and_Property (accessed March 9, 2011).

lands passed to the eldest. During much of the 19th century, inexpensive land could be had by those who migrated west (see Figure 5.5).

STATE LAND STATES

Two different systems of land allocation were used. Twenty states were *state land grant* states. These states were anchored by the 13 original colonies. To those, we can add the other New England states of Maine and Vermont. West Virginia was part of Virginia during much of the 19th century. Land systems were already well under way in Kentucky and Tennessee before the federal system was set up. Texas and Hawaii also had established land registration before they became states. To these 20 states, the federal government ceded the right to sell or otherwise distribute available land within their own boundaries. For ancestors living in these states, property records are located in these states—sometimes at the state level and sometimes at the local level.[9] The way property in these states was described in legal documents relied largely on landmarks visible at that time and the boundaries of the property then owned by others. This description of property boundaries often was not nearly as technical as the system described next, which was used when the federal government was in charge of distributing land.

A typical description for a small parcel of land might be as follows: "beginning with a corner at the intersection of two stone walls near an apple tree on the north side of Muddy Creek road one mile above the junction of Muddy and Indian Creeks, north for 150 rods to the end of the stone wall bordering the road, then northwest along a line to a large standing rock on the corner of John Smith's place, thence west 150 rods to the corner of a barn near a large oak tree, thence south to Muddy Creek road, thence down the side of the creek road to the starting point."[10]

Such descriptions are easier to visualize if one can pretend to be walking the boundary. Unfortunately, many of these landmarks, highly visible at that time, are no longer extant today.

FEDERAL LAND STATES

Thirty states were *federal land grant* states in which the initial assignment of land was under the control of the federal government. The first purchasers of tracts of land received a patent from the federal government.

The National Archives and Records Administration (NARA) is the official repository for records of the U.S. General Land Office (GLO), Bureau of Land Management, which document the transfer of ownership of public lands from the United States to private individuals. The case files generated by more than 10 million such individual land transactions are located in the National Archives.[11]

Fortunately, some of the information about this transfer of public lands to private ownership can be explored through the (GLO site without making a trip to Washington, D.C.[12] Figure 5.6 shows a record of one such 19th-century transfer. Only the first such transfer is recorded by the GLO. Subsequent transfers from one private party to another are only documented at the local level.

The legal description for this piece of property will allow motivated patrons to find exactly where these 80 acres are located. However, it will take a little bit of translation.

Most land in the 30 states, in which the federal government controlled the initial distribution of land, was divided up into townships. This system of describing land is much more fully described in a primer available at the GLO site.[13] In these states, townships were approximately six miles square (see Figure 5.7).

Remember that the property for which we found a land patent was in Section 32, which is in the lower, or southern, tier of the township in which it is located. Within the section, a different scheme is used to describe the location of the land (see Figure 5.8).

The hypothetical section shown in Figure 5.9 can be visualized as the Section 32 where the land granted to Peter Dowell was located. Often at this point, it is useful

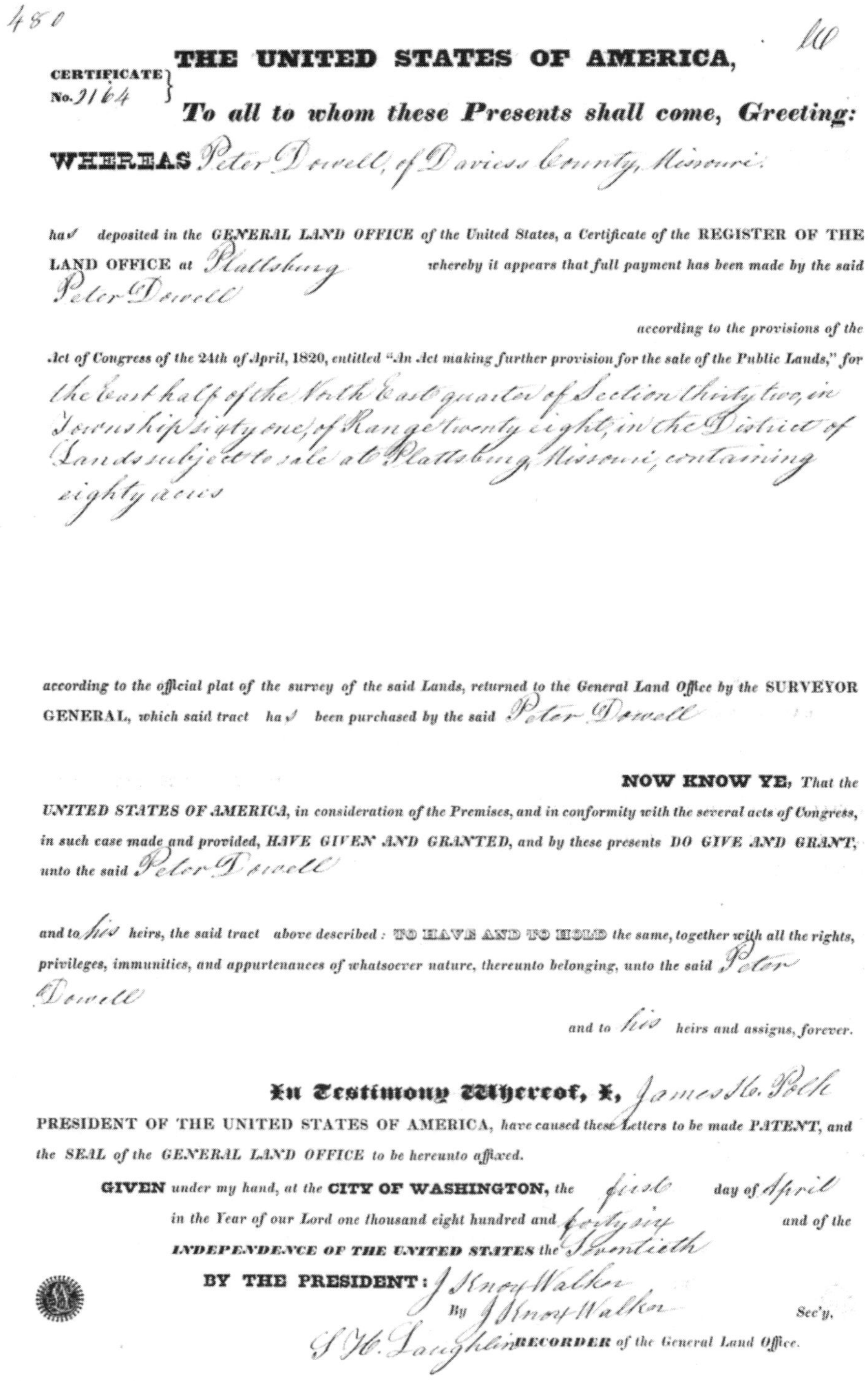

480 … 110

CERTIFICATE No. 9164

THE UNITED STATES OF AMERICA,

To all to whom these Presents shall come, Greeting:

WHEREAS Peter Dowell, of Daviess County, Missouri

has deposited in the GENERAL LAND OFFICE of the United States, a Certificate of the REGISTER OF THE LAND OFFICE *at* Plattsburg *whereby it appears that full payment has been made by the said* Peter Dowell *according to the provisions of the Act of Congress of the 24th of April, 1820, entitled "An Act making further provision for the sale of the Public Lands," for* the East half of the North East quarter of Section thirty two, in Township sixty one, of Range twenty eight, in the District of Lands subject to sale at Plattsburg, Missouri, containing eighty acres

according to the official plat of the survey of the said Lands, returned to the General Land Office by the SURVEYOR GENERAL, *which said tract has been purchased by the said* Peter Dowell

NOW KNOW YE, *That the UNITED STATES OF AMERICA, in consideration of the Premises, and in conformity with the several acts of Congress, in such case made and provided, HAVE GIVEN AND GRANTED, and by these presents DO GIVE AND GRANT, unto the said* Peter Dowell *and to* his *heirs, the said tract above described:* TO HAVE AND TO HOLD *the same, together with all the rights, privileges, immunities, and appurtenances of whatsoever nature, thereunto belonging, unto the said* Peter Dowell *and to* his *heirs and assigns, forever.*

In Testimony Whereof, I, James K. Polk PRESIDENT OF THE UNITED STATES OF AMERICA, *have caused these Letters to be made PATENT, and the SEAL of the GENERAL LAND OFFICE to be hereunto affixed.*

GIVEN *under my hand, at the* CITY OF WASHINGTON, *the* first *day of* April *in the Year of our Lord one thousand eight hundred and* forty six *and of the INDEPENDENCE OF THE UNITED STATES the* Seventieth

BY THE PRESIDENT: J Knox Walker

By J Knox Walker Sec'y.

S H Laughlin RECORDER *of the General Land Office.*

Figure 5.6: Land patent issued to Peter Dowell of Daviess County, Missouri, in 1846 for 80 acres of land located in the "East half of the North East quarter of Section thirty two, in Township sixty one, of Range twenty eight."

Source: Bureau of Land Management, General Land Office Records, Land Patent Search, http://www.glorecords.blm.gov/details/patent/default.aspx?accession=MO4420__.480&docClass=STA&sid=o32kvpsg.syd#patentDetailsTabIndex=1 (accessed March 9, 2011).

to read the legal description backward. First locate the northeast quarter in the upper right quadrant of the section. Within that quadrant, the east half of it would comprise the extreme upper right square of the entire section and the square immediately below it.

If we were in Washington Township, Daviess County, Missouri, the parcel described in the 1846 patent to Peter Dowell would be the square in the upper right hand corner of Figure 5.9 (which is subdivided into a 10-acre tract and a 30-acre tract in the illustration) and the square immediately below it labeled "SE^4 NE^4". The tract all added together made up the 80 acres covered in the original land transfer.

If we were to check the plat map maintained at the courthouse, we would discover that Peter Dowell actually had possession of the land about two and a half years before the federal records led us to believe (see Figure 5.10). Paperwork took a long time even back in the 19th century.

To follow what has subsequently happened to the ownership of this particular parcel of land, one would have to consult the property records maintained in the county courthouse in Gallatin, Missouri. If your patrons were to do so, they could follow every transfer of this property over the subsequent almost 17 decades and determine the current ownership of the land. In addition, your patron should be advised to check for other land that Peter owned nearby, the land owned by other family members, and who owned adjoining land where current or future in-laws are frequently found. From Figure 5.7 we can see that the Dowell's other immediate neighbors would have lived in Sections 28, 29, and 33 of their township. These sections are located to the northeast, north, and east of the property we have been researching. Sometimes such immediate neighbors can be in the next township, county, or even state.

When tracking 19th-century land records, you often come across the term *dower*. Often it is used as a *right of dower*. Although laws of different states varied, a wife often had the right of dower to property of a deceased husband in her lifetime as long as she did not remarry. In some old property transfer records, you will see that the wife was required to come before a magistrate and renounce her right of dower before the husband could sell property that might have become part of her right of dower should the husband predecease her. A similar document might be required to sell his land after his death because under common law a portion of the land—generally one-third—was deemed to be available for her support in her widowhood. These documents can help us verify that the woman was alive at the time the property was sold and whether she could sign her name or whether she made her mark in the presence of an official witness.

Typically, the right of dower entitled the surviving wife to one-third of the husband's estate. This is the reason why both husbands and wives are listed on deeds as sellers of property. On the other hand, husbands were not required to get the consent of their wives to buy property, so their names generally did not appear when land was purchased. Property records will continue to be important ways to trace the movements of ancestors as we continue back into colonial times.

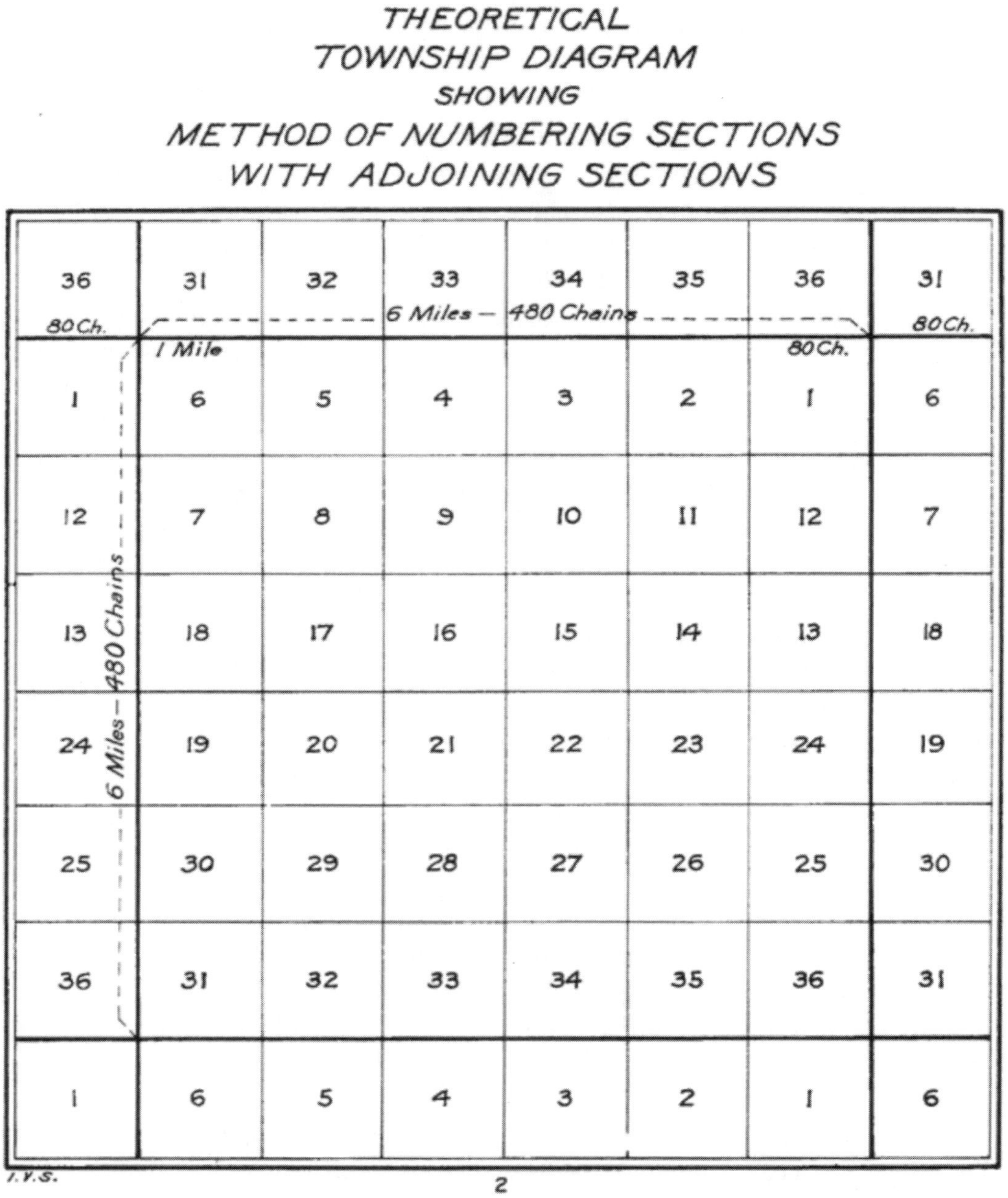

THEORETICAL
TOWNSHIP DIAGRAM
SHOWING
METHOD OF NUMBERING SECTIONS
WITH ADJOINING SECTIONS

36	31	32	33	34	35	36	31
80 Ch.	6 Miles — 480 Chains					80 Ch.	80 Ch.
1	6	5	4	3	2	1	6
12	7	8	9	10	11	12	7
13	18	17	16	15	14	13	18
24	19	20	21	22	23	24	19
25	30	29	28	27	26	25	30
36	31	32	33	34	35	36	31
1	6	5	4	3	2	1	6

I Mile — *6 Miles — 480 Chains*

I.V.S.   2

Figure 5.7: A theoretical township to demonstrate the numbering scheme for sections of land within it. Note that the numbering scheme for the sections within the township start in the upper right corner of the section and move to the left. Then the numbers wrap back and forth through the remaining part of the section.
Source: Bureau of Land Management, General Land Office Records, http://www.glorecords. blm.gov/images/page2_large.gif (accessed September 9, 2010).

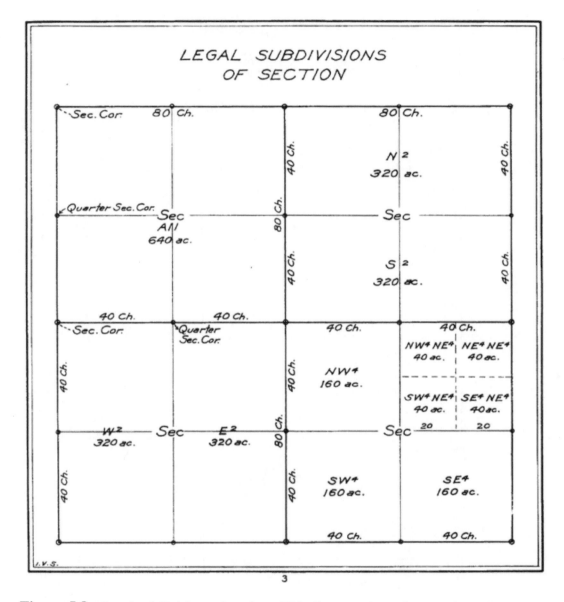

Figure 5.8: Legal subdivisions of sections. This diagram shows four sections. Each section contained 640 acres. Within a section, land was divided into quadrants of 160 acres each, and then each of those quadrants was further subdivided into 40-acre parcels.
Source: Bureau of Land Management, General Land Office Records, http://www.glorecords. blm.gov/images/page3_large.gif (accessed September 9, 2010).

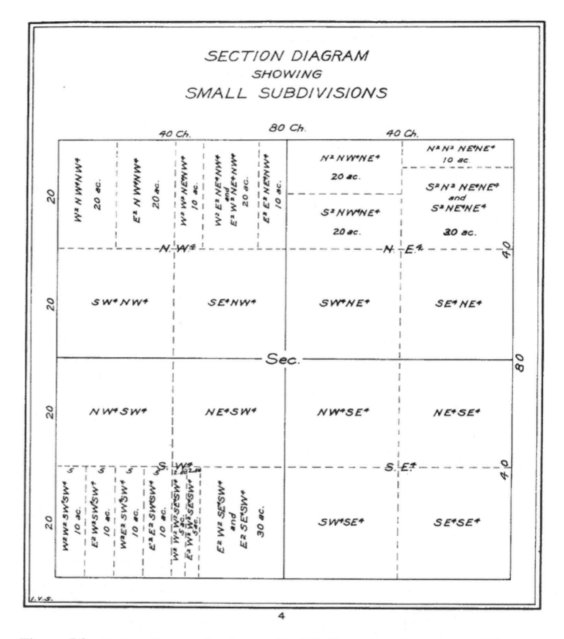

Figure 5.9: Section diagram showing small subdivisions. A single section could be subdivided in many ways, and the legal description even though precise can be very difficult to decode unless one is reading such descriptions on a regular basis.

Source: Bureau of Land Management, General Land Office Records, http://www.glorecords. blm.gov/images/page4_large.gif (accessed September 9, 2010).

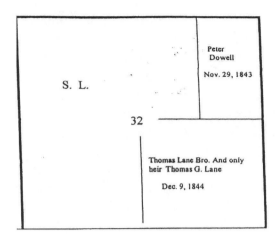

Figure 5.10: **Land ownership map of Section 32 in Washington Township, Daviess County, Missouri. Note that initially the Dowells had no neighbors to the west as that was still state land and that the Lanes bought land just to the south about a year later.**

VITAL RECORDS

Vital records generally were not recorded at the state level before the 20th century. For records of such events that occurred before that time, attention should be focused on the local level.

Twenty-first-century researchers need to keep in mind the times in which our ancestors lived. It is too easy to try to impose our own standards on them.

We must remember that the only vital events in our lives that require us to apply for official approval are marriage and divorce. We don't need to apply for a permit to be born, and we don't need one to die. The ability to clearly establish an exact date of birth for all citizens has taken on much more importance since the mid-20th century as Social Security annuities and other similar retirement benefits have become nearly universal.

When seeking vital records, always remember to check for church or other religious records as well as the secular records created by governmental bodies. The events surrounding births, marriage, and death often had much greater religious meaning than civil significance during segments of our history.

MILITARY RECORDS

Wars are the worst enemy of genealogists as they destroy records repositories. Simultaneously, they assist genealogists as they led to the creation of many records about our ancestors. Wars in the United States in the 19th century were no exception. Vast numbers of records were destroyed in eastern Virginia and other parts of the South during the Civil War. The British attack on Washington, D.C., during the War of 1812 is given as the cause of the disappearance of the 1790 U.S. census records for Delaware, Georgia, Kentucky, New Jersey, Tennessee, and Virginia.[14] On the other hand, muster rolls, draft registrations, unit histories, veterans' censuses, and pension applications often document the lives of ancestors who otherwise left few footprints.

The Civil War was responsible for the creation of documentation about men who lived and sometimes died in the middle of the 19th century: "Over 2.8 million men (and a few hundred women) served in the Union and Confederate armies during the Civil War."[15] Ancestry.com, Footnote.com, and local histories are good starting points for identifying those who served in this tragic conflict. Your first task is to help patrons identify periods of service and military units in which their ancestors may have served. Some may have had multiple enlistments in different units. A few served on both sides at different points of the war. Once men are tied to specific units at specific times, you should help your patron search for both online and in-print unit histories. If the ancestor served for any significant time, it may be productive to request his compiled military service record (CMSR) from the U.S. Archives. The NARA site is also a useful place to look for assistance in getting started in researching military records for any conflict involving U.S. troops. According to NARA, "Records relating to Confederate soldiers are typically less complete than those relating to Union soldiers because many Confederate records did not survive the war."[16]

> Most Union army soldiers or their widows or minor children later applied for a pension. In some cases, a dependent father or mother applied for a pension. The pension files are indexed by NARA microfilm publication T288, *General Index to Pension Files, 1861–1934* (544 rolls) which is also available online at Ancestry. com.[17]

Note that the pension records resulting from Civil War service extend well into the 20th century. Often Congressional acts granting pensions were only approved years and even decades after wars were completed and many of the eligible recipients who survived had died of their wounds or from totally unrelated causes. Revolutionary War pensions were still being applied for in the middle of the 19th century. From the genealogist's point of view, it is fortunate if the pension was denied or at least delayed. Those resulted in fat files of documentation. Claims that were immediately granted may have generated only a page or two of documentation.

> The pension file will often contain more information about what the soldier did during the war than the CMSR, and it may contain much medical information if he lived for a number of years afterwards. For example, in his pension file, Seth Combs of Company C, 2d Ohio Cavalry, reported: "...my left eye was injured while tearing down a building...and in pulling off a board a splinter or piece struck my eye and injured it badly...it was hurt while in the Shenandoah Valley near Winchester, Va. about Christmas 1864—a comrade who stood by me name Jim Beach is dead." In another affidavit, Seth said he "also got the Rheumatism while on duty as a dispatch bearer on detached duty."

To obtain a widow's pension, the widow had to provide proof of marriage, such as a copy of the record kept by county officials, or by affidavit from the minister or some other person. Applications on behalf of the soldier's minor children had to supply both proof of the soldier's marriage and proof of the children's birth.[18]

Once again, less information is available for Confederate troops than for those who served the Union.

NARA does not have pension files for Confederate soldiers. Pensions were granted to Confederate veterans and their widows and minor children by the States of Alabama, Arkansas, Florida, Georgia, Kentucky, Louisiana, Mississippi, Missouri, North Carolina, Oklahoma, South Carolina, Tennessee, Texas, and Virginia; these records are in the state archives or equivalent agency.[19]

SUMMARY

Nineteenth-century research presented different challenges and opportunities than that conducted in more recent times. U.S. census records became decreasingly useful, and other forms of documentary evidence were more at risk of suffering the rages of destruction due to the passage of time. In the next chapter, we will continue our trek backward in time into the colonial period.

NOTES

1. Loretto Dennis Szucs and Matthew Wright, *Finding Answers in U.S. Census Records* (Provo, UT: The Generations Network, 2001), pp. 39–40.
2. Ibid., pp. 83–84.
3. I have studied enough history to understand that it is called the War between the States in some quarters.
4. George B. Everton, *The Handybook for Genealogists: United States of America,* 11th ed. (Logan, UT: Everton Publishers, 2006).
5. Alice Eichholtz, *Red Book: American State, County and Town Sources,* 3rd ed. (Provo, UT: Ancestry, 2004); Ancestry's *Red Book* is now searchable online as part of Ancestry.com Library Edition.
6. Gold Bug Software, *AniMap Plus: County Boundary Historical Atlas for Windows,* http://www.goldbug.com/AniMap.html (accessed March 9, 2011).
7. Christine Rose, *Courthouse Research for Family Historians: Your Guide to Genealogical Treasures* (San Jose, CA: CR Publications, 2004).
8. "US Supreme Court: Land Grants," Answers.com, http://www.answers.com/topic/land-grant (accessed September 1, 2010).
9. The National Archives maintains a list of contact information for the various state archives, which can be viewed at http://www.archives.gov/research/alic/reference/state-archives.html (accessed March 9, 2011).

10. "Metes and Bounds," *Wikipedia,* http://en.wikipedia.org/wiki/Metes_and_bounds (accessed September 9, 2010).

11. National Archives and Records Administration (NARA), "Research in the Land Entry Files of the General Land Office (Record Group 49)," *General Information Leaflet* no. 67, http://www.archives.gov/publications/general-info-leaflets/67.html#intro (accessed September 8, 2010).

12. Bureau of Land Management, General Land Office Records, Land Patent Search, http://www.glorecords.blm.gov/search/default.aspx#searchTabIndex=0&searchBy TypeIndex=0 (accessed March 9, 2011).

13. "General Land Office Primer of Instructive Information Relative to Legal Subdivisions and Plats of Public Land Surveys, 1921," prepared under direction of I. P. Berthong, chief of Drafting Div., Bureau of Land Management, General Land Office Records, http://www.glorecords.blm.gov/visitors/PLSS.asp (accessed September 9, 2010).

14. Szucs and Wright, *Finding Answers in U.S. Census Records,* p. 11.

15. "Civil War Records," NARA, http://www.archives.gov/genealogy/military/civil-war/index.html (accessed September 10, 2010).

16. Ibid.

17. Ibid.

18. Ibid.

19. Ibid.

CHAPTER 6

Colonial Research

For your patrons who have ancestors living in colonial North America the focus for their research now must turn almost completely to the local level. U.S. census records are no longer available. This also means more variation from one region to another. As shown in Figure 6.1, many countries besides Great Britain controlled parts of what became the United States for significant periods of time prior to 1800. If your patrons are researching ancestors who lived in those regions at the appropriate times, this needs to be factored into their research plans.

Even within British North America, there were perceivable regional differences. Social historian David Hackett Fischer identified four distinct patterns of folkways. He traced these back to regional differences found in the regions of the British Isles from which the colonists originated.[1] His thesis, which he detailed in almost 1,000 pages, was that regional differences were transported across the Atlantic and continued in America. According to reviewer Nelson Rosit,

> Fischer brings back from recent oblivion the colorful regional stereotypes of American history. New Englanders really were puritanical; Southern gentlemen genuine aristocrats; Quakers were very pious; and Southern highland clans feuded as they had in the old country.
> According to Fischer, the foundation of American culture was formed from four mass emigrations from four different regions of Britain by four different socio-religious groups. New England's constitutional period occurred between 1629 and

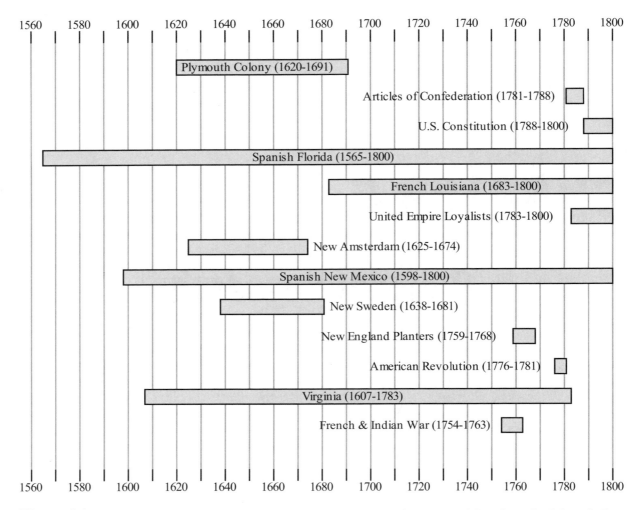

Figure 6.1: **A selected time line of events of interest to genealogists researching the colonial period.**

1640 when Puritans, most from East Anglia, settled there. The next mass migration was of southern English cavaliers and their servants to the Chesapeake Bay region between 1640 and 1675. Then, between 1675 and 1725 thousands of Quakers, led by William Penn settled the Delaware Valley. Finally, English, Scots, and Irish from the borderlands settled in Appalachia between 1717 and 1775. Each of these migrations produced a distinct regional culture which can still be seen in America today.[2]

William Dollarhide, in a much-condensed restatement, built on this thesis when he suggested that if researchers know where their immigrant British ancestors settled North America in the 17th or early 18th centuries, they would have a better than average clue to help determine from where in the British Isles they had emigrated.[3] However, that is a quest for discussion in a subsequent chapter.

Fischer's basic thesis of the impact of regional differences in Britain on the variations found in the development of American colonies is much too lengthy to be discussed comprehensively here. However, patrons should be encouraged to read the chapters that relate to the area of the United States that they are researching. This background will be useful in understanding the culture in which their ancestors lived. It will also help them with their research as Fischer lists such things as varying naming patterns that may be helpful in tracing ancestral lines.

Fischer's thesis, at the very least, reminds us that researchers need to be aware of regional differences in record keeping and retention. The basis for some of these differences did have its roots in the political and religious civil wars that plagued 17th-century England. As each period of conflict ended, it generated a wave of followers of the defeated side who immigrated to the colonies.

The culture from whence they came in Europe had a long time to wait before civil registration of vital events was to become the norm. For the most part, this did not occur until the 19th century—1837 in England. Before that time, this function was under to control of the dominant state-sanctioned church—whichever one that might be at the time. Sometimes the dominant church was responsible for registering life events of nonconformists. At other times, nonconformists could not legally get married or register other important events in their lives. The first American colonists attempted to set up a different system.

David Dearborn of the New England Historic Genealogical Society has pointed out that New Englanders rebelled against the church control of record keeping they had left in England and established the town as the focus for record keeping. This was a system that was to last in the Northeast long after the colonial period. Researchers who have colonial ancestors should give thanks if their forbearers came to New England. That region kept meticulous records and has suffered relatively less destruction of repositories than in many other areas—particularly in the South.

LINEAGE AND HEREDITARY SOCIETIES

One of the prime motivators for some of your patrons to work on their family history is to allow them to qualify for membership in a lineage or hereditary society. Not all such organizations have their roots in colonial America, but many do. These societies have their own umbrella organization—the Heredity Society Community of the United States of America (HSC). Within this community, there is a strict protocol of precedence among the societies:

> The rule of precedence for hereditary societies is based upon the chronological order of the date of founding of each society. The following is a comprehensive list of all current hereditary societies (those which qualify for an HSC listing based on membership and longevity), in the appropriate order of precedence. Society insignia should be properly mounted and publicly displayed according to the order listed.[4]

The Ancient and Honorable Artillery Company of Massachusetts, founded in 1637, gets the honor of being the first organized in North America.[5] More than 200 such societies are currently listed by the HSC. The most well-known of them is the

National Society of the Daughters of the American Revolution (DAR). The DAR is well down this list of precedence, having been founded in 1890. The demand for such societies must still be strong as more than a dozen have been formed and recognized by the HSC within the last decade. An abbreviated list of the objectives of these societies includes the following:

- We are educators.
- We are genealogists.
- We are historians.
- We promote civic duty and patriotism.
- We are a fellowship.[6]

Some have a reputation of snobbishness, and some societies make it clear that new members can join by invitation only; sometimes self-initiated contact with the society by potential members is counterproductive. Members tend to take themselves and their societies very seriously, and library workers helping researchers would do well to take them in the same manner.

It is difficult to keep these societies straight even if you consult their official websites. For example, there are four separate societies for French Huguenots alone. Many other societies have similar names and goals. You cannot be an expert on all of them. Therefore, do not hesitate to refer your interested patrons to the HSC website for definitions and for links to the sites of individual societies for the latest official information.

Lineage societies both stimulate and enable genealogical research. The stimulation part is seen in your libraries and in other venues populated by family history researchers as patrons seek to satisfy the documentation requirements for membership. Many of the societies maintain genealogy and local history libraries and other databases often resulting from the previous applications for membership. If there are such society libraries in your region, you would do well to familiarize yourself with their resources and access requirements so that you can refer your patrons as appropriate—whether or not they are actively trying to prepare applications for membership in hereditary societies.

An unusually rich genealogical resource is the Genealogical Research System (GRS). The GRS is a combination of several databases created in recent years to organize the large quantity of information that the DAR has collected since its inception. Recently, access to many of these databases have been made available online.[7]

Lines of ascent back to Revolutionary War patriots in the DAR database have more credibility than the average pedigree posted online. However, they too should be critically examined. Early membership applications were not subjected to the same scrutiny that current ones receive. In addition, the DAR still refuses to consider DNA evidence. It is understandable that Y-chromosome or mitochondrial DNA cannot be used to establish proof certain that a present-day person descended from a particular Revolutionary War patriot. However, it certainly can support documentary evidence.

On the other hand, Y-chromosome DNA can absolutely disprove such descent. To the date of this writing, the DAR still refuses to consider DNA results that would totally disprove lines of descent that it has previously accepted on documentary evidence. The author knows of two separate lines of descent for which membership has been granted despite the fact that DNA results from multiple living individuals have established that the line shown in the GRS could not possibly be correct. When such evidence was offered to the DAR's director of genealogy, she stated emphatically that DNA evidence could not be considered but that she would be happy to consider documentary evidence that would discredit a proven line.[8] Until the DAR adopts a policy of considering all credible evidence, its database will be less reliable that it otherwise might be. Again, the data found here have more credibility than some. It has had some level of review and verification by someone other than the researcher. However, it still cannot be accepted without being critically examined with other available evidence.

REVOLUTIONARY WAR PENSIONS

You might think Revolutionary War pensions were started in the late 18th century. However, in general, that was not the case. You might expect Revolutionary War pension files to provide information about the war. However, often much of the information is about more recent times. Some states did initiate payments soon after the war to disabled veterans and occasionally to others. For information about those cases, the documentation would be found mainly at the archives of the individual states. However, the majority of pensions were not awarded until the early 19th century. It was only then that the federal government got involved.

On the basis of the initial federal Pension Act of 1818 and its successors, so many pensions were approved that Congress had to appropriate additional funds to supplement those originally appropriated. However, many applications were at least initially denied. As a genealogist, you should hope that the application of your ancestor was one of the latter. Applications that were immediately approved generated very little paperwork. Denied applications, on the other hand, sometimes resulted in voluminous files of correspondence back and forth, which is often rich with genealogical information. Some of these application disputes extended well into the middle of the 19th century before they were resolved.

These federal pension application files are housed at the National Archives. The easiest way to access them is through Footnote.com. Footnote is a pay site. If your public library does not have a subscription, you should check to see if it is available at a nearby family history center of the Mormon Church. Many of them hold such subscriptions for their patrons. HeritageQuest also provides access to many pension records. Check with your local library or family history center for access to these databases.

According to a newspaper article published in the *Star* of Christchurch, New Zealand, in 1902, there were then still three widows receiving pensions based on the service of their spouses during the Revolutionary War.

> The youngest of these is Mrs [*sic*] Mary Snead, of Virginia, now 86 years old. Her husband held a commission in a Virginia regiment. He was born about 1750, and married for the first time in 1835, when eighty-five years old. His bride, who still survives as his widow, was nineteen years old at her marriage.
>
> Another of these widows, Mrs [*sic*] Rebecca Mayo, is eighty-seven years old. Her husband was a private from Virginia. His widow was his third wife, whom he married in 1834, when he was seventy-eight years old. He himself lived until he was ninety. One child was born to this couple in 1835, so that if she, an unmarried daughter, should live to the age of her father, she would in 1925 be in receipt of a pension 168 years after the death of her father, on account of services rendered by him in a war ending in 1783.
>
> The Third of these widows, Mrs [*sic*] Damon, is eighty-eight. Her husband was a private in a Massachusetts regiment throughout the whole of the Revolutionary War.[9]

Among the jewels I have found in Revolutionary War pension files is the only official confirmation I have ever seen of the parentage of my third great-grandfather, Peter Dowell, who was born in 1788. His mother initiated a request for a widow's pension in her old age. It was denied several times, but Mary persisted until her death in 1853. A few weeks after her death, a notice came that the pension had been approved. Then the amount approved for her had to be paid to her surviving children who were listed as Peter and his sister Elizabeth (Dowell) Johnson wife of Ambrose Johnson.

EXODUS TO CANADA

Much migration has taken place back and forth across the U.S.-Canadian border. This continues to this day. Some mass movements need to be understood by your patrons as they research back into colonial times. Two such relocations to Canada took place in the last part of the 18th century. These involved the Planters and the Loyalists.

The Planters were approximately 8,000 farmers and fishermen from New England who were recruited to move to Nova Scotia between 1759 and 1768. They were needed by the British to secure the Atlantic Coast of Canada as part of their worldwide strategic battle with France. The Arcadians had just been expelled from Nova Scotia because the British suspected their French sympathies. Some of them moved to the French-controlled territory of Louisiana and became the Cajuns. Others returned to Europe or moved to other French colonies. Some slipped inland and remained in Canada. To fill this strategic vacuum, Britain recruited heavily both in old England and in New England. Descendants of many of these Planter families filtered back into the United States over the next few generations.

The United Empire Loyalists were another matter. Although they had a choice in their decision to remain loyal to King George when their friends, neighbors, and even family members were revolting, most of them did not have a choice about their relocation to Canada. Most of them had their homes and farms confiscated. British land was offered to them in Ontario and Nova Scotia. Similarly to the Planters, many of the descendants of the Loyalists gradually returned to the United States over the next three or four generations. Some of them retained ties with the extended families they left behind when they fled to Canada.

WHAT CALENDAR?

September 2, 1752, was a great day in the history of sleep.

That Wednesday evening, millions of British subjects in England and the colonies went peacefully to sleep and did not wake up until twelve days later. Behind this feat of narcoleptic prowess was not some revolutionary hypnotic technique or miraculous pharmaceutical discovered in the West Indies. It was, rather, the British Calendar Act of 1751, which declared the day after Wednesday the second to be Thursday the fourteenth.

Prior to that cataleptic September evening, the official British calendar differed from that of continental Europe by eleven days—that is, September 2 in London was September 13 in Paris, Lisbon, and Berlin. The discrepancy had sprung from Britain's continued use of the Julian calendar, which had been the official calendar of Europe since its invention by Julius Caesar (after whom it was named) in 45 B.C.[10]

The impact of that change to the Gregorian calendar was far greater than on those 12 days in 1752. Prior to that, the first day of the calendar year was not January 1. Instead, it came on March 28.

Quakers refused to use those days of the week or months of the year which they saw as being derived from the names of heathen gods and goddesses. Instead, they used only numerals for those months. For those with Quaker ancestors, this creates a real dilemma when using secondary sources. You often have a difficult time understanding if someone has previously converted the date or not.

TORREY'S *NEW ENGLAND MARRIAGES*

For patrons who are fortunate enough to have identified ancestors who were living in 17th-century New England, Torrey's *New England Marriages Prior to 1700* is an excellent resource.[11] Gary Boyd Roberts calls it "the seminal compendium of seventeenth century New Englanders."[12] In compiling data covering about

1,000 pages, Torrey attempted to be comprehensive, but of course, it was not complete. Even after three supplements were added, no project like this can ever document everyone. However, I hope your library has the original volume and Sanborn's *Third Supplement.* It adds almost another 400 pages and incorporates the first two supplements as well.[13] In addition to giving one the dates and places of marriage of ancestors, this source can help sort out multiple marriages of the same individuals and show the progression of their migration from town to town. However, Sanborn points out,

> Despite its great popularity and very frequent use, most people do not appear to understand what it is that Torrey did. Some insist on using Torrey as a reference, when his work is in actuality an index to references. . . . [H]is work was a faithful index of what others discovered and published. Thus, his index contained many entries that are incorrect or contradictory; it remains for the user to evaluate the references cited.[14]

Much can be learned from reading the introductions and prefaces of such books. However, in the haste to find the names, we often miss pointers that will help us find those names efficiently and that also will help us to understand and interpret those that we find.

THE GREAT MIGRATION

One resource for those who have ancestors who arrived in New England very early is the Great Migration Project of the New England Historic Genealogical Society (NEHGS).

> The goal of the Great Migration Study Project is to create comprehensive biographical and genealogical accounts of all immigrants to New England from 1620 to 1643, from the arrival of the Mayflower to the decline of immigration resulting from the beginning of the Civil War in England. . . . The entire time period of the Great Migration has been divided into smaller chronological chunks, within which range of years the sketches are published in alphabetic order. The first series of volumes covered the immigrants who arrived in the years from 1620 through 1633 . . . contained more than nine hundred sketches. Beginning in 1634 and running until the end of that decade the annual rate of migration became much higher.[15]

Great pains have been taken to be comprehensive and accurate. However, some of the original sketches first published in 1995 have already been revised to reflect new research and to correct "those errors that had been discovered in the original research."[16] This massive project has a long way to go to complete its ambitious agenda. So far, the product has been very useful to researchers of very early New England families.

ARRIVING AT THE WATER'S EDGE

If you and your patrons have now traced their ancestors back to the water's edge, that is quite an accomplishment. It may now be time to get ready to take the research abroad, to fill in more details about the line already documented, or to pursue another branch of the family tree.

NOTES

1. David Hackett Fischer, *Albion's Seed: Four British Folkways in America* (New York: Oxford University Press, 1989).

2. Nelson Rosit, "Review: Albion's Seed: Four British Folkways in America," Institute for Historical Review, http://www.ihr.org/jhr/v12/v12p114_Rosit.html (accessed September 10, 2010).

3. William Dollarhide, *British Origins of American Colonist, 1629–1775* (Bountiful, UT: Heritage Quest Genealogical Services, 1997).

4. "Society Precedence," The Heredity Society Community, http://www.hereditary.us/precedence.htm (accessed September 21, 2010).

5. Ibid.

6. Ibid., "Overview."

7. "Online Research: The DAR Genealogical Research System (GRS)," National Society of the Daughters of the American Revolution (DAR), http://www.dar.org/library/online_research.cfm (accessed September 22, 2010).

8. Terry Ward, DAR Genealogy Director, interview with the author, June 25, 2010.

9. "Three U.S. Pensioners: American Longevity," *Star,* Christchurch, New Zealand, November 5, 1902, p. 2, on Paperspast, http://paperspast.natlib.govt.nz/cgi-bin/paperspast?a=d&cl=search&d=TS19021105.2.11&srpos=5&e=————-10—1——0Revolutionary+War+pensions—(accessed March 9, 2011).

10. Ben Snowden, "The Curious History of the Gregorian Calendar: Eleven Days That Never Were," Infoplease.com, http://www.infoplease.com/spot/gregorian1.html#axzz0zpGg7uhW (accessed September 18, 2010).

11. Clarence Almon Torrey, *New England Marriages Prior to 1700* (Baltimore: Genealogical Publishing, 1992). A new three-volume set of this classic was just announced in late 2010.

12. Ibid., p. xvi.

13. Melende Lutz Sanborn, *Third Supplement to Torrey's New England Marriages Prior to 1700* (Baltimore: Genealogical Publishing, 2003).

14. Ibid., p. vii.

15. "The Great Migration," New England Historic Genealogical Society, http://www.newenglandancestors.org/publications/great_migration.asp (accessed September 19, 2010).

16. Ibid.

CHAPTER 7

Researching People of Color

African American and Native American patrons have often been led to believe that their family history research is going to be very difficult if not nigh well impossible. Hispanic Americans may be under similar illusions. While there is some truth in these perceptions, they have been exaggerated to the point that many people of color have given up on researching their family histories even before they have begun. There is much similarity between their task and the process through which any other patron must go. As they begin their backward trek through time, there are many more similarities than differences. Researching these families of color through the 20th century is not significantly different than it is for others. Even when we progress back to the 19th century, their tasks may be no more difficult than the ones faced by the present-day descendants of many European immigrants who arrived here late in the 1800s.

Your first task may be to reassure patrons of color that they will be able to find information about their families. Not a single one of Dr. Dave's rules have been suspended when it comes to researching these families. Their descendants need to follow the steps that I hope you are beginning to feel familiar with by this point of the book. Start with what you know yourself and what you can find out from living family members. Build backward step-by-step. Use the resources that were introduced in the "Speed Dial" list in chapter 3. This should make the task less daunting. First, bridge the 20th century. There most of the processes and resources outlined in chapter 4 will be similar to those that work for other Americans. Discourage them from trying to navigate the 19th century until they come to it in the natural backward progression of their journey.

In this Crash Course book we can only do a flyover of the general genealogical process with quick snippets for subdisciplines. If the composition of your clientele is significantly weighted toward any ethnic group, you may need more than a *Crash Course in Genealogy* to become somewhat knowledgeable in that specialty. In order to become an expert resource for your patrons, much more in-depth study and practice will be necessary.

HISPANIC AMERICAN GENEALOGY

Americans of Hispanic descent are a very diverse group. In some cases, they have been within the geographic boundaries of what is now the United States longer than those of British descent. In the 16th century, there were Hispanic settlements in both present-day Florida and New Mexico. In other cases, they are among our most recent arrivals, having spent considerable time in other areas of the Americas in the intervening centuries between the departure of their ancestors from Spain or Portugal and their arrival here. Along the way, they may have blended with other ethnicities—particularly other people of color.

In order to trace Hispanic roots back through other areas of the Americas, researchers need to follow the process of taking research to another country outlined in the following chapter. Knowledge of history, geography, and culture is essential to this type family history research. One example of this kind of knowledge is naming patterns. Genealogist Kimberly Powell explains,

> Most Hispanic countries, including Spain, have a unique naming system in which children are commonly given two surnames, one from each parent. The middle name (1st surname) comes from the father's name (apellido paterno), and the last name (2nd surname) is the mother's maiden name (apellido materno). Sometimes, these two surnames may be found separated by y (meaning "and"), although this is no longer as common as it once was. Recent changes to laws in Spain mean that you may also find the two surnames reversed—first the mother's surname, and then the father's surname. Women also retain their maiden name when they get married, making it much easier to track families through multiple generations.[1]

Rich resources for Hispanic American genealogy are the records of the Catholic Church, which dominates the culture of much of Latin America as well as the Iberian Peninsula. Many of these records have been microfilmed and are available through the network of family history centers described more fully in chapter 9.

Iberian Americans, those who descend from ancestors who migrated from Spain or Portugal, often had other stops along the way. One example is that many Portuguese Americans first migrated to the Azores prior to relocating to the Americas.

AFRICAN AMERICAN RESEARCH

Examples of the snippets of information that help provide context for researching the families of subsets of Americans are the following list from the Family-Search Wiki:

Did you know?

- The first African settlers in the U.S. were indentured servants in Jamestown, Va., in 1619 (before the Pilgrims landed at Plymouth Rock) and freed after 7 years.
- African American is the most common ancestry in: Maryland, Virginia, North Carolina, South Carolina, Georgia, Alabama, Mississippi, and Louisiana.
- The Freedman's Bank and the Freedmen's Bureau were separate organizations, from different federal departments, in separate National Archives record groups.
- Ten percent of the African American population was free before the Civil War.
- Only 15 percent of freed slaves used the family name of a former owner.
- From 1865 to 1875 many African Americans changed their family name.[2]

The popularity of Alex Halley's *Roots* has broken down many of the misconceptions about the impossibility of documenting the stories of African American families. In the three decades since then, a number of resources have focused on aiding such research. The stories of Emmitt Smith and Spike Lee on NBC's *Who Do You Think You Are?* in spring 2010 destroyed even more such misconceptions. It is not my intent here to detail all of them. Google "African American genealogy" or check CyndisList for such details. There really are a lot of helpful guides out there. I will, however, mention a few of them to whet your appetite.

A great place to start is with Dee Parmer Woodtor's "African American Genealogy: An Online Interactive Guide for Beginners,"[3] which is part of the very resource-rich and award-winning website AfriGeneas: African Ancestored Genealogy from Africa to America. The FamilySearch Wiki can also be helpful as it offers more than three dozen links to sites of research interest.[4]

From the present back to about 1875, the process of documenting the family stories of African American families is roughly similar to that of documenting the stories of other American families. Prior to that time, the trail may become somewhat more challenging. In 1870 the South was still in the throes of Reconstruction following the Civil War. A lot of families, particularly African American families, were still on the move as they tried to put their lives back together and put the war behind them. This period was so chaotic for all Southerners that the U.S. Census Bureau retroactively adjusted its count upward by 1.3 million to cover the suspected undercount in the South. Social scientists still argue about whether an adjustment of this magnitude was appropriate. However, it is reasonable to assume that the undercount of blacks in the South that year approached 6 percent or 7 percent.[5]

In 1860 and 1850, slave schedules were a separate part of the census enumerations so that the South could get three-fifths credit for each individual so listed in the apportionment of seats in the House of Representatives. Generally, the names of the slave owners were given, but not the names of those enslaved. However, sometimes the given names, genders, and ages of the slaves were listed. These records can be useful to your patrons as can property records. Information about the sale of individual slaves was sometimes recorded as a business transaction. In addition, slaves were sometimes listed by given names and/or ages in the wills of their masters/mistresses.

NATIVE AMERICANS

North American Indians were sometimes relegated to reservations and sometimes integrated into the general population. This is a big distinction that will determine the appropriate research path to follow. General assumptions can lead researchers to miss some available documents.

> Every year, the staff of the Fort Worth Branch of the National Archives gets thousands of letters from people all over the United States who are trying to prove that an ancestor was an Indian. These researchers comprise what must be one of the largest "tribes" in North America, the Wantabes. People wantabe an Indian for a variety of reasons but most are not successful in their efforts to find proof and thus join the ranks of another very large "tribe", the Outalucks. Many people fail in their genealogical research because they are not familiar with the records of the Federal government which relate to the American Indian.[6]

"The National Archives holds information about American Indians who maintained their ties to Federally-recognized Tribes (1830–1970). Most records are arranged by tribe,"[7] according to the National Archives and Records Administration (NARA) website. Much of that information is housed in the National Archives branch facility in Fort Worth, Texas. Anyone doing a significant amount of research on Native American ancestors should become familiar with the holdings of this repository. The staff of the Fort Worth branch has prepared many helpful finding aids. The website describes the information useful to know before visiting that archive either virtually or in person.

Helpful information to know before searching these records includes the following:

- Name of the person
- Name of the person's federally recognized tribe

- Approximately when the person lived
- What state or territory the person lived in[8]

The Fort Worth archive is particularly useful for tracing members of the Five Civilized Tribes, which were relocated to Oklahoma Territory in the first half of the 19th century. The Five Civilized Tribes are the Cherokee, Chickasaw, Choctaw, Creek, and Seminole. Depending on the tribe being researched, your patrons may want to become familiar with the Dawes Rolls of the Five Civilized Tribes[9] or the Guion-Miller Roll of Eastern Cherokees. Many enumerations of other tribes were also conducted by the federal government at various times and may be found in the National Archives.[10]

RICH AND DIVERSE TAPESTRY

Researching the histories of families of color can lead to many surprises. Often their ancestry is much more diverse than present-day family members have been led to believe. Two clients, with whom I have worked in two different states in two different decades, illustrate this point. Both had grown up in black neighborhoods and considered themselves African Americans. After much research, we were able to document that each had three great-grandparents who appeared to be African Americans. However, both were able to discover that each had three great-grandparents who could be documented to be Cherokees. One had a great-grandfather who could be documented as Caucasian.

This illustrates three points. Native Americans sometimes owned slaves. In addition, people of color often were relegated to the fringes of white society where they came into close contact with other people of color of very different ethnicities. Finally, many people of color had a European male in their paternal ancestry.

Michael Hammer, a biotechnology research geneticist at the University of Arizona, and his colleagues have been actively studying this and similar phenomena in the last few years.

> The frequencies of non-European (3.4%) and non-Asian (4.5%) Y chromosomes are generally low in European American and Asian American populations, respectively. The frequencies of European Y chromosomes in Native-American populations range widely (i.e., 7–89%) and follow a West to East gradient, whereas they are relatively consistent in African-American populations (26.4+/–8.9%) from different locations. The European (77.8+/–9.3%) and Native-American (13.7+/–7.4%) components of the Hispanic paternal gene pool are also relatively constant among geographic regions; however, the African contribution is much higher in the Northeast (10.5+/–6.4%) than in the Southwest (1.5+/–0.9%) or Midwest (0%).[11]

All of this has implications for family history research, but it takes a while to wrap one's mind around it:

1. About 96 percent of European Americans and Asian Americans do not have male ancestors in their direct paternal line who were non-European or non-Asian.
2. From 7 percent to 89 percent of Native Americans have had at least one European male ancestor in their direct paternal lines. The highest percentage is in the East where Native Americans have long been integrated into the general population. In the West where Native Americans have long lived on reservations, this percentage is much, much lower.
3. In different locations, the percentages of African Americans who have had at least one European male ancestor in their direct paternal lines range from 17.5 percent to 35.3 percent.
4. About three-fourths of Hispanic Americans have had a European male ancestor somewhere in their direct paternal lines.
5. About 10 percent of Hispanic Americans in the Northeast are likely to have had an African male ancestor in their direct paternal lines. In the Southwest, that falls to about 1.5 percent. I would assume that this is because Hispanic Americans in the Northeast are much more likely to have migrated through the Caribbean region than are those in the Southwest.

All of these statistics are derived from the study of Y-chromosome haplotypes, which will be discussed in much greater detail in chapter 10. DNA testing can now help determine whether and how much of one's DNA came from different parts of the world several hundred years ago.

This intermixing of ethnic groups makes even more valuable such printed sources and electronic databases that include more than one group. Angela Y. Walton-Raji is an expert in this field. Her *Black Indian Genealogy Research*[12] should be read by anyone seriously interested in such ethnic mixing.

A resource for locating 18th-century people of color is the National Society of the Daughters of the American Revolution (DAR) publication *Forgotten Patriots—African American and American Indian Patriots of the Revolutionary War: A Guide to Service, Sources, and Studies.*[13] The 2008 second edition of *Forgotten Patriots*

> identifies over 6,600 names of African Americans and American Indians who contributed to American Independence. [Its] 872 pages contains details of the documented service of the listed Patriots, historical commentary on happenings of the time, an assortment of illustrations, and an extensive bibliography of research sources.... On an additional level, the hope is that it will also encourage the female descendents of these patriots to join the important volunteer and educational work of the DAR.[14]

This book is an important part of the DAR's affirmative action to mitigate its reputation, illustrated most notably by the well-documented refusal to allow famous African American contralto Marian Anderson to perform a concert before an integrated audience in its Constitution Hall just a block from the White House in 1939. Anderson was subsequently invited by First Lady Eleanor Roosevelt to hold the concert on the steps of the Lincoln Memorial.[15]

SUMMARY

This chapter has been a brief example of additional resources that may need to be explored for researchers interested in the specific ethnicity of any Americans—whether they are people of color or European Americans.

NOTES

1. Kimberly Powell, "Researching Your Hispanic Heritage: Introduction to Hispanic Genealogy," About.com Guide, http://genealogy.about.com/cs/hispanic/a/ancestry.htm (accessed March 9, 2011).
2. "African American Research," FamilySearch Wiki, https://wiki.familysearch.org/en/African_American_Research (accessed March 9, 2011).
3. Dee Parmer Woodtor, "African American Genealogy: An Online Interactive Guide for Beginners," AfriGeneas, http://www.afrigeneas.com/guide/ (accessed March 9, 2011).
4. "African American Research."
5. J. David Hacker, Steven Ruggles, Andrea R. Foroughi, and Walter L. Sargent, "Public Use Microdata Samples of the 1860 & 1870 U.S. Censuses of Population," *Integrated Public Use Microdata Series,* http://usa.ipums.org/usa/volii/4_1860–70rev.shtml (accessed November 6, 2010).
6. Kent Carter, "Wantabes and Outalucks: Searching for Indian Ancestors in Federal Records," The U.S. National Archives and Records Administration (NARA), http://www.archives.gov/research/native-americans/ancestor-search.html (accessed March 9, 2011).
7. "Native American Records at the National Archives," NARA, http://www.archives.gov/research/native-americans/index.html (accessed December 16, 2010).
8. Ibid.
9. Good overviews of the "Dawes Rolls" are provided on FamilySearch Wiki, https://wiki.familysearch.org/en/Dawes_Commission_Enrollment_Records_for_Five_U.S._Indian_Tribes; and the NARA website, http://www.archives.gov/research/native-americans/dawes/intro.html (accessed December 22, 2010).
10. "American Indians in Census Records," NARA, http://www.archives.gov/research/census/native-americans/index.html (accessed December 17, 2010).
11. Michael F. Hammer, Veronica F. Chamberlain, Veronica F. Kearney, Daryn Stover, Gina Zhang, Tatiana Karafet, Bruce Walsh, and Alan J. Redd, "Population Structure of Y Chromosome SNP Haplogroups in the United States and Forensic Implications for Constructing Y Chromosome STR Databases," *Forensic Science International,* December 1, 2006, p. 45.
12. Angela Y. Walton-Raji, *Black Indian Genealogy Research: African-American Ancestors among the Five Civilized Tribes* (Westminister, MD: Heritage Books, 2007).
13. Eric G. Grundset, *Forgotten Patriots—African American and American Indian Patriots of the Revolutionary War: A Guide to Service, Sources, and Studies* (Washington,

DC: National Society Daughters of the American Revolution, 2008), http://www.dar. org/library/publication.cfm#agr (accessed March 9, 2011).

14.   "Forgotten Patriots," National Society of the Daughters of the American Revolution (DAR), http://www.dar.org/library/fp.cfm (accessed December 22, 2010).

15.   "Marian Anderson and the DAR," DAR, http://www.dar.org/natsociety/marian_an derson_and_dar.cfm#3% (accessed December 22, 2010).

CHAPTER 8

Taking Research to Another Country

In this Crash Course book, we cannot get into detailed research guidance for every country outside the United States from which your patrons' ancestors may have come. However, I will attempt to set forth a generic template which will give general guidance for extending research into other countries. At least this chapter can serve as a checklist and can raise questions about the kinds of resources that you will need to explore. Hopefully, these may lead to answers that can be found in the specific overseas locations where your patrons' ancestors may have lived. A general methodology may help one to begin research in almost any country. However, the most appropriate tools to use in each country will vary considerably.

The search starts closer to home. It is necessary to research thoroughly records that are available here. Foreign research needs a solid starting point. It cannot be successful unless you have a specific place on which to focus your research. One more time, I must repeat some of the basic tenets of successful genealogical research. When undertaking foreign research these principles are still essential. Start from what you know and work backward in time. And location, location, location are still the three most important guidelines to get to the destinations where the desired answers may be found.

DOING YOUR *HOME* WORK

Before your patrons can be successful in extracting family information from their countries of origin, they must assemble all the clues that are available here. In this search, the patron needs to try to identify the specific town or parish from which the ancestors came as well as their religion there, their occupations, and so forth. In assembling this information, the most important steps are really not that different from those suggested earlier in this book as the most effective way to start a genealogical research project here in the United States. They would include:

1. Interviewing any family members or other individuals who may have information about the ancestors' location before they immigrated to the United States.
2. Sometimes the place of origin of the patron's ancestors may be listed on death certificates and/or in obituaries, and occasionally even on tombstones.
3. Naturalization records, particularly the statement of intent or first papers, may be helpful.
4. Immigration, transit, and emigration records can at times be extremely helpful.
   a. Emigration papers or permissions to leave were required from many countries. These might include confirmation that all taxes had been paid or that males had completed their military service obligation and that all legal debts had been satisfied.
   b. Immigration records are records created in the country of arrival. These led to permission to enter the new country and were usually created at the port of entry—occasionally at a city that we would not typically think of as a port. One example of this is that some immigrants sailed to Canadian locations and then were transported on smaller boats or by rail to U.S. locations—for example, Buffalo, New York.

   Ellis Island always comes to mind when novice family history researchers think of their immigrant ancestors. Many immigrants did use this portal to enter America. Those who did are reasonably well documented and may be researched through a free database.[1] Ship passenger arrival records for this period are also available on Ancestry. However, this immigration center was in use for a relatively short time. Ellis Island did not open until 1892. Those who arrived earlier might have used other portals, such as Castle Garden in New York, which calls itself America's First Immigration Center,[2] or might have come in through entirely different ports of entry. During the period from 1820 to the opening of Ellis Island in 1892, about 11 million immigrants entered through Castle Garden—almost as many as were to enter through Ellis Island in a much shorter period.

More than 12 million immigrants did enter the United States through Ellis Island—mostly in the three decades ending with the passage of the Immigration Act of 1924. This law greatly restricted immigration and shifted most of the screening of immigrants to U.S. embassies and consulates overseas. Also of value to family history researchers are the almost equally numerous records on nonimmigrant passengers and crew members who entered New York Harbor during the same period. For those seeking another way to search these records, Stephen Morse offers a one-step search engine for many immigrant databases.[3]

 c. Do not neglect suggesting to your patrons that ship manifests listing passengers are a separate and often rich source of information. They were created after the emigration records and before the immigration records.

  Of course, not all three of these record types may be available. In some cases, none of them may be extant. However, the search should not be abandoned until each of these three possibilities has been exhausted. Each, if available, may offer different bits of information that may help to identify the ancestor's place of origin where more information may be located. Be careful not to confuse the port of departure with the last permanent residence. Sometimes, ancestors temporarily lived in a port city while they were getting all their papers together, arranging financing and booking passage.

5. Pictures left behind also may provide clues. See the "Photo Detective," Maureen Taylor,[4] for guidance in interpreting ethnic clues in old ancestral pictures if you are fortunate enough to have access to such photos.

6. Sometimes census records can provide clues. The 1870 U.S. census was more specific than most in recording the birthplace of those enumerated—particularly those who came from areas that are now part of Germany.

PREPARATION FOR YOUR VOYAGE OF DISCOVERY

Once you have been able to help your patrons focus on a probable place of ancestral origin, they are ready to proceed to the next step of the search. Some background work will greatly increase the success of the researcher's efforts. These steps should include finding out as much as is feasible about the possible points of origin. In this effort, the following are key resources to helping researchers begin research in a country in which they have not previously conducted family history research. As a library worker, you should familiarize yourself with the kinds of resources enumerated in this chapter. First check what international resources are held in your library and then expand your investigation to include other local resources. Increasingly, authoritative geographic and historical resources are being added to websites. So when patrons' inquiries lead you into a country with which you are not familiar, check what library resources are locally available and also explore web resources. Don't hesitate to Google it, at least as a starting point.

Geographic Information

In family history research, one can never have too much geographic information. Preferably, this will include at least one map that is current and one that shows what the area was like when the ancestors lived in that area. Atlases of the country/region of origin, both current and historical, can be very useful. Gazetteers for that country can help to locate geographic locations that are out of the way or otherwise unknown to the researcher. One example for German research is the mother of all such gazetteers, *Meyers Orts,* a title much shorter and easier to remember than its original name in German.[5] This formidable 2,500-page, multivolume work contains detailed information about more than 210,000 cities, towns, villages, estates, hamlets, and other inhabited places that made up the German Empire before World War I. The data for *Meyers Orts* was collected largely toward the end of the 19th century, around a time of heavy emigration from Prussia and other Germanic areas. It is a treasure house of information about the various entities that had overlapping jurisdiction over the lives of the residents of those locations. All of them may have created records about those residents. From *Meyers Orts,* I learned that births, at least of males, were recorded by the military districts so that they could predict the number of potential soldiers there would be 18 years hence. Church parishes and schools are also listed. If your patron is researching ancestors from this area, it is important to know what religion they practiced as parish records are very important. Most would have been either Roman Catholic or Lutheran. However, smaller groups of Jews, Mennonites, Waldensians, and so forth, also lived there. You can find the complete, encyclopedic version of *Myers Orts* online in the Family History Library catalog[6] or at Ancestry.com.

HISTORIES AND HISTORICAL NOVELS

Both fictional and nonfictional accounts, set in the time just before or at the time your ancestors left their homeland, can help us understand why they migrated and the conditions under which their journeys began. They can also help researchers make sense out of the facts they uncover. For example, I was surprised to find that an ancestress of mine in New Sweden (now part of Delaware) appeared to be ethnically Finnish based on her mitochondrial DNA. However, a little historical research revealed that Finland was part of Sweden in the 17th century when New Sweden was settled. At least half of the immigrants to New Sweden are thought to have been ethnic Finns. In addition, there was once a settlement in New Sweden called Finland. In light of this information, the DNA results seemed very reasonable.

In another example, my wife's immigrant Irish ancestor came to Chicago in 1850. His immigration took on new meaning once we understood that this was right at the end of the potato famine. That catastrophic event reduced the population of Ireland to about half of its previous size through death and emigration. The resulting food shortage weakened the populace and led to widespread illnesses. His emigration was probably, at least in part, to get away from these extremely unhealthy living conditions.

RESEARCH GUIDES

Some excellent research guides have been written on getting started with genealogical research in a wide variety of countries. Familiarize yourself with any that are available in your library. An example of an excellent one is *Your Swedish Roots*.[7] Other sources of country research guides are the following:

1. FamilySearch.org
   a. FamilySearch is another place to check for background sources. The older and still the most comprehensive coverage of these guides can be found by selecting the "Research Helps" tab and then either "Articles" or "Guidance" on the dropdown menu.[8] Many of these helps can be downloaded as PDF files. You may wish to print out some of them for ready referral prompts to use when you are assisting patrons at your service desk.
   b. The relatively new FamilySearch Wiki[9] is made up of articles written, in many cases, by seasoned experts. However, since this is a volunteer effort, results vary. These articles will gradually update and replace the guides and articles in item (a). At this writing, the Wiki already contains about 40,000 articles and can be browsed by country or by other topics.
   c. FamilySearch also offers a series of videos that can be streamed and watched online. Currently, these include research classes on England, Germany, Ireland, Italy, Mexico (in Spanish), Poland, and Russia. Lessons on reading records in an even wider variety of languages including Latin are also provided. Latin is often important to researchers in many countries including the United States because church records are often the best source for birth, marriage, and death information. Often, records of Roman Catholic churches are a mix of Latin and the local vernacular—depending on which priest was recording the events. In parishes in the United States where one ethnic group dominated the community, the church records may be a mix of Latin, English, and the language native to that ethnic group.

2. Ancestry.com, under its Learning Center tab, offers a number of archived webinar sessions on European genealogical research. Archived webinars can be very helpful if one understands that they are not live and that therefore most of the interactive features are not available. Occasionally you will find webinars that do not seem to be working. Before you give up, try a different browser. Some of these were developed with a specific browser, such as Explorer, and do not perform well with others.

3. About.com offers "Genealogy by Region"[10] and the "Country Specific Genealogy Research Guides: How-To Genealogy for the Country Where Your Ancestors Once Lived." This series is edited by genealogist Kimberly Powell.

4. WorldGenWeb.org does not cover all countries.[11] For those that it does cover, the coverage ranges from very comprehensive to very sketchy. This is because it is a completely volunteer effort. When you are helping a patron research a country with which you are not familiar or where you have not researched for a while, explore GenWeb resources early in the research process.

5. Cyndi's List of Genealogy Sites on the Internet was once available also as a printed book, but the dynamic nature of the subject matter soon made this format out of date by the time it was printed. Cyndi Howells has provided more than a quarter of a million links to sites of interest to genealogists. These links can also be browsed by country and other topics. Cyndi also tells us when each topic list was last updated—often an important thing to know in this kind of research.[12]

Another means of locating resources for genealogy research in an unfamiliar country is to Google the country name along with the word *genealogy* (e.g., "Italian genealogy"). If you are looking for an ancestor of a particular ethnic group within a country, you may have success in Googling the ethnic group along with the term *genealogy*. At first, don't include too many search terms or you may narrow the search too quickly and miss useful resources. You can also broaden searches by the use of wildcards. For example, try "Swed* genealogy" to retrieve sites listed under either "Swedish genealogy" or "Sweden genealogy."

WHO CONTROLLED THE TURF?

One misconception that can lead novice researchers astray is that they tend to think countries in the Old World have always been more or less like they are today. Nothing could be further from the truth. To list but a few examples, Germany, as we have known it in our lifetimes, was not united into a single nation until about 1871; Italy, about 1849. Prior to that time, they were but a collection of small kingdoms and other independent states. In addition, Poland didn't really exist as a nation at all during a long period of time that included all of the 19th century. This is in spite of the fact that many census records list our ancestors as having been born in Poland during that period. In addition to these examples, national borders shifted frequently. The importance of this is that finding the ancestral village, while a major accomplishment, still may leave your patrons with additional work to do to discover where the repositories may be located that document the lives of their ancestors. You must know who governed that area *at the time the records were created.*

One dynamic way to acquaint yourself and your patrons with the fluidity of national boundaries in the part of the world from which most of our ancestors came is the software package Centennia Historical Atlas.

> CENTENNIA is a map-based guide to the history of Europe and the Middle East from the beginning of the 11th century to the present. It is a *dynamic, animated* historical atlas including over 9,000 border changes. The map controls evolve the map forward or backward in time bringing the static map to life. Our maps display every major war and territorial conflict displaying the status of each region at intervals of a tenth of a year. The maps reflect actual "power on the ground" rather than internationally-sanctioned or "recognized" borders.[13]

When I show the evolution of the borders of the countries we are studying in my European research class, the senior adults come alive and jockey for a good position to view the screen.

WHO KEPT THE RECORDS?

Another key fact to be discovered early in researching the records of another country is when civil registration began—that is, when did the civilian government take over responsibility for recording births, marriages, and deaths? It may take a while for those of us who have lived our lives in a country where there is no officially recognized state-sponsored religion to grasp the consequences of how this might impact the custody of various records. Such historical arrangements vary considerably from country to country. For example, although England has existed as an entity since long before the 19th century, civil registration of vital records did not begin until 1837. Prior to that, any official vital records were recorded by the state church—in this example, the Church of England. In countries that underwent religious civil wars, the official state-sanctioned church may have changed from time to time. It is also important to know what the local practice was for recording the key events in the lives of those who belonged to dissident religions. In some countries at some times, it was the responsibility of the established church officials to record the births, marriages, and deaths of all citizens. At other times and places, that was not the case. In some situations, it was even illegal for those who did not practice the official religion to be married at all.

NAMING PATTERNS

It is also important to know if our 20th-century naming patterns were being followed during the period in which your patron is trying to research. Did they have a given name (first name) and a family name (surname)? Or did they use some form of patronyms? That means they took some form of the father's given name. The most obvious example may be the Scandinavian countries of Norway, Sweden, Finland, and Denmark. There until the last half of the 19th century, it was customary for the children to take a surname based on the first name of their father. Children of John Olsen might be Oscar Johnson or Brigit Johnsdatter rather than Oscar Olsen or Brigit Olsen. The change from this naming convention to the one with which we are more familiar in the 21st century did not take place all at once. Although you can find official dates when each of the four countries legally mandated that names be recorded in our current pattern, some early adopters were using the modern naming convention a decade or two earlier, and some trailed the official mandate. Advise your patrons to be flexible in this regard.

Other naming quirks appeared in different regions. Norway for example, had naming conventions that incorporated the name of the village or farm on which the people lived. Under this system, the first name was a given name, the second was a form of family name, and the third was the farm or village name. Another variation was that in some areas, women kept their maiden names even if they married. This was the case in some parts of France during certain periods. *Wikipedia* gives a surprisingly comprehensive listing of varying usages of patronyms in a wide variety of countries.[14] This discussion of variations in naming patterns is not intended to be in any way comprehensive. Rather it is merely a heads-up that researchers need to find out what the local customs were in the place and at the time their ancestors lived.

DATES

Dates can trip up an unwary researcher. Does December 4, 1932, mean December 4 or April 12? It depends on where you are. Americans have reversed the order in which the day and month are generally recorded in Europe.

If researchers are fortunate enough to trace their lines back into the 18th century, another date format issue may arise. What calendar was in use? Was it the Julian calendar or the Gregorian calendar (both of which were discussed in chapter 6)? Was it the relatively short-lived French Republican calendar? Was it the Islamic lunar calendar? Even though Pope Gregory XIII ordered the calendar to be advanced by 10 days in 1582, we saw in chapter 6 that England did not make the adjustment for another 170 years, at which point a 12-day adjustment was necessary.

Despite the prudence of Pope Gregory's correction, many Protestant countries, including England, ignored the papal bull. Germany and the Netherlands agreed to adopt the Gregorian calendar in 1698; Russia only accepted it after the revolution of 1918, and Greece waited until 1923 to follow suit. And currently many Orthodox churches still follow the Julian calendar, which now lags 13 days behind the Gregorian.[15]

NATIONAL REPOSITORIES

Many of the national libraries and archives of Europe have well-developed websites. In addition, the national archives of some countries have well-developed digitization projects. In Europe these tend to be controlled by the government rather than being contracted out to private-sector vendors as is the case in the United States. However, users of these digitized records generally must pay for them before actually viewing them. Practice varies as to whether the search results can be viewed without paying a fee. Generally, a deposit account is required to get access to these digital collections. Users can use major credit cards to make a deposit. Amounts vary, but the equivalent of US$30 to US$50 is not uncommon. As records are viewed, the researcher's account is debited accordingly. The deposited amount is good for a limited time, which varies depending on the archive being accessed.

STATE AND REGIONAL RESOURCES

European history has resulted in a patchwork of subdivisions that vary considerably from one nation to another. Some of these are based on history and others are based on a more systematic redrawing of local administrative units. Some of the best resources are found at the local level.

The Irish Family History Foundation's county genealogy centres provide Ireland's largest genealogical research service, both online and via commissioned research services.... Its member centres are based in local communities, working with volunteers, local historical societies, local clergy, local authorities, county libraries and government agencies to build a database of genealogical records for their county.[16]

HYPHENATED AMERICAN GENEALOGY SOCIETIES

Descendants of immigrants from most other countries have organized societies to promote knowledge of and research about the cultures and families of the motherland. These exist for almost all points of origin and can be found by Googling "*-American

Genealogy Society"; or if you have a specific country in mind, you can replace the "*" in the search statement with the name of the country in which you have an interest. Some of these societies offer a wide array of information and other services—including an opportunity to make contact with other researchers who are interested in the same surnames and/or localities in which your patrons have an interest.

VOCABULARY OF GENEALOGICAL TERMS

Even if you don't know anything about the language of the country where your patron's ancestral home is located, you can still figure out some of the records if you are sufficiently motivated. The following three hints will assist you in that process:

1. Many European genealogy websites have an English version. Examine the page closely to see if there is link to such a version. It could be an icon of an American flag or of the flag of the United Kingdom.
2. Whole web pages or parts of them can be loosely translated from other languages into English by utilities like Google Translate (http://translate.google.com). While these automated translations may not be ideal, often they will allow researchers to get the general idea of the document.
3. Many genealogical glossaries are available to give researchers assistance in deciphering basic terms such as *marriage, death, birth, father, grandmother,* and so forth. With a little patient effort, those unfamiliar with a language will either find something useful or be able to determine that the records contain no relevant information. It is also important to use such glossaries even when examining a document written in languages in which the researchers believe themselves fluent—like English. Specialized terms are often different from one area to another and from one historical period to another.

    There are a number of ways to find such glossaries. The simple way is to Google something like "German genealogy glossary" (without the quotation marks). You can also consult CyndisList.com, FamilySearch, and so forth.

However, often the services of a language and/or country research specialist will need to be enlisted in order to discover all the information that is there to be found.

NO FREE LUNCH

Your patrons are always looking for free information. The information you provide them is free up to a point. Generally, there is not a meter on most library services. However, particularly after the recent economic downturn, we are reminded that even free library services must be paid for by someone—even if it is your community as a whole that shoulders the costs.

Free websites are no different. They must be paid for in some way by someone. When your patrons find a website that has a URL ending in .com, it is a commercial site. Perhaps it can pay its costs by selling advertising in the page margins. Often, some free information is offered to lure individuals to these sites in the hope that they will buy additional information, services, or products. URLs ending in .gov are operated by a governmental agency. These sites may be operated solely at taxpayer expense, but some of them also try to recover costs by selling some information or services. Sites with URLs ending in .org tend to have the aura of operating for the public good. However, they also exist to promote some cause, perhaps one that is very beneficial to society, and they also have something to sell or will solicit a contribution. There is nothing wrong with any of this, but consumers should understand that *free* sometimes comes at a cost. If the sites cannot support themselves, they will not be able to sustain and expand their information and other services.

When researchers look for free information on the Internet about genealogy in foreign countries, all of these factors are involved. In addition, another factor should be considered. Websites aimed at attracting genealogical researchers from other countries take one or both of two approaches. Some of them are designed to provide information and services through the site itself. Others are designed to entice the site visitors to come and do research in that country. Again, there is nothing wrong with either approach. The latter may be subsidized by the host government or industries that benefit from tourists' dollars. It is beneficial for researchers to understand this as they surf the web. Sites that are aimed at promoting tourism are not likely to offer a great deal of information that can be downloaded and consumed for free over the Internet. On the other hand, what could be better than to be able to research our ancestors during a visit to the land where they lived their lives?

SURNAME LOCATORS

Finding your ancestors in their country of origin if you don't have a specific location to research can be harder than finding the proverbial needle in a haystack. For some countries, the odds of finding them can be improved—particularly if your ancestors had unusual surnames. That means unusual in their country of origin. Your odds can be improved even more if you have a married couple who immigrated together, you know both of their surnames, *and* both of these names are uncommon.

Some European countries have surname distribution maps. It is better if these maps are based on data close to the time that your ancestors immigrated, but even present-day data can be helpful. If all else fails, telephone directories can be of some value. Again, it depends on how common your surnames are in that country.

Examples of such surname distribution maps are as follows:

1. Poland: http://www.moikrewni.pl/mapa/. Although this page will come up in Polish, you probably will be able to guess how to use it. You can use Google to translate it into English using Google Translate, as mentioned earlier. Easiest of all, if you are using Google Chrome as your browser, a bar will pop up at the top of the page asking you if you want the page translated into English.
2. Italy: http://gens.labo.net/.
3. France: http://www.geopatronyme.com/. This one has the advantage of allowing the researcher to choose four different historical periods to be mapped.
4. United Kingdom: http://www.britishsurnames.co.uk/. For best results on this site, enter a surname and then select the tab for distribution in the 1881 census.

This technique will not work well with common surnames. It works best when two (or more) uncommon ancestral names happen to be concentrated in the same region of the country. Even better, combine this technique with other bits of information from oral tradition and family documents. It is not a magical solution, but it may be able to help you narrow your search or to confirm other fuzzy information.

SPECIALIZED RESOURCES

Each country has its own specialized resources that may not be available for other countries, as well as specialized repositories that may be off the beaten path. Only a comprehensive guide to a particular country could include them, but to cite one example, Norwegian researchers are blessed to have *bygdeboks,* which, roughly translated, are parish books. *Bygdeboks* have been described as consisting of one or more of the following:

1. A broad "general history" (*generell historie*) covering many hundreds of years
2. A "farm history" (*gårdshistorie*), going back as far as sources exist
3. A "genealogy" part (*slektshistorie*), as a rule going back to 1600[17]

More information on *bygdeboks* can be found on RootsWeb.[18] Various libraries in the United States have *bygdeboks* in their collections. The Family History Library contains a few hundred. The University of North Dakota houses one of the largest collections of such books in the United States—approximately 1,000. The University of Minnesota libraries also own a substantial collection.

Clan records are another type of specialized records. A small library in Moultrie, Georgia, houses a very extensive collection of genealogical information about Scottish clans. These records are arranged more like an archive than a library. Records of more than 100 clans and related family organizations have been deposited in the Moultrie–

Colquitt County Library, which started its Scottish collections when it received a million-dollar bequest about two decades ago.[19]

Researchers who live in or focus their research on a given country tend to post their compiled genealogies on web-hosting sites local to that country. GenesReunited is an example of such a site based in the United Kingdom. For a modest annual fee, members can upload GEDCOM versions of their family histories and compare them with those of other members. This site allows members to have control over who has access to the information in their trees.

Bygdeboks, clan files, and compiled genealogies are just three examples of small but very rich special collections of genealogical information that are available in surprising places.

SUMMARY

This very quick overview of genealogy research beyond the borders of the United States may seem more confusing than helpful to some of you. However, the process outlined earlier for U.S. research works in other countries as well. Researchers should start with what they know, collecting all the information known to or owned by family members. Build back to the ancestral country. Create geographic and historical time lines. This may allow you to identify the specific locations of the relatives and of the records for their era. The examples sprinkled throughout this chapter are intended to whet your appetite to find similar means for exploring the genealogical records of the ancestral homes of your patrons.

NOTES

1. Ellis Island—FREE Port of New York Passenger Records Search, http://www.ellisisland.org (accessed March 9, 2011). This site requires registration but not payment for use.
2. Castle Gardens arrival records are being indexed, and that index can be searched free at http://castlegardens.org (accessed March 9, 2011).
3. Stephen Morse, "1 Step Webpages," http://stephenmorse.org (accessed March 9, 2011).
4. Maureen Taylor, http://www.maureentaylor.com/ (accessed March 9, 2011).
5. Erich Uetrecht, *Meyers Orts- und Verkehrs-Lexikon des Deutschen Reichs,* 5th ed. (Leipzig, Germany: Bibliographisches Institut, 1912–1913).
6. E. Uetricht, *Meyers Orts- und Verkehrs-Lexikon des Deutschen Reichs: auf Grund amtlicher Unterlagen von Reichs-, Landes- und Gemeindebehörden* (Leipzig: Bibliographisches Institut, 1912–1913). Family History Archives, http://contentdm.lib.byu.edu/cgi-bin/showfile.exe?CISOROOT=/FHSS&CISOPTR=36853&filename=36854.pdf (accessed March 10, 2011).

7. Per Clemensson and Kjell Anderson, *Your Swedish Roots: A Step by Step Handbook* (Provo, UT: Ancestry Publishing, 2004).

8. Research Guidance/Helps, Family Search.org, http://www.familysearch.org/eng/search/RG/frameset_rg.asp (accessed March 10, 2011).

9. FamilySearch Wiki, https://wiki.familysearch.org/en/Main_Page (accessed April 1, 2011).

10. Kimberly Powell, "Genealogy by Region," About.com, http://genealogy.about.com/od/localities/Genealogy_by_Region.htm (accessed March 10, 2011).

11. WorldGenWeb, http://www.worldgenweb.org/ (accessed March 10, 2011).

12. Cyndi's List of Genealogy Sites on the Internet, http://www.cyndislist.com/ (accessed March 10, 2011).

13. Centennia Historical Atlas, http://www.clockwk.com/centennia.html (accessed March 10, 2011).

14. "Patronyms," *Wikipedia,* http://en.wikipedia.org/wiki/Patronymic (accessed September 18, 2010).

15. "The Gregorian Calendar—History," Infoplease.com, http://www.infoplease.com/spot/gregorian1.html#ixzz0zpOYlSBQ (accessed March 10, 2011).

16. E-mail from Irish Family History Foundation (enquiries@rootsireland.ie) received by the author July 19, 2010.

17. Johan I. Borgos, "A 'Bygdesdok'—What Is That?" Slekt & historie, http://www.nndata.no/home/jborgos/bygdeen.htm (accessed March 10, 2011).

18. "Bygdeboker," RootsWeb, http://homepages.rootsweb.ancestry.com/~norway/bygdebok.html (accessed March 10, 2011).

19. "The Ellen Payne Odom Genealogy Library," ElectricScotland, http://www.electricscotland.com/familytree/about_odom.htm (accessed March 10, 2011).

CHAPTER 9

Fieldtrips

Sooner or later, your patrons will exhaust the resources of your library and the electronic resources you can help them find on the Internet. Dick Eastman reminds us there is much more out there. In a recent issue of *Eastman's Online Genealogy Newsletter,* he made the provocative statement, "I am guessing that 98% of the information of interest to genealogists has not yet been digitized."[1] So Dick's message, which I strongly endorse, is that there is a great deal of information out there to help document family histories. Much of the relevant documents are in other libraries and in courthouses or other government repositories. Cemeteries are also full of dead people waiting for their lives to be documented.

LIBRARIES

Every region of the country has libraries with strong genealogy collections. Some specialize in their own region, and others are international in scope. You will want to learn what other collections are within a reasonable traveling distance for your patrons. In this Crash Course book, I can only mention a few of the most outstanding genealogy libraries. If you don't know ones near you, start asking your patrons where they have had good experiences in their research. Local genealogy society members also are usually willing to share their experiences. Resource guides for most states are available through USGenWeb.org. The new Wiki.FamilySearch.org also has an article for most states under, for example, "Alabama Archives and Libraries." Substitute the name of your state for Alabama in this search statement.

GenWise News columnist Gena Philbert Ortega advises researchers who visit a library to take full advantage of it.

> When searching through a library, make sure to utilize all the library has to offer including online databases, periodical collections, special collections, and rare books. It's always a good idea to check out the library website prior to making a trip and noting any resources that you want to look at while there. Don't forget to talk to a reference librarian once you have arrived and ask him or her for any other resources that might be helpful.[2]

This would be good advice if they are visiting your library. Make sure you are prepared to help researchers take full advantage of all these resources when they visit your library. This comprehensive approach is particularly important when the researcher is visiting from out of the area and may not soon have another opportunity to return to examine overlooked treasures in your collections.

Ortega's advice is also a good approach for you to recommend to patrons when you refer them to larger and more specialized libraries. There it is very important to have a plan prior to arrival. Otherwise, a great deal of time can be wasted by being so overwhelmed by the vast array of possibilities that researchers can be paralyzed into inaction or at least into wasted time and effort. Generally library catalogs can be searched prior to arrival, and a list of items of interest can be identified. As a result, your patrons can become productive almost from the minute they walk in the door.

Even though Dr. Dave's Rule 7 is to have a plan, some of the best finds may be serendipitous. Researchers need to be alert for and open to unscripted opportunities as Dorcas, an otherwise anonymous researcher, reports.

> As I was leaving the Courthouse, I noticed the Historical Society across the street. I figured there wasn't much chance of finding anything, but I'd give it a try. I told the folks at the information desk what I was looking for. They said that they didn't know anything about a family of Hubbell in their county, but there was a lady from the next county who kept coming over and looking.... They gave me a telephone number.
>
> She said that she had no information on my grandfather's family, but if anyone would know it would be Clyde Hubbell in Ithica [sic], New York.... I wrote to Clyde and he quickly wrote back saying that he didn't know about my grandfather (the youngest child) but here was the information on his brother, sister, and his parents, and gave me all the information going back 12 generations, to our immigrant ancestor who was in the Great Migration. Since then I have been able to find documentation for all the data Clyde sent me. This is something I would never have been able to do if I hadn't made the trip to New York.[3]

All of your patrons will not be motivated to use their vacations to explore repositories of genealogical documents and information. However, some of them will be. This chapter includes a few of the libraries that are significant enough to be vacation destinations for dedicated genealogists. As Lauren Gamber colorfully states: "Whether your ancestors hailed from Michigan or Maine, Milan or Minsk, you're bound to make headway at one of these giant repositories."[4] My list here is in no way comprehensive and is limited to libraries with which I have had personal experience. Lists created by other genealogists would vary based on their personal experience and geographic location.

FAMILY HISTORY LIBRARY (FHL)

It is with good reason that the FHL in Salt Lake City is considered the Mecca for genealogical researchers from around the world. The sole purpose of this library is to serve family history researchers. Local hotels offer special travel packages for researchers, as do genealogy societies near and far. I have a timeshare within walking distance so that I can spend two weeks there each year. Nearby is a great staff cafeteria for which researchers can pick up a guest pass at the library information desk.

Its 142,000 square feet spread over five floors justify its claim as the largest library of its kind in the world. Some 1,500 visitors come to the library on a typical day for research and/or attend short seminars for which there is no charge. The main attractions are the collections, and statistics about them are mind-numbing: "The collection includes over 2.4 million rolls of microfilmed genealogical records; 742,000 microfiche; 310,000 books, serials, and other formats; 4,500 periodicals; 700 electronic resources."[5]

Internal databases contain hundreds of millions of names. These databases, of which the Ancestral File, the International Genealogical Index (IGI), and the Pedigree Resource File are the most prominent, are searchable remotely; however, the backup data is only available in Salt Lake City. Detailed information about these databases can be found on the FamilySearch.org website. Records are available from around the world. According to a media kit for the library: "In 2003, the collection increased monthly by an average of 4,100 rolls of film, 700 books, and 16 electronic resources. A majority of the records contain information about persons who lived before 1930."[6] While this ambitious filming of records continues, the emphasis recently has shifted from microfilming to digitization.

Its library facilities are also impressive. At last report, there were about 500 patron computers, almost as many microform readers, and a like number of reading room seats. The library has taken the lead in applying technology to the transfer of microfilm images or book scans to patron flash drives.[7]

Mormon missionaries and paid staff are available to conduct orientations, answer reference questions, and teach research classes. Some of them are country and language specialists who can be of great assistance in tracing ancestors in other countries.

Currently 100 full-time and part-time professional staff members are supplemented by approximately 700 trained volunteers.[8]

FAMILY HISTORY CENTERS

Family history centers can best be understood as remote branches of the FHL. Currently there are more than 4,500 family history centers operating in more than 100 countries. Since local family history centers are staffed by volunteers, their hours are not as extensive as researchers have come to expect at public libraries. However, about 100,000 rolls of microfilm are circulated to family history centers each month.[9]

In addition to providing a portal to the vast resources from the FHL, the local family history centers also provide access to many electronic databases to which your library may not be able to afford subscriptions. Although the array of databases will vary from time to time and perhaps from center to center, the following might be typical:

1. 19th-Century British Library Newspaper Digital Archive
2. Alexander Street Press—The American Civil War. This collection contains a research database; collections of letters and diaries; and a database of images, photographs, posters, and ephemera.
3. Ancestry.com
4. FindMyPast.com.uk
5. Footnote.com
6. The Genealogist
7. Genline.com (Swedish parish records)
8. Godfrey Memorial Library
9. HeritageQuest Online
10. Historic Map Works Library Edition
11. World Vital Records

LIBRARY OF CONGRESS (LC)

Washington, D.C., offers a trifecta of genealogical treasure houses to attract family history researchers. The U.S. National Archives was previously discussed in chapter 3. A database of the National Society of the Daughters of the American Revolution (DAR) Library was discussed in chapter 6, but other features of that institution will be discussed in this chapter. That leaves the Library of Congress (LC), the world's largest library, which among other collections, holds more than 50,000 genealogies, 100,000 local histories, 5 million maps, and extensive collections of city directories and newspapers.[10]

Many of the LC's holdings can be explored from afar. One of the most important collections is American Memory.

American Memory is a gateway to the Library of Congress's vast resources of digitized American historical materials. Comprising more than 9 million items that document U.S. history and culture, American Memory is organized into more than 100 thematic collections based on their original format, their subject matter, or who first created, assembled, or donated them to the Library.[11]

Can I find genealogy information in American Memory?

To see if information about your ancestors is included anywhere in American Memory, enter your family name in the search box at the top of each American Memory page. Serious genealogical researchers will also want to consult the bibliographies, research guides, and web links available online from the Library's *Local History and Genealogy Reading Room.*

Can I find local history content in American Memory?

To find American Memory collections specifically devoted to city, state, or regional subjects, you can browse the *collections in a variety of ways.* To find information about a specific place, enter the name in the search box at the top of any American Memory page. Also check the home pages of each of the books and other printed texts, *American Memory collections of books and other printed texts,* so that wherever possible you can search the full text of their documents.[12]

In late 2010, the LC released the beta version of a new search engine to explore its holdings more efficiently. You can try it at search.loc.gov.

Visiting the LC for the first time can be incredibly intimidating. The facilities cover three square blocks, and there are various reading rooms in each of the buildings. All of this is connected by underground tunnels, which at first are a bit of a challenge to navigate. At least two cafeterias provide nourishment for researchers and staff alike. LC is a closed-stacks facility, which means patrons must fill out request slips for most items they wish to examine. Before your patrons attempt to use this facility for genealogy research, you should strongly encourage them to print out and carry with them a copy of "Genealogy Research at the Library of Congress."[13] This 10-page guide may be the difference between a productive trip and a failed one. The guide is one of the more than 30 bibliographies and guides written by the reference librarians of the Local History and Genealogy Reading Room that can be downloaded and examined prior to a visit.[14] That reading room should be the place where they start their research.

DAR LIBRARY

While the LC is near the U.S. Capitol building where Congress conducts business, the DAR Library is just off the Capitol Mall near the White House. Compared to the LC, the DAR Library is cozy. Its open-stacks arrangement allows researchers to browse the shelves and retrieve their own materials. When using the library, it is obvious this lovely building was not built for a library of this size, as the shelving sequences are sometimes difficult to follow as they wind through the various alcoves. There is a modest fee for researchers who are not DAR members. A quick lunch can be found in the American Red Cross complex across the street.

> This... library was founded as a collection of genealogical and historical publications used to verify application papers for society membership. It now houses those applications and supporting files plus biographies, genealogies, cemetery records, Bible records, church records, city directories, periodicals and manuscripts—making it an especially great resource for tracing your ancestry to the Revolutionary War.[15]
>
> The DAR Library is one of the largest genealogical research centers in the United States. Since its founding in 1896, the library has grown into a specialized collection of American genealogical and historical manuscripts and publications and recently added powerful on-site ancestry databases to its collection. The DAR Library collection contains over 180,000 books, 300,000 research files, thousands of manuscript items, and special collections on Native American, African American and women's history, genealogy and culture. Nearly 30,000 family histories and genealogies comprise a major portion of the book collection, many of which are unique or available in only a few libraries in the country.[16]

NEW ENGLAND HISTORIC GENEALOGICAL SOCIETY (NEHGS) LIBRARY

"Hist. Gen," as it is called by some, is located in the Back Bay section of Boston. Since 1847 the society has published the venerable *New England Historical and Genealogical Register.* It also publishes a slicker, more graphically appealing periodical, which until recently was called *New England Ancestors.* In keeping with recognition that the scope of its collections and interests are much wider than New England, the title of the latter publication was recently changed to *American Ancestors.* Databases offered to members include indexes to an expanding number of journals not published by the society as well as town guides and early vital records for New England. Gamber describes the facility as, "Eight floors hold unpublished genealogies, Bible records, family associations' papers, diaries, journals, photographs, cemetery records and other rarities."[17] As with most society libraries, a small researchers' fee is charged to non-members. There are a variety of nice lunch spots just down the block.

ALLEN COUNTY PUBLIC LIBRARY

"This Fort Wayne, Ind., library's claim to fame," according to Gamber, "is the Periodical Source Index which catalogs thousands of genealogical and historical periodicals published since 1800. Staff have collected more than 10,000 titles.

You can access PERSI from any library that has a HeritageQuest Online subscription."[18]

Dick Eastman describes a more recent development: "The new web site, located at www.genealogycenter.org, includes several free databases and portals including the African American Gateway, Family Bible Records and Our Military Heritage that have been developed by the Genealogy Center."[19]

The library specializes in Canadian, British Isles, African American, and American Indian research. Its collection comprises 588,645 microfilms and microfiches, 55,804 volumes of family history books, 206,366 volumes of local history books, 28,575 microfilm reels of historical newspapers, thousands of maps and gazetteers, and more.[20] There is a small deli/snack bar on the premises.

MIDWEST GENEALOGY CENTER

This library is almost unique among top genealogy libraries because of its location and new facility. Located in a suburb of Kansas City, it is easily approached by I-70 and has ample free parking. I'm afraid I do not have any lunch tips as I have not been there at mealtime. Gamber describes this facility's collections:

> *Mid-Continent Public Library Midwest Genealogy Center:* The new Midwest Genealogy Center in Independence, Mo., accommodates the library's 80,000 family history books, 100,000 local history items, 565,000 rolls of microfilm and microfiche, and 7,000 maps.
>
> It earns high marks for its complete US. census collection, many immigration and naturalization records, manuscripts pertaining to the American slave trade and the Antebellum South, and focus on the Southeast, Mid-Atlantic, Midwest and Plains states.[21]

NEWBERRY LIBRARY

The Newberry on the Near North Side of Chicago is an outstanding private research library that specializes in the humanities. One of the strengths of the collection is its

> over 17,000 published genealogies. The collection's coverage of colonial America and New England is particularly strong. Many rare titles covering gentry and noble families of the British Isles are also included.
>
> The local history collection includes county, city, town, church, and other local histories from all regions of the United States, as well as from Canada and the British Isles. The Newberry holds a comprehensive collection of New England town histories, as well as a strong collection of county histories from the Midwest

and Mid-Atlantic states. The collection of local histories from the British Isles is also noteworthy.[22]

In recent years, the Newberry has created a number of electronic resources that can be of great value to researchers whether or not they are able to visit Chicago. Among these are the notable resource ChicagoAncestors.org and a broad collection of pathfinders, which can be accessed through the library's website.[23]

OTHER LIBRARIES

Other areas of the country have their own go-to genealogy libraries. The Los Angeles area has a collection of public and private libraries each with their own collection strengths. These include the downtown LA Public Library and the recently renovated and enhanced Church of Jesus Christ of Latter-Day Saints Family History Center in West Los Angeles. Nearby are the Sons of the Revolution Library in Glendale, the Southern California Genealogical Society Library and the Immigrants Library in Burbank, as well as the U.S. National Archives and Records Administration (NARA) branch archive in Orange County.

The San Francisco Bay area offers the Sutro Library, a branch of the California State Library located on the edge of the San Francisco State University campus. The Sutro specializes in the genealogy of the 49 states other than California. This resource is supplemented by a NARA branch archive in San Bruno, near the San Francisco airport, and the California Genealogical Society Library in Oakland.

Other areas of the country also have great libraries worth a genealogical field trip. Send me a description of your favorite genealogy library. If you provide a compelling description, I'll publish it on my blog.

COURTHOUSES

As important as libraries are in genealogical research, we as library workers need to keep in mind that the original records are generally only found in archives. For many records, that means a trip to a courthouse is required to view and copy these records. Libraries often have indexes, abstracts, and transcriptions. However, even the most careful indexer, abstractor, or transcriber adds the element of human error—particularly when they are dealing with interpreting poor penmanship, damaged pages, and fading ink. Sometimes only the original document can clear up ambiguities or correct misconceptions.

Christine Rose has distilled her wisdom gained from more than 500 courthouse visits in an entire book on how to succeed in courthouse research—starting with preparation that begins before the researcher leaves home. Her guidance starts with a discussion of whether one needs to actually visit the repository.[24] Her first tip seems obvious but is sometimes overlooked. Researchers should make sure they are going to the right repository.[25] To find the rest of the story, see her book. Anecdotes of what can be found in courthouse research can be found in Diane Rapaport's regular column in *American Ancestry*.[26] Courthouses have a wide variety of records that document all kinds of transactions your ancestors had with their local government, including but not limited to the following:

1. Vital records
2. Probate records
3. Tax records
4. Property records
5. Voting records

Other repositories that may be valuable to family researchers are state archives, university archives, manuscript collections and historical society collections, churches, schools, and last but not least, cemeteries.

RANDOM ACTS OF GENEALOGICAL KINDNESS

If a road trip cannot be fit into your clients' calendars and they cannot afford to hire a professional genealogist at the remote location where their ancestors lived, Random Acts of Genealogical Kindness™ (RAOGK) may meet their needs. The RAOGK website explains, "Our volunteers have agreed to do a free genealogy research task at least once per month in their local area as an act of kindness."[27] While the time of the volunteer is free, you will be charged for any incidental expenses such as copying fees. One way for you and your patrons to pay back this generous service is to become volunteers in your own area.

Other sites like Find-a-Grave operate on similar principles but have a more limited focus. In this example, the services of Find-a-Grave volunteers are limited to photographing tombstones. It purports to already have 55 million searchable grave records online.[28]

SUMMARY

In addition to the documents that may be unearthed, descendants also can get a feel for the original places their ancestors inhabited by walking the same land and viewing the same sights. In the next chapter, we will explore another way to get better acquainted with ancestors through examining their DNA.

NOTES

1. Dick Eastman, "Are You Missing Most of the Available Genealogy Information?" *Eastman's Online Genealogy Newsletter,* October 20, 2010, http://www.eogn.com/wp/lastweek.htm#-_Are_You_Missing_Most_of_the_Available (accessed November 3, 2010).
2. Gena Philibert Ortega, "Great Library Finds from Members," *GenWise News,* July 28, 2010.
3. Dorcas A, "Great Library Finds from Members," *GenWise News,* July 28, 2010.
4. Lauren Gamber, "9 Genealogy Libraries to Visit Before You Die," *Family Tree Magazine,* September 28, 2009, http://www.familytreemagazine.com/article/9-libraries (accessed March 11, 2011).
5. "Media Kit for the Family History Library," FamilySearch, http://www.familysearch.org/eng/Home/News/frameset_news.asp?PAGE = Press/fhl_library_facts.asp (accessed September 15, 2010).
6. Ibid.
7. Ibid.
8. Ibid.
9. Ibid.
10. Gamber, "9 Genealogy Libraries to Visit Before You Die."
11. "About American Memory," Library of Congress, http://memory.loc.gov/ammem/about/about.html (accessed November 4, 2010).
12. "Frequently Asked Questions: Genealogy/Local History," Library of Congress, http://memory.loc.gov/ammem/help/faq.html#local (accessed November 4, 2010).
13. Local History and Genealogy Reading Room, Library of Congress, "Genealogical Research at the Library of Congress," http://www.loc.gov/rr/genealogy/bib_guid/research.pdf (accessed November 4, 2010).
14. "Bibliographies and Guides," Library of Congress, http://www.loc.gov/rr/genealogy/bib_guid/bibguide.html (accessed November 4, 2010).
15. Gamber, "9 Genealogy Libraries to Visit Before You Die."
16. National Society of the Daughters of the American Revolution, http://www.dar.org/natsociety/content.cfm?ID = 828&hd = n (accessed September 22, 2010).
17. Gamber, "9 Genealogy Libraries to Visit Before You Die."
18. Ibid.
19. Dick Eastman, "New Genealogy Site: http://www.genealogycenter.org," *Eastman's Online Genealogy Newsletter,* http://blog.eogn.com/eastmans_online_genealogy/2010/10/new-genealogy-site-httpwwwgenealogycenterorg.html, October 12, 2010 (accessed October 11, 2010).
20. Gamber, "9 Genealogy Libraries to Visit Before You Die."
21. Ibid.
22. "Overview of Newberry Library's Genealogy Collections," The Newberry Library, http://www.newberry.org/genealogy/overview.html (accessed December 10, 2010).
23. Ibid.
24. Christine Rose, *Courthouse Research for Family Historians: Your Guide to Genealogical Treasures* (San Jose, CA: CR Publications, 2004), p. xvii.

25. Ibid., pp. 1–3.
26. Diane Rapaport, "Tales from the Courthouse," a regular column in *American Ancestry* (prior to 2010, *New England Ancestry*).
27. Random Acts of Genealogical Kindness, http://www.raogk.org/ (accessed September 24, 2010).
28. Find a Grave, http://www.findagrave.com/ (accessed March 11, 2011).

CHAPTER 10

Incorporating DNA Research

He's back! That hyperactive oral learner from chapter 1 is standing in front of you again. This time, he is clutching a 9" x 11-1/2" white envelope. In it, he quickly tells you, are his DNA lab test results. He proudly produces an impressive looking chart that shows his 12-marker results; then he demands that you tell him what they mean. Your patron has just employed the latest genealogical tool to research his genome to find his family tree. He has an impressive looking chart that looks suitable for framing, but what does it all mean? On the surface, it tells him nothing about his family history. He was under the impression that if he swabbed the inside of his cheek and sent the sample to the lab, they would be able to tell him his entire family history.

DNA is an important new tool for 21st-century genealogists. Someone has said DNA testing is "putting the gene: back in genealogy."[1] However, it is a supplement to and not a replacement for traditional family history research. Wrapping your mind around the information in this chapter will take some time and probably require some rereading. You are not being asked to become a geneticist. Rather, you are being given some information on how to apply DNA research to the traditional process of family history research.

There are several separate and distinct kinds of DNA research. Some of them are as follows:

1. Crime scene investigation (CSI) forensic identification of a specific individual.
2. Medical testing for specific genes that may have an impact on various health risks.

143

3. Paternity testing to establish the father and/or mother of a specific individual.
4. Haplotype testing for deep ancestry which may have sociological value in identifying one's ancient clan or tribe.
5. Genealogical testing to establish or eliminate possible family relationships.

It is the latter two types of testing that will be discussed in this chapter.

> Today the number of families tested has reached the mass required to define the migration patterns of our ancient past. The results will rewrite the first chapter of every family history and expand genealogy into a whole new realm, that of one's *deep ancestry*—determining where and when these…ancestors lived…Imagine uncovering which ancestors have Greco-Roman, central Asian, or Mid-Eastern ancestry. Imagine discovering that one's family shares a DNA signature with the ancient Hebrews or the ancient Egyptians. Imagine finding a common ancestry among the indigenous tribes of India, the Chaldeans of the Tigris and Euphrates, or the ancient peoples of East Africa. Today family historians, through the interpretation of genealogically based DNA testing, can not only speculate origins prior to written records but prove family connections back thousands of years.
> DNA is nature's biological road map to understand our deep past.[2]

Test results for an individual are meaningless in isolation. They take on meaning only when they are compared with databases containing the results of many people. In this case, big is definitely better. The larger the database against which your patron can compare his results, the more likely he will learn something useful about his family history.

Genetics is a relatively young field. It is currently one of the most dynamic areas of scientific research. New discoveries are made constantly. What one thinks one knows today is likely to change within a few months as more is discovered in the labs.

Y-CHROMOSOME TESTING

For the first decade of the 21st century, the most potent use of DNA in genealogy research has been for Y-chromosome comparisons. Only males have Y chromosomes. Therefore, only males can be tested for Y-chromosome DNA. Men pass a copy of their Y-chromosome genes to each of their male offspring. In a vast majority of these intergenerational transfers, the markers on the Y-chromosome genes are copied exactly. This allows researchers to follow lines of ascent backward in time. However, in a very small percentage of transmissions, a mistake or mutation is made in the marker-copying process. This small number of mutations is what allows us to differentiate between different family lines. While Y-chromosome results are useful, the test results only apply to a small part of a male's family tree.

In Figure 10.1 note that the Y-chromosome test results only give information concerning 1 of the 8 great-grandparents. This small fraction of ancestors that can be

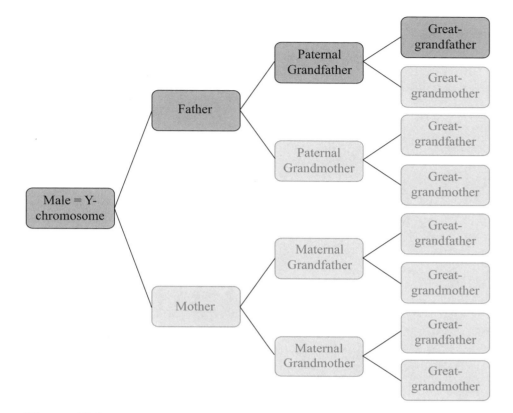

Figure 10.1: **Y-chromosome DNA testing can help men trace their paternal line.**

illuminated based on Y-chromosome results shrinks significantly with each preceding generation to 1 of 16 great-great-grandparents and 1 of 32 great-great-great-grandparents, and so forth.

MITOCHONDRIAL TESTING

Mitochondrial DNA is passed from the mother to each of her children whether they are male or female (Figure 10.2). Both genders can be tested for mitochondrial DNA. Mothers, even after they give birth, continue to provide a safe environment for and nourishment of every cell in the body of each of their offspring through this transfer of mitochondrial DNA. Although it is not important that you understand mitochondria from the perspective of a geneticist, perhaps you should know that these organelles are not chromosomes. In my own nonscientific understanding, I view mitochondria as the battery packs contained in each human cell to provide the energy needed for that cell to operate. In this analogy, the nucleus of the cell containing the chromosomes draws energy from the surrounding mitochondria. Both mitochondrion and chromosomes

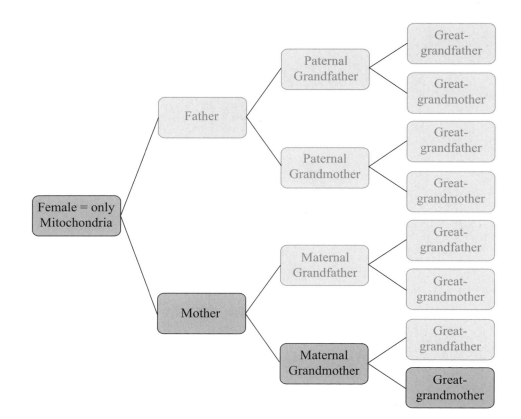

Figure 10.2: **Mitochondrial DNA can help both women and men trace their maternal line.**

have DNA that can be examined. I hope geneticists reading this description are not gritting their teeth.

Mitochondrial DNA is more stable than Y-chromosome DNA. That means there are fewer mutations (copying errors) between generations in mitochondrial DNA than Y-chromosome DNA. Mitochondria generally remain identical through many, many generations. Therefore, mitochondrial DNA is more useful for tracing deep ancestry back hundreds or even tens of thousands of years than it is for differentiating among different family lines in genealogical time. In this sense, genealogical time means the last few centuries when most families have had surnames. For example, a mitochondrial match at the lowest testing level may only indicate that there is a 50 percent chance of a common female ancestress within the last 52 generations or so. That is much too far back to have meaning in most family trees. Higher levels of testing might have raised that precision up to a 50 percent chance of a common female ancestress within the last 20 generations; but that still is not too helpful for genealogical purposes. Until mid-2009, I was actively discouraging students and clients from testing their mitochondria unless they had a specific situation in which it could be useful. For example, it might have eliminated the possibility of a close match or it might have given a clue about some deep ethnic origin, but it would not have been useful in identifying specific ancestors.

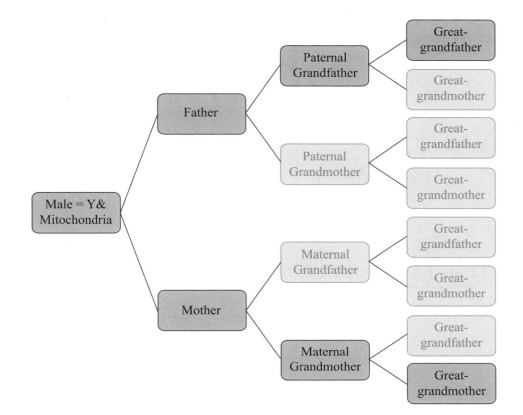

Figure 10.3: Men can use Y-chromosome DNA testing to trace their paternal line as well as mitochondrial DNA testing for their maternal line.

At the risk of being redundant, women cannot be tested for Y-chromosome DNA. On the other hand, men can be tested for both mitochondrial and Y-chromosome DNA. This gender difference may not seem fair, but there really is a genetic difference between girls and boys. Therefore, a male, if he is tested for both, can find information about both of his parents, half of his grandparents, but only 2 of his 8 great-great-grandparents, and so forth (see Figure 10.3).

The precision of mitochondrial testing for the consumer genealogy market changed radically in 2009. This was brought about by the introduction of mtFullSequence testing to the masses at an almost affordable price. Heretofore, only small fragments of mitochondrial DNA had been tested—generally, a sequence at the beginning (HVR2) and a sequence at the end (HVR1). The mtFullSequence test (briefly called FGS at first) is billed as the last mitochondrial test one would ever have to have because it tests the entire mitochondrial genome—some 16,569 values.

Most of the previous limitations remained. Only the direct maternal line could be traced backward in time. However, more mutations could be detected because they had previously been outside the area being examined. Therefore, more branching of the human tree could be identified. As a result, the ancient tribes or haplogroups (see discussion later in this chapter) could be divided into smaller and more homogeneously useful subgroups.

The downside for the short term is that relatively few individuals have tested at the mtFullSequence level. It will take time—perhaps a few years—for the databases of tested individuals to grow large enough so that most of those who have tested to this level can expect to find meaningful matches to aid their genealogical research. It is too early to know if this level of exploration will ever be as useful as a 67-marker Y-chromosome test now is for tracing paternal lines. Only a few more years of accumulated experience will tell.

To maximize the power of DNA research, one needs to participate in a DNA project that includes many potential or actual extended family members. If family members are strategically chosen and can be recruited to be tested, DNA can be a powerful tool in genealogical research.

TESTING FAMILY MEMBERS AS SURROGATES

It is quite common for women to recruit a brother, father, male cousin, or nephew to act as a surrogate donor of a Y-chromosome DNA sample for testing to establish paternal lineages. Other ingenious uses of surrogates can be made to test specific hypotheses. For example, surname DNA projects often test a carefully selected sample of the present-day male descendants of a family patriarch who lived long ago. This can lead to information that is very helpful in grouping his descendants and separating out nondescendants.

In like manner, surrogate donors can be useful for mitochondrial testing. For example, my paper research trail indicated that a sixth great-grandfather, Henry Stedham, had taken as his third wife a woman reportedly named Marjory Owens. I have only found her surname in one marriage document. Generally, Owens is considered to be a surname of Welsh origin. There are known to have been Owens from Wales in nearby Maryland around that time—early 1700s. However, Henry and Marjory lived in an area that had been settled in the 17th century as New Sweden and now is part of present-day Delaware. Henry's father had come as a child from Sweden along with his family. So I was left to wrestle with the question of whether Marjory was of Swedish or Welsh ancestry.

Marjory was a direct maternal ancestress of my grandmother. Unfortunately, it was the wrong grandmother. I could not use my mitochondrial DNA sample to test for a relationship because Marjory was an ancestor of my father through his mother, and my father was deceased. My father could not pass on his mother's mitochondrial DNA. Only mothers can provide mitochondrial DNA to their descendants. To explore this relationship, I recruited a first cousin who is the daughter of my father's sister (Figure 10.4).

My cousin is a descendant back to Marjory in an unbroken female line of eight generations (two of which are shown in Figure 10.4). My cousin's mitochondrial sample was subjected to a mtFullSequence test. This test is still pricey, but lower-level tests are not precise enough to return genealogically useful results that would have been useful in addressing my research question. Since mitochondrial tests at the mtFullSequence

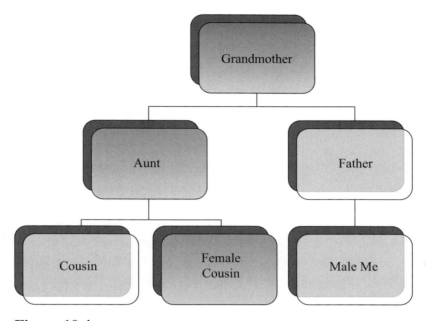

Figure 10.4: **Female cousin gives surrogate mitochondrial DNA sample to test to help a male test his paternal grandmother's line.**

level have just recently come on the market, the databases of tested individuals are still very small. However, I was fortunate to have my cousin exactly match four individuals in the database of Family Tree DNA (FTDNA). Two of these four matches live in Finland, and the others are believed to be of Finnish American descent.

Now it was time to go back to more traditional family history research. I learned that at the time of the colonization of New Sweden in the 17th century, Sweden included most of what is now Finland. In addition, there was an enclave of ethnic Finns in central Sweden. There was even a settlement in New Sweden at one time that was called Finland. By combining traditional family history research with targeted DNA testing, I learned something about my family that I had previously been unable to unravel. I am still exploring how a surname like Owens got to the colony of New Sweden. My theory for now is that it was originally something slightly different that got anglicized into Owens on this side of the Atlantic. This is but one example of the many genealogical hypotheses that can be tested by ingeniously choosing the right relative or relatives and then persuading them to swab their cheeks or spit into sample tubes.

INTERPRETING Y-CHROMOSOME TEST RESULTS

Meanwhile, your excited patron is waving something in your face that has the information shown in Figure 10.5.

Just as you don't need to be an aeronautical engineer to be able to fly in an airplane, you don't need to have a degree in genetics to be able to interpret such information for

PANEL 1 (1-12)											
Locus	1	2	3	4	5	6	7	8	9	10	11	12
DYS#	393	390	19*	391	385a	385b	426	388	439	389-1	392	389-2
Alleles	13	25	14	11	11	14	12	12	11	13	13	29

Figure 10.5: The author's 12-marker Y-chromosome DNA test results.

genealogical purposes. It's not the data itself that is important. The row for "Locus" in Figure 10.5 is only the numerical sequence of the markers being examined. For example, Locus 1, or the first result reported in Figure 10.5, is for DNA Y-chromosome segment number (DYS#) 393. While DYS# 393 may be very exciting to a geneticist, the only significance it has to you and your patron is that it has a value of 13, which can be compared with the value other individuals have for the same DYS#. The value of 13 has no known significance on its own. It is not better than or worse than a value of 12 or 14. It is just the first result for the tested person. The lab in this instance was FTDNA. Although there is increasing standardization among the reporting schemes from labs that analyze DNA, this field is too new and dynamic to allow automatic and easy cross-lab comparison of results.

The actual areas of DNA used for Y-chromosome and mitochondrial analysis are from parts of one's DNA called junk DNA. As far as we know now, these particular parts of our DNA have no known purpose in the passing of characteristics from one generation to the next. These DYS# numbers do not determine whether one will have blue eyes or brown, be tall or short, or be likely to get breast cancer. Therefore, individuals can compare their results with others without fear of inadvertently disclosing information that some might want to keep private.

Taken in combination, the Y-chromosome values can indicate whether two individuals are likely to have a common male ancestor within the genealogical era—the period in which most families have had surnames. Therefore, it is by comparing these results with others that they take on value. It can help two individuals, or a group of individuals, to determine whether they are closely related. If two individuals have the same exact 12-marker values *and* the same (or a close derivate) surname, this would probably indicate that they had shared a common male ancestor sometime within the last few hundred years. If there is a single mismatch and a similar surname, a close relationship is also possible. A 12-marker test is very minimal. Several mismatches would rule out a close familial match. Note in Figure 10.6 that the author and another male of the same surname mismatch at locations 6, 9, and 11. This is called a genetic distance of 3.

Subsequent extensions of these tests confirmed that we were not closely related and that in fact our closest common male ancestor probably lived between 3,000 and 3,500 years ago. In most cases, at least 37 markers would be needed to have any confidence in confirming a match.

Such DNA information, taken alone, is not nearly as useful as it can become when combined with the results of traditional genealogical research. I have a very

Locus	1	2	3	4	5	6	7	8	9	10	11	12
DYS #	393	390	19	391	385a	385b	426	388	429	389-1	392	389-2
Me	13	25	14	11	11	**14**	12	12	**11**	13	**13**	29
Another Dowell	13	25	14	11	11	**13**	12	12	**12**	13	**14**	29

Figure 10.6: **Comparison of first 12 markers of the author and another Dowell.**

Generations Back to a Common Male Ancestor	Likelihood of a Common Male Ancestor	
	Based Only on DNA Results	Combining DNA with Family History Information
4	22.22%	NA
8	66.55%	22.42%
12	90.00%	76.81%
16	97.58%	94.38%
20	99.48%	98.81%
24	99.90%	99.77%

Figure 10.7: **Sample probabilities of the number of generations back to find a common male ancestor for two men based on their Y-chromosome DNA results.**

close DNA match with several men whose surname is McDaniel. Based on DNA evidence alone, there would be a statistical probability of almost two chances in three that I shared a common male ancestor with them within the last 8 generations. This is approximately the length of time we each have established our ancestors have been on this side of the Atlantic. In addition, we have established through the triangulation of the DNA results of living Dowell distant cousins and living McDaniel distant cousins that the DNA of the common ancestor in each surname has not mutated in some of the living descendants for almost three centuries. That means our ancestors almost 300 years ago were as far apart in their DNA markers as many of their descendants living today. Therefore, when we take this information into account, we must adjust the probability timeline back to when we were likely to have had a common ancestor.

When I entered the information from traditional genealogy research that there was no common ancestor in at least the last 8 generations, the projected probabilities were adjusted (see Figure 10.7).[3]

A very good probability (94%) exists that we share a common male ancestor within 16 generations. There is a better than a coin-flip probability (50%) that the match occurred within the last 11 or 12 generations. A common male ancestor becomes almost a statistical certainty well in excess of a 99 percent probability within 24 generations. However, that long ago, 600 to 800 years ago, surnames were not in common use, and North America was inhabited only by Native Americans.

Y-CHROMOSOME DNA SURNAME PROJECT

During most of the last several years, the most productive application of DNA to genealogy has been in Y-chromosome surname projects. Figure 10.8 is an example of one such project. This did not start out to be a project of descendants of Philip Dowell. It started out as part of the McDowell surname project. Almost every branch of the Dowell family had an oral tradition that they originally were called McDowell but that at some point the *Mc* had been dropped. If you think about it, this is counter intuitive. *Mc* means "son of." So it is more logical to have originally been a Dowell and then to have become a McDowell. However, DNA results soon put this mental exercise to a merciful death. So far, no Dowell DNA has come close to matching any McDowell DNA. That was our first nugget of new learning from DNA testing.

The next finding was more jolting. We had assumed that all Dowells were related in some way. There were some Dowell researchers who could trace their ancestry back to early Virginia and some who could trace their roots back to early Maryland. No big deal. Back then, people traveled by water when they could. Roads were barely passable at best. It appeared obvious that some Dowell had gone down the James River in Virginia and up the Chesapeake Bay in Maryland. These were the paths that goods took when they came from England and that tobacco took when it was exported. It would have been a relatively easy trip from central Virginia to southern Maryland. But it didn't happen like that. DNA results have established that the Maryland Dowells and the Virginia Dowells have not had a common male ancestor for at least 3,000 years—a period that would extend far earlier than when surnames like Dowell were in use. The names had grown up simultaneously in two separate locations.

Along the way, we proved an oral tradition that a Bartley woman had children with a Dowell man, had never married, and had given her children the surname Bartley, which they still carry a couple of hundred years later. We also got another surprise. One branch of the supposed Virginia Dowells was genetically identical to DNA of group of Martins—at least on their paternal side. Dowells lived next door to Martins

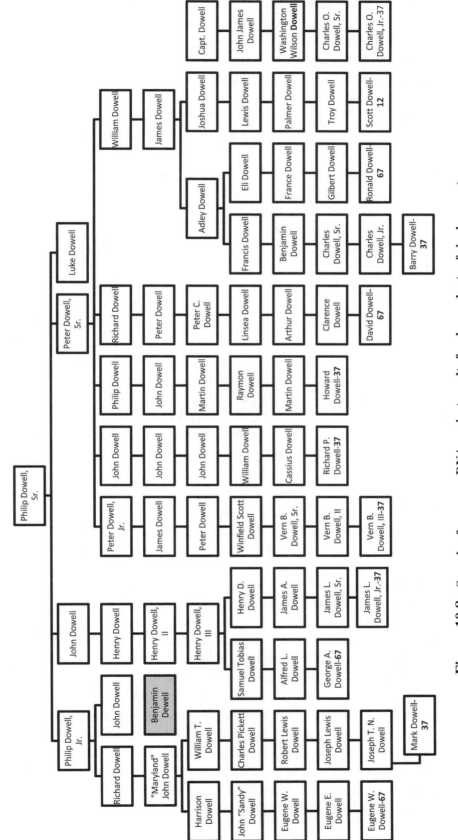

Figure 10.8: Sample of surname DNA project results for descendants of single ancestor.

in mid-18th-century Virginia. Now we are trying to figure out a way to determine whether these folks who have carried the surname Dowell since a generation prior to the Revolutionary War could be connected from the main group of Virginia Dowells on their maternal side of the family.

And then there is the Dewell line. Printed genealogies at least for the last 80 years have attributed the Dewell line of Maryland and Ohio to a branch of the Maryland Dowells who were alleged to have changed the first vowel of their name somewhere along the line. Many examples can be found of people who were clearly the same individuals who were listed as "Dowell" some of the time and "Dewell" some of the time. It didn't happen that way even though the National Society of the Daughters of the American Revolution has granted membership to some Dewells based on their alleged connection to a Dowell who had provided service during the Revolutionary War. However, DNA tests of Dewell gentlemen show them to be related to each other, but they are much further removed genetically than the Virginia Dowells are from the Maryland Dowells. Isn't DNA fun? We have learned all this in about 5 years.

We have developed a descendant tree that is based on testing at least two living descendants of three of the sons of Philip Dowell Sr., the earliest Maryland Dowell who can be clearly documented. By triangulating their results, we have established that most of the currently living descendants of the third son still have the exact same 67 Y-chromosome marker values that Philip carried. Most of the descendants of the oldest son have mutated on 1 or 2 markers over the ensuing generations. Descendants of the second son show mutations on as many as 4 markers of 67 tested over the three centuries since Philip Sr. lived. If nothing were known of their paper trail, the lab reports there would be a 45 percent probability of common ancestor. In this case, the match would appear to be correct even though the odds are slightly against it. It is good to keep in mind that probabilities are averages. Other information needs to be combined with DNA results in order to arrive at the best genealogical answers. No documented living descendants have yet been identified for son number four, although he is known to have had children who survived him at his death in 1750.

Note in the chart in Figure 10.9 that both descendants of the first son share one mutation at marker 447. Both descendants of the second son share mutations on markers 576 and CDYb. None of the descendants of the third son have had mutations. The shared mutations occurred further back in time and would be inherited by any subsequent descendants. In addition to the shared mutations, some show more recent mutations that occurred after their line of descent split off from their nearest cousin. Of the three undocumented family members, it is possible that one or more of them descends from the fourth son or that some of them descend from a so far unidentified brother or cousin of Philip Sr. They could also have descended from one of the first three sons. More work will have to be done before they can be placed with confidence.

Maryland

Dowell DNA	393	390	19	391	385a	385b	426	388	439	389I	389II	392	458	459a	459b	455	454	447	437	448	449	464a	464b	464c	464d	460	H4	YCAa	YCAb	456	607	576	570	CDYa	CDYb	442	438
1st son	13	25	14	11	11	14	12	11	11	13	29	13	17	9	10	11	11	25	15	19	28	14	15	15	17	11	10	19	23	16	15	18	16	37	37	12	12
1st son	14	25	14	11	11	14	12	11	11	13	29	13	17	9	10	11	11	25	15	19	28	14	15	15	17	11	10	19	23	16	15	18	16	37	37	12	12
2nd son	13	26	14	11	11	14	12	11	11	13	29	13	17	9	10	11	11	26	15	19	28	14	15	15	17	11	10	19	23	16	15	19	16	37	38	12	12
2nd son	13	25	14	11	11	14	12	11	11	13	29	13	17	9	10	11	11	26	15	19	28	14	15	15	17	11	10	19	23	16	15	19	16	38	38	12	12
3rd son	13	25	14	11	11	14	12	11	11	13	29	13	17	9	10	11	11	26	15	19	28	14	15	15	17	11	10	19	23	16	15	18	16	37	37	12	12
3rd son	13	25	14	11	11	14	12	11	11	13	29	13	17	9	10	11	11	26	15	19	28	14	15	15	17	11	10	19	23	16	15	18	16	37	37	12	12
3rd son	13	25	14	11	11	14	12	11	11	13	29	13	17	9	10	11	11	26	15	19	28	14	15	15	17	11	10	19	23	16	15	18	16	37	37	12	12
3rd son	13	25	14	11	11	14	12	11	11	13	29	13	17	9	10	11	11	26	15	19	28	14	15	15	17	11	10	19	23	16	15	18	16	37	37	12	12
3rd son	13	25	14	11	11	14	12	11	11	13	29	13	17	9	10	11	11	26	15	19	28	14	15	15	17	11	10	19	23	16	15	18	16	37	37	12	12
3rd son	13	25	14	11	11	14	12	11	11	13	29																										
3rd son	13	25	14	11	11	14	12	11	11	13	29	13	17	9	10	11	11	26	15	19	28	14	15	15	17	11	10	19	23	16	15	18	16	37	37	12	12
undocumented	13	25	14	11	11	14	12	11	11	13	29	13	17	9	10	11	11	26	15	19	28	14	15	15	17	11	10	19	23	16	15	18	16	37	37	12	12
undocumented	13	25	14	11	11	14	12	11	11	13	29	13	17	9	10	11	11	26	15	19	28	14	15	15	16	9	10	19	23	16	15	18	16	37	37	12	12
undocumented	14	26	14	11	11	14	12	11	11	13	29	13	17	9	10	11	11	26	15	19	28	14	15	15	17	11	10	19	23	16	15	18	16	37	37	12	12

Figure 10.9: Y-chromosome results for men in a surname DNA study of descendants of a common ancestor.

INTERPRETING MITOCHONDRIAL TEST RESULTS

The results in Figure 10.10 of a mitochondrial test look very different from those of the Y-chromosome tests shown already.

Mitochondrial results are not reported in an absolute value like Y-chromosome results. Rather, they are reported in terms of the locations in which they vary from the Cambridge Reference Sequence (CRS). This is an arbitrary point of departure. Much like Greenwich mean time is the standard for the time zones of the world, CRS is the standard for measuring deviations of mitochondrial DNA. It exists because a lab in Cambridge was the first to identify values for all 16,569 locations on the mitochondrial genome. Since then, all other mitochondrial tests have measured their results based on which of those locations vary from those of the first mitochondria sequenced at Cambridge. About the only significance these mutations have is that the less British a person is in their maternal line, the more variance they are likely to have from the CRS.

If persons only have a low-resolution test, they will get results for the last 569 locations on the mitochondrial genome (16001–16569). In the example given, there was only a variance from the CRS at location 16519. To reach a high-resolution test, locations 00001 to 00574 would also need to be tested. (Don't try to remember all these numbers, they will not be on an exam!) In this example, four additional variances were

Hypervariable Region (HVR)1 differences from Cambridge Reference Sequence (CRS)	Hypervariable Region (HVR)2 differences from Cambridge Reference Sequence (CRS)	Coding Region (CR) differences from Cambridge Reference Sequence (CRS)	
16519C	152C	750G	8860G
	263G	1438G	13326C
	309.1C	2259T	13680T
	315.1C	4745G	14872T
		4769G	15326G
		7337A	

Figure 10.10: Sample mitochondrial DNA results for a person who has tested at the mtFullSequence level.

identified in hypervariable region 2, or HVR2. When the entire remaining locations (00575 to 16000) were tested, several additional variations were found.

The significance of this pattern of variations, or the person's mitochondrial signature, is in matching with others who have an identical or almost identical mitochondrial signature. Such matching can identify deep ancestry and trace the migration patterns of human populations.

HAPLOGROUPS

Both Y-chromosome and mitochondrial DNA provide information about deep ancestry. Generally, this is beyond genealogical time or before humans commonly used surnames. However, while we may not be able to trace specific surnames, we can determine the haplotypes of our ancestors. These haplotypes allow us to assign our forbearers to haplogroups, or their ancient clans. It is important to remember that maternal haplogroups (traced by mitochondria) and paternal haplogroups (traced by the Y chromosome) are classified by two different schemes. Therefore, maternal haplogroups cannot be compared with paternal haplogroups. I cannot state this strongly enough. Haplogroup A for women is in no way related to haplogroup A for men. Haplogroup A for men indicates African American ancestry, while haplogroup A for women indicates Native American heritage. The actual designations are in no way related to each other. The two schemes might as well have been developed on separate planets.

To me, the male haplogroup classification makes more sense. The earliest haplogroup was labeled haplogroup A. It originated in East Africa. After the first mutation occurred, the men who carried that mutation forward are classified as belonging to haplogroup B. Then followed another mutation, and haplogroup C resulted. In other words, the paternal classification scheme was originally alphabetical based on the next available letter after each branching occurred. Many of the mutations that define smaller and smaller branches have only recently been discovered. Rather than assign a new letter, they are grouped under the original letter with a suffix added. Geneticists continue to uncover more every few months. As this happens, the classification scheme, which had a logical and intuitive beginning, has become much more complex, somewhat parallel to what has happened to library classification schemes. For example, one of the most common haplogroups of men originating in western Europe is at this writing now known as R1b1b2a1*b5,* or is it R1b1b2a1*a2f*?

Those of you who are really into classification schemes will note that the first eight characters, reading from left to right, are identical. It is what is going on at the extreme right of this haplogroup designation that seems to be different. Actually, what is happening is that different labs have more or less simultaneously discovered new subdivisions of the main haplogroup. These two designations are actually two different ways of defining the very same haplogroup. By the time you are reading this book, standardization will have set in, and one of these designations will have prevailed. My reason for belaboring the point is not for you to remember either one of these designations. Rather, it is to remind you of how fast the science of genetics and genetic genealogy is advancing. In some ways, the application of genetics to genealogy is now a process of "Ready, fire, aim!" We cannot stop progress in the lab until we come up with the perfect classification scheme—particularly when we cannot predict what will be discovered next.

HAPLOGROUP MIGRATIONS OF Y-CHROMOSOME DNA

The map in Figure 10.11 shows the gradual mutations of the Y chromosomes of males over thousands of years as they moved out of East Africa to populate the

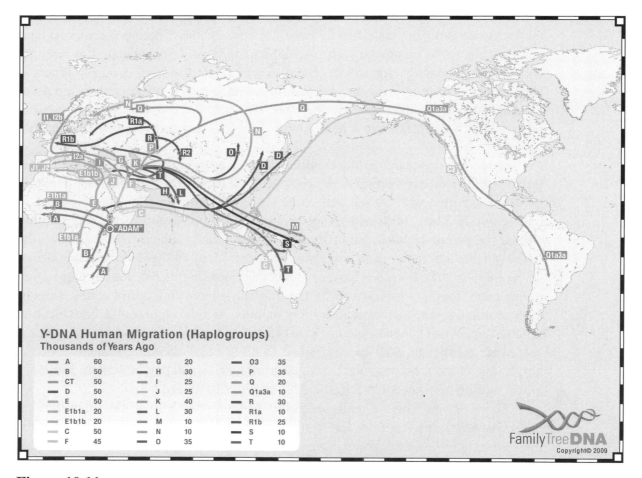

Figure 10.11: **Map showing the migration of Y chromosome DNA (men) out of Africa to populate the world. (Courtesy of Family Tree DNA)**

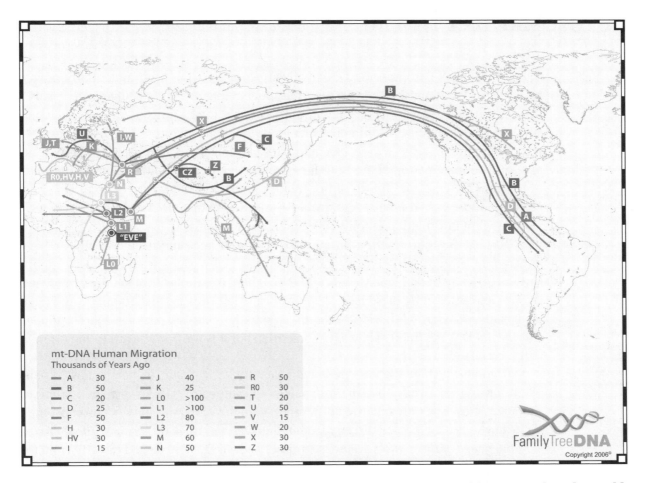

Figure 10.12: **Map of the mitochondrial DNA (female) migration out of Africa to populate the world.** **(Courtesy of Family Tree DNA)**

earth. Distinct haplogroups emerged along the migration paths as mutations occurred in the Y chromosomes over multiple generations. The letters along the migration paths changed as new DNA patterns emerged.

HAPLOGROUP MIGRATION OF MITOCHONDRIAL DNA

Of course, females followed parallel migration paths to those of the men. However, the classification scheme that has been assigned to the evolution of mitochondrial DNA, as it gradually mutated over the centuries, assigns different letters to this branching process than was the scheme used to describe a similar mutation and migration pattern for men (Figure 10.12).[4] Of course, the mutations that led to a distinctly new grouping occurred at different times for women than for men.

AUTOSOMAL DNA TESTING

Although Y-chromosome DNA and mitochondrial DNA are potentially powerful tools in breaking through barriers that documents research is unable to resolve, these tools only address a very small part of one's total family tree. As researchers succeed in discovering additional generations of their ancestors, the fraction of the next generation that these tools can help with plummets precipitously. While they can give a male information about both his parents, they return information on only half of his grandparents, one-fourth of his great-grandparents, and one-eighth of his great-great-grandparents. You will recall from our discussion that DNA samples provided by women yield information on only half that many ancestors.

To help find information on all the grayed-out ancestors in the middle of your family tree (Figure 10.13), testing of autosomal DNA was introduced to the public early in 2010 by both 23andMe and FTDNA. There is quite a bit of similarity between the services offered by these labs: 23andMe calls its software that compares individuals Relative Finder, while FTDNA calls its parallel analysis package Family Finder. Autosomal DNA certainly shows real potential, but it is too early to tell if that promise will be realized.

If you have studied a little genetics, you may know that each person has 23 pairs of chromosomes. Twenty-two of those pairs—the autosomal DNA—give us our unique characteristics. They are inherited differently than the 23rd pair, the sex chromosomes. Y chromosomes are passed directly from fathers to their male offspring *without mixing with the genes of the mother.* Likewise, mitochondrial DNA is passed directly from the mother to all her offspring *without mixing with the genes of the father.* In this direct transmission, both can pass down unaltered through many generations. That is the norm. The rare copying errors in these intergenerational transfers are what allow us to trace different branches of the human family.

The transfer of the 22 pairs of chromosomes, or autosomal DNA, from one generation to the next is quite a different process. Visualize a mixing bowl on the counter. Both the father and the mother contribute their DNA to the bowl. Then the DNA in the bowl is mixed around. Next, some of the resulting mix from the bowl is taken out and passed on to their baby. In this process, about half of the DNA received by the child will be segments from the mother and about half from the father. But, which segments of each parent's DNA are they?

If this couple has another baby, the mixing process is repeated again. Again each parent contributes to the process. However, after this mixing process is completed, the segments of DNA that are passed on to the second child may be quite different. Hence, we have the difference between siblings.

This mixing and passing down goes on generation after generation. During this process, some strands of DNA remain intact, and others are jumbled up into new sequences. Autosomal DNA testing, for genealogical purposes, is looking for intact strands of DNA that are similar between individuals. The more of these strands that

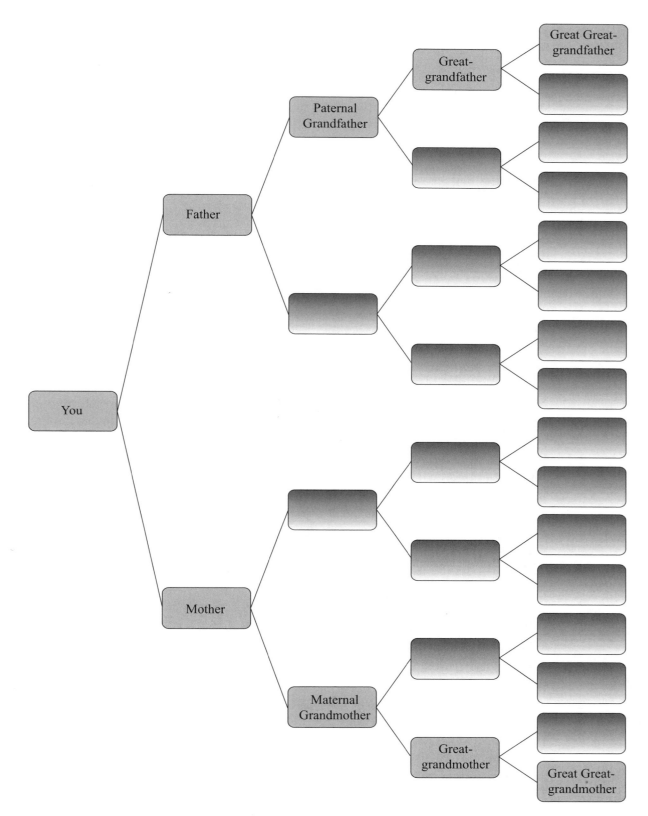

Figure 10.13: Autosomal DNA helps find matches that cannot be discovered by Y-chromosome or mitochondrial testing since it potentially provides information on every ancestor within several generations who contributed DNA to a person.

are shared by two individuals, the closer their biological relationship is thought to be. Of particular interest is the length of the longest intact identical segment that is shared between two individuals. Children share about half of the genes contributed by each parent. With each succeeding generation of remixing the genes, the longest intact surviving segment in the autosomal chromosomes from the original ancestor gets shorter and shorter. The labs use the length of the longest common segment and the total amount of matching segments to estimate the number of generations two individuals are from a shared common ancestor.

As mentioned earlier, autosomal DNA testing, for genealogical purposes was first offered to the public in 2010. Therefore, we are still in the early stages of learning how to best apply it to advance our family history research. It is predicted that such testing may be able to identify some relationships as far back as fifth cousins. In this kind of testing, men and women are on a level playing field. One thing is becoming clear in the early days of testing. Early reports indicate that this kind of testing relies even more heavily on well-researched family trees than have the earlier types of testing. No longer can one assume that a match lies on the paternal line as is the case in Y-chromosome testing. Likewise, one cannot assume that a match lies on the maternal line as is the case in mitochondrial testing. It can be on either of those lines *or on any line in between.* Once a shared segment is discovered, it is now time to look for shared surnames and the locations where they lived. That information can only be compiled and documented by traditional genealogical research. In some ways, autosomal research, at least in its early days, seems to be saying, "There is a common ancestor approximately x generations back on one of your lines. Now go find it."

If autosomal testing turns out to live up to the promotional promises of testing labs, most of us will have a hard time taking full advantage of the power we are being offered. Rather than being the magic bullet that by itself reveals our family trees, it reemphasizes the need for traditional genealogy research. Experienced genetic genealogist Larry Vick states it this way, "Whether we use Relative Finder, Family Finder, or both most of us need to do a much better job on our pedigrees to get more value from either test. I plan to spend a week at the Family History Library this summer beefing up my pedigree."[5] In my own experience, many of my autosomal matches are adoptees or others who know little about their family histories. For them and for those of us who discover genetic matches with them, learning how we might be related is a very frustrating process.

What is the probability that patrons will share enough DNA with a relative that it will be detected by autosomal testing? If you are related within four generations (third or more recent cousins), then autosomal testing is almost sure to detect your relationship. Testing may also detect many fourth cousins and a few fifth and more distant cousins. Combining the early experience with autosomal testing by both FTDNA and 23andMe, the chances of finding a match within the last few generations (shown in Figure 10.14) appear likely.[6]

So if someone is a fourth cousin or closer, there is a good chance they will be detected in autosomal testing. Detection of matchers further back is a long shot but is still possible. The main problem is that even those of us with well-researched pedigree

Relationship	Probability of Detecting Common Segment
2nd cousins or closer	99%
3rd cousin	90%
4th cousin	45-50%
5th cousin	10-15%
6th cousin and more distant	5% or less

Figure 10.14: **The probability of detecting a common segment of DNA between two related individuals based on early autosomal test results from 23andMe and Family Tree DNA (FTDNA) labs.**

charts rarely know who all our 32 great-great-great-grandparents are. They would be the ancestors we have in common with a potential fourth cousin. In addition, our potential fourth cousin (with whom we have determined we share an autosomal segment) would also need to have documented who their 32 great-great-great-grandparents were as well. Beyond this generation, some matches will occur. In fact, many will show up in the results of an autosomal test because we have many more potential living cousins as we go back further a generation or two. However, the likelihood of identifying a connecting ancestor becomes increasingly remote.

SUMMARY

In the past decade, DNA has become an important instrument in the tool kit of well-prepared genealogical researchers. It has the power to verify or refute many kinds of hypothesized relationships. It does not replace traditional research—in fact, it sometimes makes document searching even more important. The fast pace of scientific discoveries in genetics labs makes the application of this tool a very dynamic and rapidly evolving area of genealogical practice.

NOTES

1. The earliest use of this phrase I have been able to find was by Rebecca Skloot in the post "Putting the Gene Back in Genealogy," POPSCI, http://www.popsci.com/scitech/article/2003–12/putting-gene-back-genealogy (accessed December 24, 2010).

2. Darvin L. Martin, "Unveiling the Deep Ancestry of Swiss Anabaptist Forebears," *Pennsylvania Mennonite Heritage* 33, no. 3 (July 2010): 2.

3. The results in the following table were generated by FTDNATiP™, which is a proprietary program of Family Tree DNA.

4. A quite readable and informative book on the arrival of different mitochondrial haplogroups in Europe is the best seller by Bryan Sykes, *The Seven Daughters of Eve* (New York: W.W. Norton, 2001).

5. James L. Vick, "Family Finder Price Increase," post to International Society of Genetic Genealogy Listserv, April 15, 2010.

6. "Family Finder: Questions about Family Finder," FTDNA, https://www.familytreedna. com/FAQ/answers/17.aspx#628 (accessed April 20, 2010); FAQs "I know that a particular person is my relative. What's the probability that we share a sufficient amount of DNA to be detected by Relative Finder?" 23andMe, https://www.23andme.com/ you/faqwin/rfprobability/ (accessed May 10, 2010).

CHAPTER 11

Keeping Up to Date

Now you have taken a big step on your path to become more proficient in serving the family historians who come into your library. What can you do next? Many opportunities exist to continue to build your skills as you continue to evolve into a person who will be valued by your local genealogical community. New genealogical tools become available all the time. If you are not keeping up, you are actually allowing your knowledge and skill level to fall behind. Your geographic location, personal learning style, budget, and amount of available time will guide your choice. Some of these activities include but are not limited to the following:

1. Follow blogs and other social media that feature genealogical information.
2. Join a Listserv of interest.
3. Become a researcher yourself.
4. Take a class.
5. Prepare pathfinders.
6. Develop or update a genealogy web page for your library.
7. Attend conferences.
8. Join your local genealogy society.
9. Read periodicals.
10. Take online tutorials.
11. Be proactive in managing the genealogy collection in your library.

12. Teach a class.
13. Create your own blog or other social media to keep your patrons up to date with new developments.
14. Go on a family history fieldtrip of your own.
15. Attend conferences and seminars.
16. Read other books.

Many of these activities are available at no cost or at a low cost in terms of dollars. All of them require an investment of another precious resource—your time. However, if you were not willing to invest the latter, you probably would not be reading this book. If it is important to you to develop the professional skills that will make you a go-to resource for your patrons, you will make the time available. However, genealogy research can be habit forming. You may become addicted just as completely as some of your more intense patrons.

BLOGS

Literally hundreds of blogs focus primarily on genealogical topics. Some are very general, and some are narrowly focused. I have my own called *Dr D Digs Up Ancestors.* It is fairly general and can be found at http://blog.ddowell.com. An example of a more narrowly focused one is CeCe Moore's *Your Genetic Genealogist.*[1] As you might guess, she focuses on developments related to the application of DNA to genealogy research. An extensive but in no way exhaustive list can be found at several places on the web. Thomas MacEntee's Geneablogers.com is a very comprehensive list of genealogy blogs. At this writing, about 1,500 are listed. No matter what your focus may be, if you are interested in family history research, you will find blogs on MacEntee's list that will be of interest. Check it out. It has surname-focused blogs, geographically focused blogs, and blogs focused on type of research. One search engine on his site searches all of them.

If you find one you like, you can become a follower so that you will be notified when new posts are added. Kimberly Powell offers "Genealogy Blogs 101" for those of you who want more information about how to find, read, and subscribe to one.[2] You may even be inspired to start your own blog as a way to share new developments with your patrons and others. If you do, I can tell you from personal experience that you will learn more in the process than your readers will. And that is a good thing!

LISTSERVS

As you know Listservs exist on almost any imaginable topic. While blogs generally have a single author, Listservs spread the joy of authorship around. Any member of a list can post on topics within the scope of that particular list. As with blogs, some genealogical lists are general, but most have a particular niche. One with which you should become familiar is Genealib. The welcoming message to new members describes its scope: "This list is intended as a communications tool for the benefit of genealogy librarians. We encourage postings by practicing librarians, retired librarians, vendors, and others who have contributions that can assist practicing genealogy librarians in the performance of their duties." To subscribe, send an e-mail to lyris@ lists.acomp.usf.edu with the following (without the quotation marks) in the body of the message "subscribe genealib your_full_name." Even if you don't think you are ready to start posting, you can learn a lot as a lurker.

Also in parallel with lists of blogs, there are lists of lists. RootsWeb.com hosts many of these lists. The two big categories are surname lists and locality lists. You certainly should find out if there is such a list covering the area in which your library is located. To find out if there is already such a list, RootsWeb hosts a list search engine at http://bigfile. rootsweb.ancestry.com/cgi-bin/listsearch. Generally, you will want to enter your local county. However, you will get responses that include lists for surnames that are common in your location. The search engine is good for recall and not as good for precision. However, precision can be improved by grouping search terms with quotation marks.

In addition, there are about 60 uncategorized lists on such topics as the RVing-Genealogist, which is a place for discussing the "conducting of genealogy while traveling in a recreational vehicle," and the Record-Keeping-Methodology list, which provides a virtual place for the "discussion and sharing of information regarding the storing, filing, archiving and recording of genealogical data collected by both physical and electronic means."[3]

Lists on RootsWeb can be experienced in at least three ways. The more conventional way is to subscribe and receive posts directly in your mailbox as they are posted. This would be your choice if you are actively involved in ongoing discussions. However, if you are primarily lurking, you may choose to receive the messages in batch (digest) mode and minimize the number of interruptions that may result daily on busy lists. A third option is to not subscribe at all but to occasionally visit the archives of the list to browse or to search for a specific topic.

RESEARCH YOUR OWN FAMILY

You can learn to help others research by doing genealogy yourself. Although your own family research may not lead you down the same paths that your patrons need to explore, you will learn from personal experience many lessons that you will be able to pass on to other researchers.

TAKE A CLASS

A more formal learning environment is provided for you if you enroll in a class. Depending on your goal, this class may be for academic credit, for continuing education units (CEUs), or solely for the structured learning activity. Among the institutions of higher education and professional associations that offer courses are Brigham Young University, Boston University, the National Genealogical Society (NGS), and the Reference and User Services (RUSA) Division of the American Library Association (ALA). Some offer one course and others a complete curriculum. Some courses are face-to-face, and some are online. Some of these programs would offer you a chance not only to get some book learning but also to start or complete some projects that would be useful on the job. The following is a list of possible projects for students who enroll in some of the online courses of the National Institute for Genealogical Studies in Toronto:

- a small booklet for your own relatives on a portion of their ancestry;
- a newsletter you produce for a family association;
- a (volunteer) answer to a query letter for your society;
- a (work-related) response to a query coming to your library or archives;
- a paragraph for your own or family benefit where you describe a process by which you reached a genealogical conclusion from conflicting or difficult sources (this is a proof argument);
- a full fledged descending or ascending genealogy;
- a direct-line pedigree study;
- an article you want to write for a peer journal;
- any projects involving software, making allowance for proper citations;
- preparing a talk or lecture for a public forum; and
- creating a genealogical workshop or ongoing instructional program.[4]

Other programs offer similar opportunities for work-related take homes.

PREPARE PATHFINDERS AND OTHER HANDOUTS

There are all kinds of opportunities to prepare pathfinders and other handouts that would be helpful to family history researchers who come into your library. A supply of blank pedigree charts, family group sheets, and templates for the various U.S. census enumerations would be a good start. Information about local resources should also be useful. Analyze the most repetitive and/or the most time-consuming questions. Take your queue from your analysis and investigate if you can prepare a handout that would help patrons get started when you are too busy to spend significant time with them.

CREATE OR UPDATE A WEBSITE

If something is useful enough to cause you to want to make a handout, it may also be a useful addition to your library's genealogy page. In addition, you can add links to various in library databases and other local resources.

ATTEND CONFERENCES

Lots of opportunities exist for attending genealogy conferences and seminars. Conferences are held all over the country. They are sponsored by local, state, and national organizations. Some are a single day, and some are multiday events. Some local societies bring in expert speakers for presentations. Even national organizations may offer half-day or all-day learning opportunities for library workers. These are usually the lead-in day for a larger genealogical or library conference. Examples of these are the librarians' day sponsored by the NGS and the Association of Genealogical Societies (AGS). These provide quality speakers who are in town for the follow-on conference. Often these events are free due to vendor sponsorship. Similar learning opportunities are offered by regional societies such as the annual Genealogy Jamboree of the Southern California Genealogical Society.

If you are fortunate enough to be able to attend such librarians' day activities, try to include a tour of the vendor and society exhibits, which will probably be available free or for a minimal charge. If you are on a budget, you can learn a lot just by walking through the exhibits. Even if it is your first time, do not hesitate to stop and talk to vendors and to ask them questions. Of course, the most ideal scenario would be to attend the full conference if your staff development budget can be stretched that far.

The History Section of the RUSA Division of the ALA sponsors two all-day preconferences for those who provide assistance to genealogy researchers in libraries. These are scheduled the day before the opening of the ALA's Midwinter and Annual Conferences. Again, try to take advantage of the exhibitors' area and any other programs you can attend.

JOIN YOUR LOCAL GENEALOGY SOCIETY AND/OR HISTORICAL SOCIETY

This activity has three things going for it. You will learn from participating. Equally important, you will make contacts that will be able to mentor you in aspects of their specialties, and you will create goodwill for your library.

READ PERIODICALS

Genealogy periodicals can be found in a variety of ways. Of course, they can come as personal subscriptions. Others result from personal membership in genealogy societies. In addition, your library may subscribe to many or have family newsletters donated. Increasingly, vendor-produced periodicals are being distributed only in electronic form from the publishers' websites. Often older issues are available online even if current ones are not. Frequently, the older ones are just as valuable to read.

TAKE ONLINE TUTORIALS

A plethora of genealogy tutorials are offered online, and the number and quality seem to be growing daily. FamilySearch, Ancestry, and many others are developing robust offerings—often with audio and video. Use your browser to search for "genealogy tutorials," and add a more specialized term to refine your search to meet your specific learning needs.

PROACTIVELY MANAGE THE GENEALOGY COLLECTION IN YOUR LIBRARY

Just going through the process of managing the genealogy collection, however large or small, in your own library can greatly expand your useful knowledge. Not only will you be better prepared to refer patrons, but you will experience much serendipitous learning. Read the flyers and other catalog offerings from publishers who specialize in the genealogy market. Think through whether any of their offerings should receive some of your meager book budget. Even make a list, ranked in priority order, of books you believe will most strengthen your collection to meet the needs of your patrons.

TEACH A CLASS

Yes, I know that may be a scary thought. However, by the time you finish this book, you should know enough to teach a short introductory course for your patrons who are just starting their research. I will guarantee that you will learn far more from your preparation than they will from your delivery.

CREATE YOUR OWN BLOG OR OTHER SOCIAL MEDIA

Blogs and other social media can be an effective way to keep your patrons up to date with new developments. Much of the technology needed to support such an endeavor requires only a small learning curve for most library workers. Help is available in several places. One of them is Fbbootcamp.blogspot.com. The primary site author is Thomas MacEntee. Although there are some good technical pointers on this site, it appears that most of MacEntee's energy is going into Geneablogers.com. You will probably find more recent blogging tips there.

Pick your own means of expression that is comfortable for you. Concentrate on the content. That is where you will learn the most and where you will make the greatest contribution to your readers.

TAKE A FAMILY HISTORY FIELDTRIP

Your first field trips should be to any family history centers, historical societies, and genealogy societies in your community or surrounding communities. Next you should visit your county courthouse and other repositories of vital, probate, and property records. You should also visit local funeral homes to inquire about records they keep and their ability and willingness to receive referrals. Similarly, investigate whether local cemeteries have records that can be consulted or whether tombstone inscriptions have been recorded by volunteers.

After you are familiar with the local resources to which you can refer library patrons, you can broaden your scope to include the kinds of family research magnets that were discussed in chapter 9.

READ OTHER BOOKS

Many fine books are available that will extend what you have learned from this brief Crash Course book. Your choice will be driven by the needs of your patrons, your own interests, and the availability of the books. A list of possible next-step books is listed at the end of the chapter. Historical fiction titles are a very good way to get a feel for what life was like back in the time your patrons are researching. It can often help you and them to understand why the ancestors migrated or made other decisions that shaped their lives.

NOTES

1. CeCe Moore, "Your Genetic Genealogist," http://yourgeneticgenealogist.com (accessed March 12, 2011).
2. Kimberly Powell, "Genealogy Blogs 101," About.com: Genealogy, http://genealogy.about.com/od/blogs/a/rss.htm (accessed March 12, 2011).

3. "Genealogy Resources on the Internet: Uncategorized Mailing Lists," Genealogy on the Internet, http://www.rootsweb.ancestry.com/~jfuller/gen_mail_general.html (accessed March 12, 2011).

4. National Institute for Genealogical Studies, http://www.genealogicalstudies.com/ (March 12, 2011).

Further Reading

In addition to the books listed here, you can read any historical fiction that accurately describes earlier time periods.

Clemensson, Per, and Kjell Anderson. *Your Swedish Roots: A Step by Step Handbook.* Provo, UT: Ancestry Publishing, 2004.

Dollarhide, William. *British Origins of American Colonist, 1629–1775.* Bountiful, UT: Heritage Quest Genealogical Services, 1997.

Eichholtz, Alice. *Red Book: American State, County and Town Sources.* 3rd ed. Provo, UT: Ancestry, 2004. Also available at: http://www.ancestry.com/wiki/index.php?title= Red_Book:_American_State,_County,_and_Town_Sources. Accessed March 13, 2011.

Everton, George B. *The Handybook for Genealogists: United States of America.* 11th ed. Logan, UT: Everton Publishers, 2006.

Fischer, David Hackett. *Albion's Seed: Four British Folkways in America.* New York: Oxford University Press, 1989.

Fitzpatrick, Colleen, and Andrew Yeiser. *DNA & Genealogy.* Fountain Valley, CA: Rice Book Press, 2005.

Halley, Alex. *Roots.* Garden City, NY: Doubleday, 1976.

Larsen, Paul. *Crash Course in Family History, Fourth Edition.* St. George, UT: EasyFamilyHistory.com, 2010, p. 85.

Lynch, Daniel M. *Google Your Family Tree: Unlock The Hidden Power of Google.* Provo, UT: FamilyLink.com, 2008.

Morgan, George G. *How to Do Everything: Genealogy.* 2nd ed. New York: McGraw Hill, 2008.

Morgan, George G. *The Official Guide to Ancestry.com.* 2nd ed. Provo, UT: Ancestry. com, 2008.

Rose, Christine. *Courthouse Research for Family Historians: Your Guide to Genealogical Treasures.* San Jose, CA: CR Publications, 2004.

Simpson, Jack. *Basics of Genealogy Reference: A Librarian's Guide.* Westport, CT: Libraries Unlimited, 2008.

Smith, Drew. *Social Networking for Genealogists.* Baltimore: Genealogical Publishing, 2009.

Smolenyak, Megan, and Ann Turner. *Trace Your Roots with DNA: Using Genetic Tests to Explore Your Family Tree.* Emmaus, PA: Rodale, 2004.

Sykes, Bryan. *Saxons, Vikings, and Celts: The Genetic Roots of Britain and Ireland.* New York: W.W. Norton & Co., 2006.

Sykes, Bryan. *The Seven Daughters of Eve.* New York: Norton, 2001.

Szucs, Loretto Dennis, and Sandra Hargreaves Luebking. *The Source: A Guidebook to American Genealogy.* Provo, UT: Ancestry, 2006. Also available online: http://www.ancestry.com/wiki/index.php?title=The_Source:_A_Guidebook_to_American_Genealogy. Accessed March 13, 2011.

Szucs, Loretto Dennis, and Matthew Wright. *Finding Answers in U.S. Census Records.* Provo, UT: The Generations Network, 2001, pp. 39–40.

Taylor, Maureen. *Through the Eyes of Your Ancestors: A Step-by-Step Guide to Uncovering Your Family's History.* Boston: Houghton Mifflin, 1999.

Taylor, Maureen. *Uncovering Your Ancestry through Family Photographs.* 2nd ed. Cincinnati, OH: Family Tree Books, 2005.

Vanderpool Gromley, Myra, and Tana Pedersen Lord. *The Official Guide to rootsweb.com.* Provo, UT: Ancestry Publishing, 2007.

Walton-Raji, Angela Y. *Black Indian Genealogy Research: African-American Ancestors among the Five Civilized Tribes.* Westminister, MD: Heritage Books, 2007.

CHAPTER 12

Concluding Thoughts

LEARNING

What motivates you as a professional—as a person? As part of a management training course years ago, from a list of 100 or more, I had to pick 10 terms that motivated me as a manager. That was relatively easy. It became harder when we had to cut that list of 10 down to 5. It was really difficult to narrow the remaining terms to 3. It was excruciating to select the top 1. However, that process gave me insight into myself as a manager, as a librarian, and as a person. My top motivator was learning. Additional reflection led me to realize that a corollary for me was to help others learn. That is one reason I write books.

A colleague of mine at a university at which I previously worked was a fairly well-known physicist. He once remarked that when he gave a scientific paper at a conference, people were reluctant to point out errors to him. He welcomed such feedback because he said he only learned new things when he or someone else disproved one of his hypotheses. I am the same way with my genealogy research. I am happy when someone corrects or extends one of my family trees because that is one of the ways I learn new things.

Such an exercise as I took in the management training course would probably lead you to a different number one motivator. However, learning is somewhat

175

important to you or you would not be reading this book. The importance to you of learning and of helping others to learn will determine how you respond to the patrons in your library.

Decades ago, I helped a woman at the reference desk. The next day, she returned and left a note thanking me for my assistance. She said that she had asked me to give her a fish and I had taught her how to become a fisherman. When you help someone at your reference desk, do you give them a fish or help them become fishers? Do you give them an answer to the question they asked, or do you help them learn techniques so that they will be able to find answers to similar questions they have in the future? There really is no single right answer to this. Your answer will probably be, "It depends." It depends on how much time you have, your personal philosophy, and the policy of your library. It also depends on the aptitude of your patron to learn.

AT THE SERVICE DESK

Back to the hyperenergized gentleman we met at your service desk in chapter 1. I hope you are now feeling more self-assured but just slightly apprehensive as you respond to him and your other patrons. My college speech teacher told us, "If you ever get up to give a presentation and you are not feeling a slight bit nervous, sit down before you embarrass yourself." To give you confidence, you now have at your command:

- Dr. Dave's 10 Rules
- A picture in your mind of what events were generating records in the time period on which you wish to focus
- An idea of where those records might be now
- Several online tools in mind in addition to the physical resources in your collection
- Ideas of other libraries and archives to which you can refer patrons for additional information

Now return your focus to the particular patron in front of you. In a policy statement about a genealogy reference interview, the American Library Association/Reference and User Services Association reminds us of additional things to keep in mind.

4.1 Librarians should know how to ascertain the skill level of their patrons in regards to genealogical research, and how to provide to the patron both an appropriate orientation to the collection and services provided by the library and instruction in the evaluation of information.

4.2 Librarians should know how to produce instructional materials, such as pathfinders, and how to make educational presentations to groups on issues relating to using the library for genealogical research.

4.3 During the reference interview, the librarian should learn the answers to the following questions from the patron, as appropriate: What are the research goals? What is known about the target ancestor—their name, children, parents, birth, marriage, death dates/places, etc.? Does the patron have pedigree and family group forms that include the target ancestor? Which sources has the patron already consulted?

4.4 As a result of the reference interview, the librarian should analyze the information needed by the patron (names, dates, places, etc.) and determine the types of sources that will provide the required data.[1]

Years ago, I had a little plaque on my office shelf that said, "Nothing is more dangerous than an idea if it is the only one you have." This is a good thing to keep in mind as you help researchers. It is good to have a favorite database, a favorite approach to answering questions. However, a single-minded approach does not answer all genealogy questions. No single library collection, database, or even library staff member will be able to solve all such mysteries. Sometimes, it is necessary to explore a different path or refer a patron to another repository or even to a colleague in your own library. A fresh set of eyes and mind can often be just what is needed. It is not a sign of weakness. Quite the contrary, it is a sign of confidence and shows that you understand that everyone cannot possibly know everything.

REFRIGERATOR ART

New researchers need to have success—even a little one. Initially, that probably means finding a few names—or at least a name—that they didn't know when they came into your library. Better yet would be finding a document they can copy or print out and take home. "Refrigerator art," I would call it if it were my grandchildren doing a project. That will excite and motivate them to keep going. So it's okay to go for low-hanging fruit. Give them something. If you do, they will think you are great and will come back for more later. It will also give you an ego boost that you were able to make their day. You may not have turned them into accomplished genealogists, but you have given them a taste of success. That's a good thing. As the old proverb says, "A trip of a thousand miles begins with one step." Enable them to have a good feeling about the first step, and what comes next is up to them.

I will close with the thoughts with which we began this book. Genealogy is the study of multigenerational family history: "[F]amily history research fulfills a need to belong or feel connected. Each new discovery into our family history provides immense satisfaction. What we learn can expand family relationships in the present and helps us better understand ourselves as we realize our ancestors struggled with similar or greater challenges."[2] "The more we know, the more we want to know. Curiosity is accelerative. There really is no such thing as the past. No one really lived in the past. They lived in the present, their present."[3] As library workers, we are privileged to help our patrons discover the present of their ancestors.

NOTES

1. Reference and User Services Association, "Guidelines for a Unit or Course of Instruction in Genealogical Research at Schools of Library and Information Science," American Library Association, http://www.ala.org/ala/mgrps/divs/rusa/resources/guidelines/guidelinesunit.cfm#foot (accessed November 5, 2010).
2. KCSG Television, "A Celebration of Family History Delights Thousands of Genealogy Enthusiasts," April 29, 2010, http://www.kcsg.com/view/full_story/7263938/article-%E2%80%9CA-Celebration-of-Family-History%E2%80%9D-Delights-Thousands-of-Genealogy-Enthusiasts?instance = home_stories1 (accessed December 16, 2010).
3. Ibid.

APPENDIX

Pedigree charts and family group sheets are the basic building blocks of any serious family history. Census templates are invaluable when you and you patrons are trying to decipher column headings for census images that have been reproduced from microfilm. Figures A-1, A-2, and A-4 through A-17 are reproduced courtesy of Ancestry. com. Figure A-13 is from the U.S. National Archives.

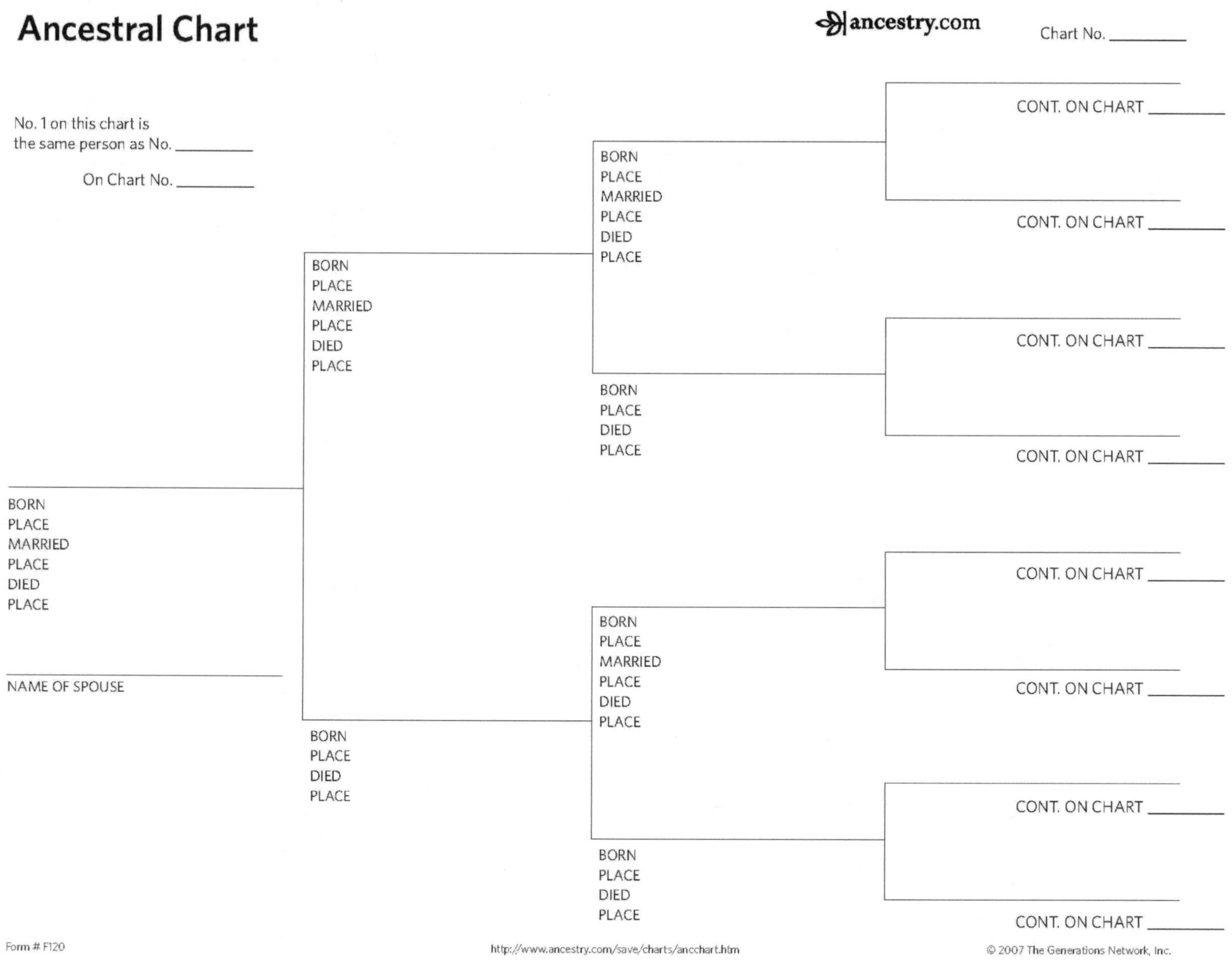

Ancestral Chart

No. 1 on this chart is
the same person as No. _____
On Chart No. _____

ancestry.com

Chart No. _____

BORN
PLACE
MARRIED
PLACE
DIED
PLACE

NAME OF SPOUSE

BORN
PLACE
DIED
PLACE

BORN
PLACE
MARRIED
PLACE
DIED
PLACE

BORN
PLACE
DIED
PLACE

BORN
PLACE
MARRIED
PLACE
DIED
PLACE

BORN
PLACE
MARRIED
PLACE
DIED
PLACE

BORN
PLACE
DIED
PLACE

BORN
PLACE
DIED
PLACE

CONT. ON CHART _____

CONT. ON CHART _____

CONT. ON CHART _____

CONT. ON CHART _____

CONT. ON CHART _____

CONT. ON CHART _____

CONT. ON CHART _____

CONT. ON CHART _____

Form # FI20

© 2007 The Generations Network, Inc.

http://www.ancestry.com/save/charts/ancchart.htm

Figure A-1. Ancestral Chart.

Family Group Record

ancestry.com

Prepared By _____ Relationship to Preparer _____

Address _____ Date _____ Ancestral Chart # _____ Family Unit # _____

Husband _____

Occupation(s) _____ Religion _____

	Date—Day, Month, Year	City	County	State or Country
Born				
Christened				Name of Church
Married				Name of Church
Died				Cause of Death
Buried	Cem./Place			
				Date Will Written/Proved

Father _____
Mother _____ Other Wives

Wife maiden name _____

Occupation(s) _____ Religion _____

Born				
Christened				Name of Church
Died				Cause of Death
Buried	Cem./Place			
				Date Will Written/Proved

Father _____
Mother _____ Other Husbands

Children	Sex M-F	Birth Day Month Year	Birthplace City	County	St./Ctry.	Date of first marriage/Place Name of Spouse	Date of Death/Cause City	County	State/Country	Computer I.D. #
Given Names										
1										
2										
3										
4										
5										
6										
7										
8										
9										
10										
11										
12										

NOTE=Direct Ancestor   Form # F106   http://www.ancestry.com/save/charts/familysheet.htm   © 2007 The Generations Network, Inc.

Figure A-2. Family Group Record.

1940 Federal Census

STATE
COUNTY
TOWNSHIP OR OTHER DIVISION OF COUNTY
INCORPORATED PLACE
WARD OF CITY

ENUMERATION DISTRICT NO.
SUPERVISOR'S DISTRICT NO.
SHEET NO.
ENUMERATED BY ME ON , 1940
, ENUMERATOR
INSTITUTION

BLOCK NO. UNINCORPORATED PLACE

LOCATION
- Street, Avenue, road, etc. (1)
- House Number (2)

HOUSEHOLD DATA
- No. of Household in order of visitation (3)
- Home owned (O) or rented (R) (4)
- Value of home or Monthly rental if rented. (5)
- Farm? (Yes or No) (6)

NAME (7)
Name of each person whose *usual* place of residence on April 1, 1940, was in this household.

BE SURE TO INCLUDE:
1. Persons temporarily absent from household. Write "Ab" after the names of such persons.
2. Children under 1 year of age. Write "Infant" if child has not been given a first name.
Enter ⊙ after name of person furnishing information.

RELATION (8)
Relationship of this person to the head of the household, as wife, daughter, father, mother-in-law, grandson, lodger, lodger's wife, servant, hired hand, etc.

CODE (Leave Blank) (A)

PERSONAL DESCRIPTION
- Sex (9)
- Color or Race (10)
- Age at Last Birthday (11)
- Marital Status (12)

EDUCATION
- Attended school or college at any time since March 1, 1940? (13)
- Highest grade of school completed (14)

CODE (Leave Blank) (B)

PLACE OF BIRTH (15)
If born in U.S. give state, territory or possession.
If foreign born, give country in which birthplace was situated on Jan. 1, 1937.
Distinguish: Canada-French from Canada-English and Irish Free State from Northern Ireland.

CODE (Leave Blank) (C)

CITIZENSHIP
- Citizenship of the foreign born. (16)

RESIDENCE, APRIL 1, 1935
In what place did this person live on April 1, 1935?
For a person who lived in a different place, enter city or town, county, and State.
- City, town, or village having 2,600 or more inhabitants If less, enter "R". (17)
- County (18)
- State (or Territory or foreign country) (19)
- On a Farm? (Y or N) (20)

CODE (Leave Blank) (D)

Line No.

PERSONS 14 YEARS OLD AND OVER – EMPLOYMENT STATUS

- Was this person AT WORK for pay or profit in private or nonemergency Govt. work during week of March 24-30? (Y or N) (21)
- If not, was he at work on, or assigned to, public EMERGENCY WORK (WPA, NYA, CCC, etc.) during week of March 24-30? (Y or N) (22)
- Was this person SEEKING WORK? (Y or N) (23)
- If not seeking work, did he HAVE A JOB, business, etc.? (Y or N) (24)
- For persons answering "No" to questions 21-24. Indicate whether engaged in home housework (H), in school (S), unable to work (U), or other (O). (25)

CODE (25a)

- If at private or nonemergency Govt. work. Number of hours worked during week of March 24-30, 1940. (26)
- If seeking work or assigned to public emergency work. Duration of unemployment up to March 30, 1940—in weeks. "Yes" in col. 22 or 23 (27)

OCCUPATION, INDUSTRY, AND CLASS OF WORKER
For a person at work, assigned to public emergency work, or with a job ("Yes" in col. 21, 22, or 24), enter present occupation, industry, and class of worker.
For a person seeking work ("Yes" in col. 23: (a) if he has previous work experience, enter last occupation, industry, and class of worker; or (b) if he does not have previous work experience, enter "New worker" in Col. 28, and leave Cols. 29-30 blank.

- OCCUPATION (28)
  Trade, profession, or particular kind of work, as—
  Frame spinner
  Salesman
  Laborer
  Rivet heater
  Music teacher
- INDUSTRY (29)
  Industry or business, as—
  Cotton mill
  Retail grocery
  Farm
  Shipyard
  Public school
- Class of Worker (30)

CODE (leave blank) (F)

INCOME IN 1939 (12 months ending Dec. 31, 1939.)
- Number of weeks worked in 1939 (Equivalent full-time weeks) (31)
- Amount of money, wages or salary received (including commissions) (32)
- Did this person receive income of $50 or more from sources other than money wages or salary? (Y or N) (33)

Number of Farm Schedule (34)

Line No. 1. 2. 3. 4. 5. 6. 7.

NA 14129 (6-09)
NARA's web site is http://www.archives.gov
National Archives and Records Administration

182

Figure A-3. 1940 Federal Census.

SUPPLEMENTARY QUESTIONS		FOR PERSONS OF ALL AGES										FOR PERSONS 14 YEARS OLD AND OVER							FOR ALL WOMEN WHO ARE OR HAVE BEEN MARRIED		
For Persons Enumerated on Lines 14 and 29.		PLACE OF BIRTH OF FATHER AND MOTHER: If born in U.S. give state, territory or possession. If foreign born, give country in which birthplace was situated on Jan. 1, 1937. Distinguish: Canada-French from Canada-English and Irish Free State from Northern Ireland.			MOTHER TONGUE		VETERANS: Is this person a veteran of the United States military forces: or the wife, widow, or under 18-year-old child of a veteran?				SOCIAL SECURITY			USUAL OCCUPATION, INDUSTRY, AND CLASS OF WORKER: Enter that occupation which the person regards as his usual occupation and at which he is physically able to work. If the person is unable to determine this, enter that occupation at which he has worked longest during the past 10 years and at which he is physically able to work. Enter also usual industry and usual class of worker.						
Line No.	Name	Father	Mother	CODE (leave blank)	Language spoken in home in earliest childhood.	CODE (leave blank)	If so enter "Yes"	If child, is veteran-father dead? (Y or N)	War or Military Service	CODE (leave blank)	Does this person have a Federal Social Security Number? (Yes or No)	Where deductions for Federal Old-Age Insurance or Railroad Retirement made from this persons wages or salary in 1939? (Yes or No)	If so, were deductions made from all, ½ or more, part but less than ½, of wages or salary?	Usual Occupation	Usual Industry	Usual class of worker	CODE (leave blank)	Has this woman been married more than once? (Yes or No)	Age at first marriage.	Number of children ever born. (Do not include stillbirths.)
	35	36	37	G	38	H	39	40	41	I	42	43	44	45	46	47	J	48	49	50
14																				
29																				

SYMBOLS AND EXPLANATORY NOTES

Col. 5 VALUE OF HOME, IF OWNED:

Where owner's household occupies only a part of a structure, estimate value of portion occupied by owner's household. Thus the value of the unit occupied by the owner of a two-family house might be approximately one-half the total value of the structure.

Col. 10 COLOR OR RACE:

White	W
Negro	Neg
Indian	In
Chinese	Chi
Japanese	Jp
Filipino	Fil
Hindu	Hin
Korean	Kor

Other races, spell out in full.

Col. 11 AGE AT LAST BIRTHDAY:

Enter age of children born on or after April 1, 1939, as follows. Born in:

April 1939	11/12
May 1939	10/12
June 1939	9/12
July 1939	8/12
August 1939	7/12
September 1939	6/12
October 1939	5/12
November 1939	4/12
December 1939	3/12
January 1940	2/12
February 1940	1/12
March 1940	0/12

(Do not include children born on or after April 1, 1940.

Col. 14 HIGHEST GRADE OF SCHOOL COMPLETED:

None	0
Elementary school, 1st – 8th	1, 2, 3, 4, 5, 6, 7, 8
High school, 1st – 4th year	H-1, H-2, H-3, H-4
College, 1st – 4th year	C-1, C-2, C-3, C-4
College, 5th or subsequent year	C-5

Col. 16 CITIZENSHIP OF THE FOREIGN BORN:

Naturalized	Na
Having first papers	Pa
Alien	Al
American citizen born abroad	Am Cit

Col. 21 WAS THIS PERSON AT WORK ?

Enter "Yes" for persons at work for pay or profit in private or nonemergency Government work. Include unpaid family workers – that is, related members of the family working without money wages or salary on work (other then housework or incidental chores) which contributed to the family income.

Col. 24 DID THIS PERSON HAVE A JOB ?

Enter "Yes" for a person (not seeking work) who had a job, business, or professional enterprise, but did not work during week of March 24–30 for any of the following reasons: Vacation; temporary illness; industrial dispute; layoff not exceeding 4 weeks with instructions to return to work at a specific date; layoff due to temporarily bad

Cols. 30 and 47 CLASS OF WORKER:

Wage or salary worker in private work	PW
Wage or salary worker in Gov't work	GW
Employer	E
Working on own account	OA
Unpaid family worker	NP

Col. 41 WAR OR MILITARY SERVICE:

World War	W
Spanish -American War; Philippine Insurrection or Boxer Rebellion	S
Spanish-American War & World War	SW
Regular establishment (Army, Navy or Marine Corps) Peace-Time Service only	R
Other war or expedition	Ot

National Archives and Records Administration

NARA's web site is http://www.archives.gov

NA 14129 (6-09)

Figure A-3. Continued.

1930 United States Federal Census

State: _____
County: _____
City, township: _____
Enumeration District: _____
Sheet Number: _____
Call Number/URL: _____
Enumeration Date: _____

NOTES:

Figure A-4. 1930 United States Federal Census.

1920 United States Federal Census

State: _____ County: _____ City / Township: _____

Call Number/URL: _____ Enumeration District: _____ Sheet Number: _____ Enumeration Date: _____

Place of Abode				Name of each person whose place of abode on January 1, 1920 was in this family	Relation	Tenure		Personal Description				Citizenship			Education		
Street, avenue, road, etc.	House number or farm	Dwelling number	Number of family, in order of visitation		Relationship of this person to the head of the family	Home owned or rented	If owned, free or mortgaged	Sex	Color or Race	Age at last birthday	Single, married, widowed or divorced	Naturalized or alien	Year of immigration to the United States	If naturalized, year of naturalization	Attended school anytime since Sept. 1, 1919	Able to read	Able to write
1	2	3	4	5	6	7	8	9	10	11	12	13	14	15	16	17	18

Line Number

Nativity and Mother Tongue

Place of birth of each person and parents of each person enumerated. If born in the United States, give state or territory. If foreign birth, give the place of birth, and, in addition, the mother tongue.

Person		Father		Mother		Occupation				
Place of Birth	Mother Tongue	Place of Birth	Mother Tongue	Place of Birth	Mother Tongue	Able to speak english	Trade, profession or particular kind of work done	Industry, business or establishment of work done	Employer, salary or wage worker, or working on own account	No. of farm schedule
19	20	21	22	23	24	25	26	27	28	29

Line Number

Ancestry® Census Form 014

To search the 1920 census online, visit www.ancestry.com

©The Generations Network, Inc. 2007

Figure A-5. 1920 United States Federal Census.

185

1910 United States Federal Census

State: _____
County: _____
City, township: _____

Enumeration District: _____
Sheet Number: _____
Call Number/URL: _____
Enumeration Date: _____

Location

Line number	
Street, avenue, road, etc.	
House number or farm	
1 Dwelling Number	
2 Number of family in order of visitation	

Name

3 — Name of each person whose place of abode on April 15, 1910, was in this family.

Enter surname first, then the given name and middle initial, if any.

Include every person living on April 15, 1910.
Omit children born since April 15, 1910.

Relation

4 — Relationship of this person to the head of the family.

Personal Description

5 Sex	6 Color or Race	7 Age at last birthday	8 Whether single, married, widowed, or divorced	9 Number of years of present marriage

Mother of how many children
10 Number born	11 Number now living

Nativity

Place of birth of each person and parents of each person enumerated. If born in United States, give state or territory. If foreign birth, give the country.

12 Place of birth of this person.	13 Place of birth of Father of this person.	14 Place of birth of Mother of this person.

Citizenship

15 Year of immigration to the U.S.	16 Whether naturalized or Alien

Occupation

17 Whether able to speak English; or, if not, give language spoken.	18 Trade or profession of, or particular kind of work done by this person.	19 General nature of industry, business, or establishment in which this person works.	20 Whether an employer, employee, or working on own account

If an employee—
21 Whether out of work on April 15, 1910	22 Number of weeks out of work during 1909

Education

23 Whether able to read	24 Whether able to write	25 Attended school any time since Sept. 1, 1909

Ownership of Home

26 Owned or Rented	27 Owned free or mortgaged	28 Farm or house	29 Number of farm schedule

30 Whether a survivor of the Union or Confederate Army or Navy	31 Whether blind (both eyes)	32 Whether deaf and dumb

Line number

To search the 1910 census online, visit www.ancestry.com

Ancestry Census Form 013

Figure A-6. 1910 United States Federal Census.

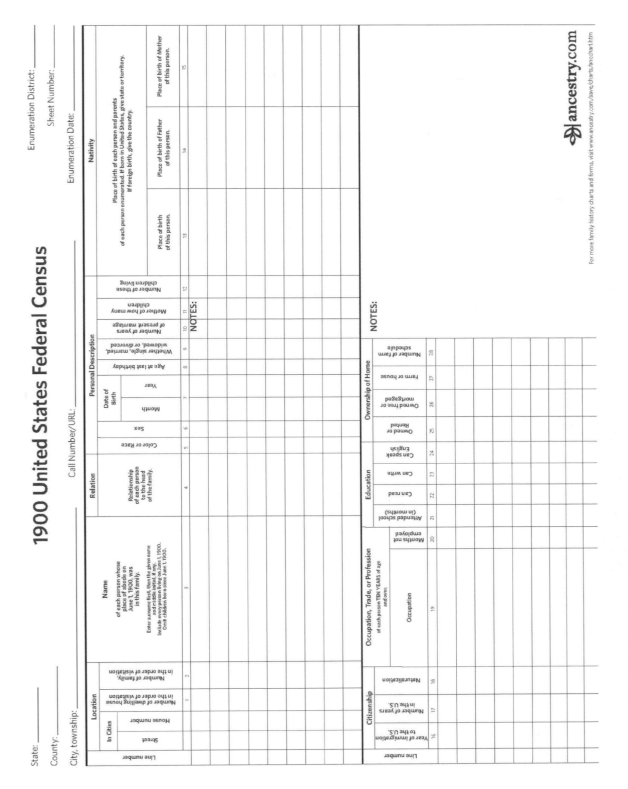

Figure A-7. 1900 United States Federal Census.

187

1880 United States Federal Census

For more family history charts and forms,
visit www.ancestry.com/save/charts/ancchart.htm

State: _____ County: _____ City: _____ Page: _____ E.D.: _____ Call #/URL: _____ Enumeration Date: _____

Figure A-8. 1880 United States Federal Census.

1870 United States Federal Census

Page: _____ State: _____ County: _____ City: _____ Call Number/URL: _____ Enumeration Date: _____

Dwelling-houses numbered in the order of visitation	Families numbered in the order of visitation	The Name of every Person whose place of abode on the first day of June, 1870, was in this family	Age at last birth-day. If under 1 year, give months in fractions, thus 3/12	Description			Profession, Occupation, or Trade of each Male Person over 15 years of age	Value of Real Estate owned		Place of Birth Naming the State, Territory, or Country	Parentage		If born within the year, state month (Jan., &c.)	If married within the year, state month (Jan., &c.)	Attended School within the year	Education		Whether deaf and dumb, blind, insane, idiotic, pauper, or convict	Constitutional Relations	
				Sex—Male (M), Female (F).	Color—White (W); Black (B); Mulatto (M); Chinese, (C); Indian, (I).			Value of Real Estate	Value of Personal Estate		Father of Foreign born	Mother of Foreign born				Cannot read	Cannot write		Male Citizens of U.S., of 21 years of age and upwards	Male Citizens of U.S. of 21 years of age and upwards where rights to vote is denied on other grounds than rebellion or other crime
1	2	3	4	5	6		7	8	9	10	11	12	13	14	15	16	17	18	19	20

Figure A-9. 1870 United States Federal Census.

1860 United States Federal Census

ancestry.com

Page: ____________ State: ____________ County: ____________ City: ____________
Call Number/URL: ____________ Enumeration Date: ____________

Dwelling-houses numbered in the order of visitation	Families numbered in the order of visitation	The Name of every Person whose usual place of abode on the first day of June, 1860, was in this family	Description: Age	Description: Sex	Description: Color (White, Black or Mulatto)	Profession, Occupation or Trade of each Male Person over 15 years of age	Value of Real Estate	Value of Personal Estate	Place of Birth Naming the State, Territory or County	Married within the year	Attended School within the year	Persons over 20 years of age who cannot read & write	Whether deaf and dumb, blind, insane, idiotic, pauper or convict
1	2	3	4	5	6	7	8	9	10	11	12	13	14

Ancestry® Census Form 008

To search the 1860 census online, visit www.ancestry.com

Figure A-10. **1860 United States Federal Census.**

1850 United States Federal Census

ancestry.com

Page: ____________ State: ____________ County: ____________ City: ____________

Call Number/URL: ____________ Enumeration Date: ____________

Dwelling- houses numbered in the order of visitation	Families numbered in the order of visitation	The Name of every Person whose usual place of abode on the first day of June, 1850, was in this family	Description			Profession, Occupation or Trade of each Male Person over 15 years of age	Value of Real Estate owned	Place of Birth Naming the State, Territory or County	Married within the year	Attended School within the year	Persons over 20 years of age who cannot read & write	Whether deaf and dumb, blind, insane, idiotic, pauper or convict
			Age	Sex	Color (White, Black or Mulatto)							
1	2	3	4	5	6	7	8	9	10	11	12	13

Ancestry® Census Form 007

To search the 1850 census online, visit www.ancestry.com

Figure A-11. 1850 United States Federal Census.

Figure A-12. 1840 United States Federal Census.

For more family history charts and forms,
visit www.ancestry.com/save/charts/ancchart.htm

Page: _____ State: _____ County: _____ Call Number/URL: _____ Enumeration Date: _____

FREE WHITE PERSONS, (INCLUDING HEADS OF FAMILIES).

Males.
- Under five years of age. | under 5
- Of five and under ten. | 5 to 10
- Of ten and under fifteen. | 10 to 15
- Of fifteen and under twenty. | 15 to 20
- Of twenty and under thirty. | 20 to 30
- Of thirty and under forty. | 30 to 40
- Of forty and under fifty. | 40 to 50
- Of fifty and under sixty. | 50 to 60
- Of sixty and under seventy. | 60 to 70
- Of seventy and under eighty. | 70 to 80
- Of eighty and under ninety. | 80 to 90
- Of ninety and under one hundred. | 90 to 100
- Of one hundred and upward. | 100 &c

Females.
- Under five years of age. | under 5
- Of five and under ten. | 5 to 10
- Of ten and under fifteen. | 10 to 15
- Of fifteen and under twenty. | 15 to 20
- Of twenty and under thirty. | 20 to 30
- Of thirty and under forty. | 30 to 40
- Of forty and under fifty. | 40 to 50
- Of fifty and under sixty. | 50 to 60
- Of sixty and under seventy. | 60 to 70
- Of seventy and under eighty. | 70 to 80
- Of eighty and under ninety. | 80 to 90
- Of ninety and under one hundred. | 90 to 100
- Of one hundred and upward. | 100 &c

Names of Heads of Families

Name of the county, city, ward, town, township, parish, precinct, hundred, or district.

LINE NUMBER

Slaves.

Males.
- Under ten years of age. | under 10
- Of ten and under twenty-four. | 10 to 24
- Of twenty-four and under thirty-six. | 24 to 36
- Of thirty-six and under fifty-five. | 36 to 55
- Of fifty-five and under one hundred. | 55 to 100
- Of one hundred and upwards. | 100 &c

Females.
- Under ten years of age. | under 10
- Of ten and under twenty-four. | 10 to 24
- Of twenty-four and under thirty-six. | 24 to 36
- Of thirty-six and under fifty-five. | 36 to 55
- Of fifty-five and under one hundred. | 55 to 100
- Of one hundred and upwards. | 100 &c

Freed Colored Persons.

Males.
- Under ten years of age. | under 10
- Of ten and under twenty-four. | 10 to 24
- Of twenty-four and under thirty-six. | 24 to 36
- Of thirty-six and under fifty-five. | 36 to 55
- Of fifty-five and under one hundred. | 55 to 100
- Of one hundred and upwards. | 100 &c

Females.
- Under ten years of age. | under 10
- Of ten and under twenty-four. | 10 to 24
- Of twenty-four and under thirty-six. | 24 to 36
- Of thirty-six and under fifty-five. | 36 to 55
- Of fifty-five and under one hundred. | 55 to 100
- Of one hundred and upwards. | 100 &c

LINE NUMBER

WHITE PERSONS included in foregoing.
- Who are Deaf and Dumb, under fourteen years of age. | under 14
- Who are Deaf and Dumb, of the age of fourteen and under 25. | 14 to 25
- Who are Deaf twenty-five and upwards. | 25 &c
- Who are blind.
- ALIENS—Foreigners not naturalized

SLAVES AND COLORED PERSONS, included in foregoing.
- Who are Deaf and Dumb, under fourteen years of age. | under 14
- Who are Deaf and Dumb, of the age of fourteen and under 25. | 14 to 25
- Who are Deaf twenty-five and upwards. | 25 &c
- Who are blind.

TOTAL

To search the 1830 census online, visit www.ancestry.com

© The Generations Network 2007

Ancestry Census Form 005

Figure A-13. 1830 United States Federal Census.

1820 United States Federal Census

ancestry.com

For more family history charts and forms,
visit www.ancestry.com/save/charts/ancchart.htm

Page: _____ State: _____ County: _____ Call Number/URL: _____

Enumeration Date: _____

Name of the county, parish, township, town, or city where the family resides	Names of heads of families	Free White Males						Free White Females						Foreigners not naturalized	Numbers of persons engaged in Agriculture	Numbers of persons engaged in Commerce	Numbers of persons engaged in Manufactures	Slaves								Free Colored Persons								All other persons except Indians not taxed
		Free white males under ten years (to 10)	Free white males of ten and under sixteen (10 to 16)	Free white males between sixteen and eighteen (16 to 18)	Free white males of sixteen and under twenty-six, including heads of families (16 to 26)	Free white males of twenty-six and under forty-five, including heads of families (26 to 45)	Free white males of forty five and upwards, including heads of families (45 & c.)	Free white females under ten years (to 10)	Free white females of ten and under sixteen (10 to 16)	Free white females of sixteen and under twenty-six, including heads of families (16 to 26)	Free white females of twenty-six and under forty-five, including heads of families (26 to 45)	Free white females of forty five and upwards, including heads of families (45 & c.)					Males under fourteen (to 14)	Males of fourteen and under twenty-six (to 26)	Males of twenty-six and under forty-five (to 45)	Males of forty-five and upwards (45 & c.)	Females under fourteen (to 14)	Females of fourteen and under twenty-six (to 26)	Females of twenty-six and under forty-five (to 45)	Females of forty-five and upwards (45 & c.)	Males under fourteen (to 14)	Males of fourteen and under twenty-six (to 26)	Males of twenty-six and under forty-five (to 45)	Males of forty-five and upwards (45 & c.)	Females under fourteen (to 14)	Females of fourteen and under twenty-six (to 26)	Females of twenty-six and under forty-five (to 45)	Females of forty-five and upwards (45 & c.)	

Figure A-14. 1820 United States Federal Census.

State: _____   Call Number/URL: _____   Enumeration Date: _____

County	Page	Names of Heads of Families	Free White Males					Free White Females					All other Free Persons	Slaves
			Under 10	10 thru 15	16 thru 25	26 thru 44	45 and over	Under 10	10 thru 15	16 thru 25	26 thru 44	45 and over		

Ancestry® Census Form 003

To search the 1800 census online, visit www.ancestry.com

©The Generations Network, Inc. 2007

Figure A-15. 1810 United States Federal Census.

1800 United States Federal Census

State: _____   Call Number/URL: _____   Enumeration Date: _____   ⟨ancestry.com

County	County	Page	Names of Heads of Families	Free White Males					Free White Females					All other Free Persons	Slaves
				Under 10	10 thru 15	16 thru 25	26 thru 44	45 and over	Under 10	10 thru 15	16 thru 25	26 thru 44	45 and over		

Ancestry® Census Form 002   To search the 1800 census online, visit www.ancestry.com   ©The Generations Network, Inc. 2007

Figure A-16. 1800 United States Federal Census.

ancestry.com — 1790 United States Federal Census

For more family history charts and forms, visit www.ancestry.com/save/charts/ancchart.htm

State: _____ Call Number/URL: _____

Enumeration Date: _____

county	city	page	names of heads of families	free white males of 16 years & upwards, including heads of families	free white males under 16 years	free white females including heads of families	all other free persons	slaves

Figure A-17. 1790 United States Federal Census.

197

QUESTIONS ASKED ON THE 1940 CENSUS[1]

The questions recorded on the 1940 census schedules are similar to the questions found on earlier census schedules. As the enumerators went door-to-door they recorded the *location* of the household and provided additional *household data,* such as the names for each member of the household and their relationships to the head of the household. Enumerators also recorded a *personal description* for each member of the household, which included their age and sex; information about each individual's *education;* their *birthplace and naturalization status;* and a unique question asking about their *residence on April 1, 1935.*

In addition, all individuals over the age of 14 were asked questions about their *employment,* and 5% of the population were asked fifteen supplementary questions. This sample survey included questions about their *parents birthplace; earliest language spoken* in the household; questions relating to *veterans, social security; occupation;* and a final section specifically for women, which recorded *marital status* and *number of children born.*

Location

- Street, avenue, road, etc.
- House number (in cities and towns).

Household Data

- Number of household in order of visitation.
- Home owned (O) or rented (R).
- Value of home, if owned, or monthly rental, if rented.
- Does this household live on a farm? (Yes or No).

Name

- Name of each person whose *usual place of residence* on April 1, 1940, was in this household. Be sure to include:
  - Persons temporarily absent from household. Write "Ab" after names of such persons.
  - Children under 1 year of age. Write "Infant" if child has not been given a first name.
  - Enter X after name of person furnishing information.

Relation

- Relationship of this person to the head of the household, as wife, daughter, father, mother-in-law, grandson, lodger, lodger's wife, servant, hired hand, etc....

Personal Description

- Sex—Male (M), Female (F).
- Color or race.
- Age at last birthday.
- Marital status—Single (S), Married (M), Widowed (Wd), Divorced (D).

Education

- Attended school or college any time since March 1, 1940? (Yes or No)
- Highest grade of school completed.

Place of Birth

- If born in the United States, give State, Territory, or possession. If foreign born, give country in which birthplace was situated on January 1, 1937. Distinguish Canada-French from Canada-English and Irish Free State (Eire) from Northern Ireland.

Citizenship

- Citizenship of the foreign born.

Residence, April 1, 1935

IN WHAT PLACE DID THIS PERSON LIVE ON April 1, 1935? For a person who, on April 1, 1935, was living in the same house as at present, enter in Col. 17 "Same house," and for one living in a different house but in the same city or town, enter "Same place," leaving Cols. 18, 19, and 20 blank, in both instances. For a person who lived in a different place, enter city or town, county, and State, as directed in the Instructions. (Enter actual place of residence, which may differ from mail address.)

- City, town, or village having 2,500 or more inhabitants. Enter "R" for all other places.
- County.
- State (or Territory or foreign country).
- On a farm? (Yes or No)

Persons 14 Years Old and Over—Employment Status

- Was this person AT WORK for pay or profit in private or nonemergency Gov't work during week of March 24–30? (Yes or No)

- If not, was he at work on, or assigned to, public EMERGENCY WORK (WPA, NYA, CCC, etc.) during week of March 24–30? (Yes or No)

If neither at work nor assigned to public emergency work. ("No" in Cols. 21 and 22)

- Was this person SEEKING WORK? (Yes or No)
- If not seeking work, did he HAVE A JOB, business, etc.? (Yes or No)

For persons answering "No" to question 21, 22, 23 and 24.

- Indicate whether engaged in home housework (H), in school (S), unable to work (U), or other (Ot).

If at private or nonemergency Govt. work. "Yes" in col. 21.

- Number of hours worked during week of March 24–30, 1940.

If seeking work or assigned to public emergency work. ("Yes" in Col. 22 or 23)

- Duration of unemployment up to March 30, 1940—in weeks.

Occupation, Industry and Class of Worker

For a person *at work, assigned to public emergency work, or with a job* ("Yes" in Col. 21, 22, or 24), enter *present* occupation, industry, and class of worker. For a person seeking work ("Yes" in Col. 23): a) if he has previous work experience, enter *last* occupation, industry, and class of worker; or b) if he does not have previous work experience, enter "New worker" in Col. 28, and leave Cols. 29 and 30 blank.

- Occupation: Trade, profession, or particular kind of work, as *frame spinner, salesman, laborer, rivet heater, music teacher.*
- Industry: Industry or business, as *cotton mill, retail grocery, farm, shipyard, public school.*
- Class of Worker.
- Number of weeks worked in 1939 (Equivalent full-time weeks).

Income in 1939 (12 months ended December 31, 1939)

- Amount of money wages or salary received (including commissions).
- Did this person receive income of $50 or more from sources other than money wages or salary? (Yes or No)
- Number of Farm Schedule.

Supplementary Questions 35–50

For persons enumerated on lines 14 and 29 [about a 5% sample of the population]

- Name.

For Persons of All Ages

Place of Birth of Father and Mother

If born in the United States, give State, Territory, or possession. If foreign born, give country in which birthplace was situated on January 1, 1937. Distinguish: Canada-French from Canada-English and Irish Free State from Northern Ireland.

- Father.
- Mother.

Mother Tongue (or Native Language)

- Language spoken in home in earliest childhood.

Veterans

Is this person a veteran of the United States military forces; or the wife, widow, or under-18-year-old child of a veteran?

- If so, enter "Yes."
- If child, is veteran-father dead? (Yes or No)
- War or military service.

Social Security

- Does this person have a Federal Social Security Number? (Yes or No)
- Were deductions for Federal Old-Age Insurance or Railroad Retirement made from this person's wages or salary in 1939? (Yes or No)
- If so, were deductions made from (1) all, (2) one-half or more, (3) part, but less than half, of wages or salary?

Usual Occupation, Industry, and Class of Worker

Enter that occupation which the person regards as his usual occupation and at which he is physically able to work. If the person is unable to determine this, enter that occupation at which he has worked longest during the past 10 years and at which he is physically able to work. Enter also usual industry and usual class of worker. For a person without previous work experience, enter "None" in column 45 and leave columns 46 and 47 blank.

- Usual occupation.
- Usual industry.
- Usual class of worker.

For All Women Who Are or Have Been Married

- Has this woman been married more than once? (Yes or No)
- Age at first marriage.
- Number of children ever born (do not include stillbirths).

Symbols and Explanatory Notes

Census takers were given specific instructions and codes to use when entering data on the census schedules. Below you will find a list of instructions for some of the census questions.

To see a chart to help decipher the symbols used on the 1940 census please click here.

Table A1

Column Number and Heading	Codes Used	Code Meaning
Column 10:	W	White
Color or Race	Neg	Negro
	In	Indian
Other races, spell out in full.	Chi	Chinese
	Jp	Japanese
	Fil	Filipino
	Hin	Hindu
	Kor	Korean
Column 11:	11/12	April 1939
Age at Last Birthday	10/12	May 1939
	9/12	June 1939
(Do not include children born	8/12	July 1939
on or after April 1, 1940.)	7/12	August 1939
	6/12	September 1939
	5/12	October 1939
	4/12	November 1939
	3/12	December 1939
	2/12	January 1940
	1/12	February 1940
	0/12	March 1940

Column 14: Highest Grade of School Completed	0	None
	1 to 8	Elementary School, 1st to 8th
	H-1 to H-4	High School, 1st to 4th year
	C1 to C4	College, 1st to 4th year
	C-5	College, 5th year or more
Column 16: Citizenship of the Foreign Born	Na	Naturalized
	Pa	Having First Papers
	Al	Alien
	Am Cit	American Citizen Born Abroad
Columns 30 and 47: Class of Worker	PW	Wage/Salary Worker in Private Work
	GW	Wage/Salary Worker in Gov't Work
	E	Employer
	OA	Working on Own Account
	NP	Unpaid Family Worker
Column 41: War or Military Service	W	World War
	S	Spanish-American War; Philippine Insurrection or Boxer Rebellion
	SW	Spanish-American War & World War
	R	Regular Establishment or Peace-Time Service
	Ot	Other War or Expedition

- *Column 5:* Value of Home, If Owned.
  - Where owner's household occupies only a part of a structure, estimate value of portion occupied by owner's household. Thus the value of the unit occupied by the owner of a two-family house might be approximately one-half the total value of the structure.

- *Column 11:* Age at Last Birthday.
  - Enter age of children born on or after April 1, 1939, as follows. Born in: (see chart [Table A1, above]).

- *Column 21:* Was This Person at Work?
  - Enter "Yes" for persons at work for pay or profit in private or nonemergency Government work. Include unpaid family workers—that is, related members of the family working without money wages or salary on work (other then housework or incidental chores) which contributed to the family income.

- *Column 24:* Did This Person Have A Job?
  - Enter "Yes" for a person (not seeking work) who had a job, business, or professional enterprise, but did not work during week of March 24–30 for any of the following reasons: Vacation; temporary illness; industrial dispute; layoff not exceeding 4 weeks with instructions to return to work at a specific date; layoff due to temporarily bad weather conditions.

20TH-CENTURY U.S. CENSUSES[2]

1940

Address; home owned or rented; value or monthly rental; whether on a farm; name; relationship to household head; sex; race; age; marital status; school attendance; educational attainment; birthplace; citizenship of foreign born; location of residence 5 years ago and whether on a farm; employment status; if at work, whether in private or nonemergency government work or in public emergency work (WPA, CCC, NYA, etc.); if in private work, hours worked in week; if seeking work or on public emergency work, duration of unemployment; occupation, industry, and class of worker; weeks worked last year, income last year.

1930

Address; name; relationship to family head; home owned or rented; value or monthly rental; radio set; whether on a farm; sex; race; age; marital status; age at first marriage; school attendance; literacy; birthplace of person and parents; if foreign born, language spoken in home before coming to U.S., year of immigration, whether naturalized, and ability to speak English; occupation, industry, and class of worker; whether at work previous day (or last regular working day); veteran status; for Indians, whether of full or mixed blood, and tribal affiliation.

1920

Address; name; relationship to family head; sex; race; age; marital status; if foreign born, year of immigration to the U.S., whether naturalized and year of naturalization; school attendance; literacy; birthplace of person and parents; mother tongue of foreign born; ability to speak English; occupation, industry, and class of worker; home owned or rented; if owned, whether free or mortgaged.

1910

Address; name; relationship to family head; sex; race; age; marital status; number of years of present marriage for women, number of children born and number now living; birthplace and mother tongue of person and parents; if foreign born, year of immigration, whether naturalized, and whether able to speak English, or if not, language spoken; occupation, industry, and class of worker; if an employee, whether out of work during year; literacy; school attendance; home owned or rented; if owned, whether mortgaged; whether farm or house; whether a survivor of Union or Confederate Army or Navy; whether blind or deaf and dumb.

1900

Address; name; relationship to family head; sex; race; age; marital status; number of years married; for women, number of children born and number now living; birthplace of person and parents; if foreign born, year of immigration and whether naturalized; occupation; months not employed; school attendance; literacy; ability to speak English; whether on a farm; home owned or rented and, if owned, whether mortgaged.

NOTES

1. This section is taken from "Questions Asked on the 1940 Census," http://www. archives.gov/research/census/1940/general-info.html#questions/T(accessedMarch14, 2011).
2. This section is taken from "Population Census Items 1790–2000," *Factfinder for the Nation,* U.S Census Bureau, June 2008, p. 3. http://www.census.gov/prod/2000pubs/ cff-2.pdf (accessed March 14, 2011).

GLOSSARY OF GENEALOGICAL TERMS

The following is provided freely for redistribution by Dan Burrows, author of "Glossary of Genealogical Terms," Digby County GenWeb, http://www.rootsweb. ancestry.com/~nsdigby/lists/glossary.htm. Burrows has created a number of other specialized guides and lists that may also be of interest as you help family history researchers. These include "Names of Old Time Illnesses," "Names of Old Time Occupations," and "Wars, Battle and Other North American Skirmishes."[1]

Abstract   Summary of important points of a given text, especially deeds and wills.

Acre   See measurements.

Administration (of estate)   The collection, management and distribution of an estate by proper legal process.

Administrator (of estate)   Person appointed to manage or divide the estate of a deceased person.

Administratrix   A female administrator.

Affidavit   A statement in writing, sworn to before proper authority.

Alien   Foreigner.

American Revolution   U.S. war for independence from Great Britain 1775–1783.

Ancestor   A person from whom you are descended; a forefather.

Ante   Latin prefix meaning "before," such as in antebellum South, "the South before the war."

Apprentice   One who is bound by indentures or by legal agreement or by any means to serve another person for a certain time, with a view of learning an art or trade.

Appurtenance   That which belongs to something else such as a building, orchard, right of way, and so forth.

Archives   Records of a government, organization, institution; the place where records are stored.

Attest   To affirm; to certify by signature or oath.

Banns   Public announcement of intended marriage.

Beneficiary   One who receives benefit of trust or property.

Bequeath   To give personal property to a person in a will. Noun—bequest.

Bond   Written, signed, witnessed agreement requiring payment of a specified amount of money on or before a given date.

Bounty Land Warrant   A right to obtain land, specific number of acres of unallocated public land, granted for military service.

Census   Official enumeration, listing or counting of citizens.

Certified Copy   A copy made and attested to by officers having charge of the original and authorized to give copies.

Chain   See *Measurements.*

Chattel   Personal property, which can include animate as well as inanimate properties.

Christen   To receive or initiate into the visible church by baptism; to name at baptism; to give a name to.

Circa   About, near, or approximate—usually referring to a date.

Civil War   War between the states; war between North and South, 1861–1865.

Codicil   Addition to a will.

Collateral Ancestor   Belong to the same ancestral stock but not in direct line of descent; opposed to lineal such as aunts, uncles, and cousins.

Common Ancestor   Ancestor shared by any two people.

Confederate   Pertaining to the Southern states, which seceded from the United States in 1860–1861, their government and their citizens.

Consanguinity   Blood relationship.

Consort   Usually, a wife whose husband is living.

Conveyance   See *Deed.*

Cousin   Relative descended from a common ancestor, but not a brother or sister.

Daughter-in-Law   Wife of one's son.

Deceased   Dead.

Decedent   A deceased person.

Declaration of Intention   First paper, sworn to and filed in court, by an alien stating that he wants to become a citizen.

Deed   A document by which title in real property is transferred from one party to another.

Deposition   A testifying or testimony taken down in writing under oath of affirmation in reply to interrogatories, before a competent officer to replace the oral testimony of a witness.

Devise   Gift of real property by will.

Devisee   One to whom real property (land) is given in a will.

Devisor   One who gives real property in a will.

Dissenter   One who did not belong to the established church, especially the Church of England in the American colonies.

District Land Office Plat Book   Books or rather maps that show the location of the land patentee.

District Land Office Tract Book   Books that list individual entries by range and township.

Double Dating   A system of double dating used in England and America from 1582 to 1752, because it was not clear as to whether the year commenced January 1 or March 25.

Dower   Legal right or share that a wife acquired by marriage in the real estate of her husband, allotted to her after his death for her lifetime.

Emigrant   One leaving a country and moving to another.

Enumeration   Listing or counting, such as a census.

Epitaph   An inscription on or at a tomb or grave in memory of the one buried there.

Escheat   The reversion of property to the state when there are no qualified heirs.

Estate   All property and debts belonging to a person.

Et al.   Latin for "and others."

Et ux.   Latin for "and wife."

Et uxor   And his wife. Sometimes written simply *et ux.*

Executor   One appointed in a will to carry out its provisions. Female—executrix.

Father-in-Law   Father of one's spouse.

Fee   An estate of inheritance in land, being either fee simple or fee tail. An estate in land held of a feudal lord on condition of the performing of certain services.

Fee Simple   An absolute ownership without restriction.

Fee Tail   An estate of inheritance limited to lineal descendant heirs of a person to whom it was granted.

Franklin, State of   An area once known but never officially recognized and was under consideration from 1784 to 1788 from the western part of North Carolina.

Fraternity   Group of men (or women) sharing a common purpose or interest.

Free Hold   An estate in fee simple, in fee tail, or for life.

Friend   Member of the Religious Society of Friends; a Quaker.

Furlong   See *Measurements.*

Gazetteer   A geographic dictionary; a book giving names and descriptions of places usually in alphabetical order.

Genealogy   Study of family history and descent.

Gentleman   A man well born.

Given Name   Name given to a person at birth or baptism, one's first and middle names.

Glebe   Land belonging to a parish church.

Grantee   One who buys property or receives a grant.

Grantor   One who sells property or makes a grant.

Great-Aunt   Sister of one's grandparent

Great-Uncle   Brother of one's grandparent.

Guardian   Person appointed to care for and manage property of a minor orphan or an adult incompetent of managing her own affairs.

Half Brother/Half Sister   Child by another marriage of one's mother or father; the relationship of two people who have only one parent in common.

Heirs   Those entitled by law or by the terms of a will to inherit property from another.

Holographic Will   One written entirely in the testator's own handwriting.

Homestead Act   Law passed by Congress in 1862 allowing a head of a family to obtain title to 160 acres of public land after clearing and improving it for 5 years.

Huguenot   A French Protestant in the 16th and 17th centuries. One of the reformed or Calvinistic communion who were driven by the thousands into exile in England, Holland, Germany, and America.

Illegitimate   Born to a mother who was not married to the child's father.

Immigrant   One moving into a country from another.

Indenture   Today it means a contract in two or more copies. Originally made in two parts by cutting or tearing a single sheet across the middle in a jagged line so the two parts may later be matched.

Indentured Servant   One who bound himself into service of another person for a specified number of years, often in return for transportation to this country.

Infant   Any person not of full age; a minor.

Instant   Of or pertaining to the current month. (Abbreviated *inst.*)

Intestate   One who dies without a will or dying without a will.

Inventory   An account, catalog, or schedule made by an executor or administrator of all the goods and chattels and sometimes of the real estate of a deceased person.

Issue   Offspring; children; lineal descendants of a common ancestor.

Late   Recently deceased.

Lease   An agreement that creates a landlord–tenant situation.

Legacy   Property or money left to someone in a will

Legislature   Lawmaking branch of state or national government; elected group of lawmakers.

Lien   A claim against property as security for payment of a debt.

Lineage   Ancestry; direct descent from a specific ancestor.

Lineal   Consisting of or being in a direct line of ancestry or descendants; descended in a direct line.

Link   See *Measurements.*

Lis pendens   Pending court action; usually applies to land title claims.

Lodge   A chapter or meeting hall of a fraternal organization.

Loyalist   Tory, an American colonist who supported the British side during the American Revolution.

Maiden Name   A girl's last name or surname before she marries.

Manuscript   A composition written with the hand as an ancient book or a nonprinted modern book or music.

Marriage Bond   A financial guarantee that no impediment to the marriage existed, furnished by the intended bridegroom or by his friends.

Maternal   Related through one's mother, such as a maternal grandmother being the mother's mother.

Measurements

    Link—7.92 inches

    Chain—100 links or 66 feet

    Furlong—1,000 links or 660 feet

    Rod—5½ yards or 16½ feet (also called a perch or pole)

    Rood—from 5½ yards to 8 yards, depending on locality

    Acre—43,560 square feet or 160 square rods

Messuage   A dwelling house.

Metes & Bounds   Property described by natural boundaries, such as three notches in a white oak tree, and so forth.

Microfiche   Sheet of microfilm with greatly reduced images of pages of documents.

Microfilm   Reproduction of documents on film at reduced size.

Migrant   Person who moves from place to place, usually in search of work.

Migrate   To move from one country or state or region to another. Noun—migration.

Militia   Citizens of a state who are not part of the national military forces but who can be called into military service in an emergency; a citizen army, apart from the regular military forces.

Minor   One who is under legal age; not yet a legal adult.

Mister   In early times, a title of respect given only to those who held important civil officer or who were of gentle blood.

Moiety   A half; an indefinite portion.

Mortality   Death; death rate.

Mortality Schedules   Enumeration of persons who died during the year prior to June 1 of 1850, 1860, 1870, and 1880 in each state of the United States; conducted by the Bureau of Census.

Mortgage   A conditional transfer of title to real property as security for payment of a debt.

Mother-in-Law   Mother of one's spouse.

Namesake   Person named after another person.

Necrology   Listing or record of persons who have died recently.

Nee   Used to identify a woman's maiden name; born with the surname of.

Nephew   Son of one's brother or sister.

Niece   Daughter of one's brother or sister.

Nuncupative Will   One declared or dictated by the testator, usually for persons in last sickness, sudden illness, or military.

Orphan   Child whose parents are dead; sometimes, a child who has lost one parent by death.

Orphan's Court   Orphans being recognized as wards of the states, provisions were made for them in special courts.

Passenger List   A ships list of passengers, usually referring to those ships arriving in the United States or Canada from Europe.

Patent   Grant of land from a government to an individual.

Paternal   Related to one's father. Paternal grandmother is the father's mother.

Patriot   One who loves his country and supports its interests.

Pedigree   Family tree; ancestry.

Pension   Money paid regularly to an individual, especially by a government as reward for military service during wartime or upon retirement from government service.

Pensioner   One who receives a pension.

Perch   See *Measurements.*

Pole   See *Measurements.*

Poll   List or record of persons, especially for taxing or voting.

Post   Prefix meaning "after," as in postwar economy.

Posterity   Descendants; those who come after.

Power of Attorney   When a person is unable to act for herself, she appoints another to act in her behalf.

Pre   Prefix meaning "before," as in prewar military buildup.

Preemotion Rights   Right given by the federal government to citizens to buy a quarter section of land or less.

Probate   Having to do with wills and the administration of estates.

Progenitor   A direct ancestor.

Progeny   Descendants of a common ancestor; issue.

Proved Will   A will established as genuine by probate court.

Provost   A person appointed to superintend, or preside over something.

Proximo   In the following month; in the month after the present one.

Public Domain   Land owned by the government.

Quaker   Member of the Religious Society of Friends.

Quitclaim   A deed conveying the interest of the party at that time.

Rector   A clergyman; the ruler or governor of a country.

Relict   Widow; surviving spouse when one has died, husband or wife.

Republic   Government in which supreme authority lies with the people or their elected representatives.

Revolutionary War   U.S. war for independence from Great Britain, 1775–1783.

Rod   See *Measurements.*

Rood   See *Measurements.*

Shaker   Member of a religious group formed in 1747 that practiced communal living and celibacy.

Sibling   Person having one or both parents in common with another; a brother or sister.

Sic   Latin meaning "thus"; copied exactly as the original reads. Often suggests a mistake or surprise in the original.

Son-in-Law   Husband of one's daughter.

Spinster   A woman still unmarried; or one who spins.

Sponsor   A bondsman; surety.

Spouse   Husband or wife.

Statute   Law.

Stepbrother/Stepsister   Child of one's stepfather or stepmother.

Stepchild   Child of one's husband or wife from a previous marriage.

Stepfather   Husband of one's mother by a later marriage.

Stepmother   Wife of one's father by a later marriage.

Surname   Family name or last name.

Territory   Area of land owned by a country, not a state or province, but having its own legislature and governor.

Testamentary   Pertaining to a will.

Testate   A person who dies leaving a valid will.

Testator   A person who makes a valid will before his death.

Tithable   Taxable.

Tithe   Formerly, money due as a tax for support of the clergy or church.

Tory   Loyalist; one who supported the British side in the American Revolution.

Township   A division of U.S. public land that contained 36 sections, or 36 square miles. Also a subdivision of the county in many northeastern and midwestern states of the United States.

Tradition   The handing down of statements, beliefs, legends, customs, genealogies, and so forth, from generation to generation, especially by word of mouth.

Transcribe   To make a copy in writing.

Ultimo   In the month before this one.

Union   The United States; also the North during the Civil War, the states that did not secede.

Verbatim   Word for word; in the same words, verbally.

Vital Records   Records of birth, death, marriage, or divorce.

Vital Statistics   Data dealing with birth, death, marriage, or divorce.

War between the States   U.S. Civil War, 1861–1865.

Ward   Chiefly the division of a city for election purposes.

Will   Document declaring how a person wants her property divided after her death.

Witness   One who is present at a transaction, such as a sale of land or signing of a will, who can testify or affirm that it actually took place.

WPA Historical Records Survey   A program undertaken by the U.S. government from 1935 to 1936, in which inventories were compiled of historical material.

Yeoman   A servant, an attendant, or subordinate official in a royal household; a subordinate of a sheriff; an independent farmer.

NOTE

1.   "Genealogy Definitions," Genealogy Records Service, http://www.obcgs.com/definitions.pdf (accessed March 14, 2011).

INDEX

ABOUT THE AUTHOR

DAVID R. DOWELL has two degrees in history and two in library science, as well as 35 years of experience as a librarian and 4 years as a special investigative officer in the U.S. Air Force. He has taught courses in U.S. genealogy research and European genealogy research since his retirement in 2007 and has researched his family history for four decades. He is a member of the National Genealogical Society, New England Historic Genealogical Society, Southern California Genealogy Society, and the San Luis Obispo County Genealogical Society. He is co-coordinator of two surname DNA projects and currently chairs the Genealogy Committee of the American Library Association. He has coauthored *Libraries in the Information Age: An Introduction and Career Guide* and *It's All About Student Learning: Management Issues in Community and Other College Libraries.* Check out his blog Dr D. Diggs Up Ancestors at http://blog.ddowell.com and his more complete resume at http://ddowell.com/dave/resume.pdf.

ML   12/11

ML   12/11